CBT Workbook

3rd Edition

by Rob Willson, PhD and
Rhena Branch, BSc, MSc, Dip CBT

for dummies®
A Wiley Brand

CBT Workbook For Dummies®, 3rd Edition

Published by: **John Wiley & Sons, Inc.,** 111 River Street, Hoboken, NJ 07030-5774, www.wiley.com

For general information on our other products and services, please contact our Customer Care Department within the U.S. at 877-762-2974, outside the U.S. at 317-572-3993, or fax 317-572-4002. For technical support, please visit https://hub.wiley.com/community/support/dummies.

Wiley publishes in a variety of print and electronic formats and by print-on-demand. Some material included with standard print versions of this book may not be included in e-books or in print-on-demand. If this book refers to media that is not included in the version you purchased, you may download this material at http://booksupport.wiley.com. For more information about Wiley products, visit www.wiley.com.

Library of Congress Control Number is available from the publisher.

ISBN 978-1-394-43111-3 (pbk); ISBN 978-1-394-43113-7 (ebk); ISBN 978-1-394-43112-0 (ebk)

SKY10166441_082126

Contents at a Glance

Table of Contents

Introduction

Welcome to *CBT Workbook For Dummies*, 3rd Edition. Cognitive behavioral therapy (CBT) is a form of psychotherapy found to be effective with depression, anxiety, and many other types of problems.

Quite often, people accept a physical illness or accident that impairs their daily functioning but may fail to accept that they struggle with a mental health problem. Every human being — regardless of culture, creed, class, background, race, or any other distinguishing characteristic — is likely to experience some form of emotional or mental difficulty during the course of their lives. The good news is that it's totally normal to experience emotional problems and it's absolutely possible to recover. CBT can really help.

We've written this book to bring you the types of CBT exercises we use in our work with clients. We know that CBT works because we've seen it work! And we want it to work for you, too. Whatever your problem, we hope that you'll find this book useful and informative.

About This Book

This book gives you an arsenal of skills and tools to help you beat a range of psychological problems. We try to give you just enough theoretical information to enable you to do the exercises contained in each chapter. All the worksheets and tasks in this workbook are indicative of the types of work we do with our clients in one-on-one CBT therapy.

You can use this workbook on your own to help you become your own CBT therapist. Or you can use it alongside a course of CBT treatment with a qualified professional. Unfortunately, we can't cover every type of psychological difficulty in depth in this book, or it would be encyclopedic in length! So, we've chosen to touch on the most common disorders that CBT has been proved effective at resolving. You can use this book as a jumping-off point to better understand your particular problems and how to battle them. If you think you need some additional professional input, don't hesitate to get it!

Yep, it's a workbook, and that means it involves — you guessed it — work. But if you really put your energy into doing the work and regular practice, you'll get benefits. Is it worth it to you to sweat and struggle in order to feel and function better? If so, roll up your sleeves, do some preliminary stretches, put on your sweatbands and hurl yourself into the process!

Foolish Assumptions

We assume that if you're reading this book, you're interested in using CBT techniques on yourself. We're guessing that you've heard of CBT before or had it recommended to you by a friend or professional. We're also guessing that you have one or two psychological problems that you'd like to be free from.

But even if our assumptions are completely wrong (or indeed foolish), this book may be of interest to you. You may have a friend or family member who you're concerned about and you want to learn more about CBT treatment. You may be feeling okay but still have an interest in CBT and how it may be able to further your enjoyment of life. So, we assume, foolishly or not, that you'll get something of use out of this book, whatever your reasons for buying it.

Icons Used in This Book

We use icons throughout this workbook to bring different types of information to your attention and to clearly guide you through the book.

EXAMPLE

The Example icon highlights examples that help illustrate a point.

TIP

The Tip alerts you to information you can use to better understand a concept or complete a worksheet.

REMEMBER

The Remember icon marks the information that's especially important to know. To siphon off the most important information in each chapter, just skim through these icons.

WARNING

The Warning icon tells you to watch out! It denotes possible pitfalls, common errors, or potential dangers.

Beyond the Book

In addition to what you're reading right now, this book comes with a free access-anywhere Cheat Sheet that includes tips and tricks for getting more out of CBT. To get this Cheat Sheet, simply go to `www.dummies.com` and type **CBT Workbook For Dummies Cheat Sheet** in the Search box.

Throughout the book there are worksheets that you may want to complete more than once. Go to `www.dummies.com/go/cbtworkbookfd3e` to download blank versions that you can print and use. Note: After going to the page, click "Related Resources" to access the content.

Where to Go from Here

This workbook is designed to be a hands-on practical approach to using CBT. It contains lots of worksheets and tasks to get you moving along the road to recovery. Because it's a workbook, we don't go into great depth about theoretical CBT concepts and principles. We focus more on action. For more about background CBT theory, check out *CBT For Dummies*, 4th Edition (Wiley).

If you're not sure where to start, head to Chapter 6 to get a sense of changes in behavior and emotion that CBT can be great at helping people achieve. Next work on Chapter 8 and define the goals you have for improving your psychological well-being. After you've worked through Part 1 to cover the basics, you can choose the chapters that are most relevant to you.

1

Getting Started with CBT

IN THIS PART . . .

We show you what cognitive behavioral therapy (CBT) is all about and how it applies to common problems. We also show you how to recognize your problematic thinking patterns, how to get on top of toxic thinking, and how to find better ways of thinking for the future.

You also get to act like a scientist in the interest of improving your emotional and mental health. Finally, we introduce mindfulness and other techniques for directing your focus of attention.

IN THIS CHAPTER

- Seeing the science and the sense of CBT
- Making CBT work for you
- Understanding your personal events
- Putting problems into an A-B-C format

Chapter 1

Exploring the Basics of CBT

Usually people respond to negative, difficult, or downright bad life events with negative emotions such as sadness or anger (to name but two). It is both natural and normal to feel distressed when bad things happen. The degree of distress you feel depends partly on the severity of the bad event. But the key word here is *partly*. Often the meanings you attach to given events can take a bad situation and make it worse. The way you *think* about aspects of your current life or past experiences can move you from healthy, normal distress to more problematic psychological disturbance. Feelings of depression, anxiety, rage, or guilt, for example, are painful and can lead to further difficulties in your life.

Fortunately, the situation's not all doom and gloom! You can learn to recognize how your thoughts, beliefs, and attitudes impact your feelings. When you understand this principle, you can work on changing your thinking and behavior to help you take bad situations and make them better.

In this chapter, we introduce the main theoretical stuff you need to know about cognitive behavioral therapy (CBT) to get you started.

Understanding the Nuts and Bolts of CBT

As the name implies, CBT is a form of psychotherapy that focuses on *cognition* (thoughts) and *behavior* (actions). One way of summing up CBT is to say, "You feel the way you think." But CBT also looks closely at behavior, because the way you act is often determined by how you feel. Furthermore, the way you act can have either a positive influence or a negative influence on your feelings. Without necessarily realizing it, you may be acting in ways that are actually fueling your bad feelings.

The interaction between thoughts, feelings, and behaviors is at the core of CBT. Therefore, CBT looks closely at how you think and act in order to help you overcome both behavioral and emotional difficulties.

Blinding you with the science of CBT

CBT practitioners are interested not only in helping people *feel* better in the short term but also in using scientifically proven strategies to help people *get* better and stay better in the long term. CBT has been tested and developed through many scientific studies, far more than any other form of psychotherapy. Because of CBT's scientific basis, it invites you to take a more scientific approach to both understanding and resolving your problems.

A big component of CBT involves helping people become their own therapists through the continued practice of specific techniques. This self-directed element is probably one of the reasons people who have had CBT relapse less frequently than those treated using other psychotherapeutic approaches or medications without CBT.

This is a good place to clarify a few terms. Like many professions, psychology and psychotherapy use a lot of jargon. Sometimes in this book we use weird words, and other times we use more everyday words but *weirdly.* The following definitions help to make your reading more straightforward:

- **Cognitive:** Refers to your thoughts, beliefs, memories, images, as well as your focus of attention, problem-solving, and other activities you carry out in your mind.
- **Behavior:** Includes everything that you do and all the things you choose *not* to do, such as avoiding situations or sulking instead of speaking.
- **Therapy:** Describes a method of treating a problem, whether physical, mental, or emotional. We use it mainly to refer to *talking therapies* such as CBT and other types of psychotherapy.
- **Belief:** Refers to your personal thinking styles and your way of understanding the world and your experiences. In CBT, we are interested not only in what you think or believe, but in how strongly you hold a belief (often measured on a scale from 0 to 100 percent).
- **Rules and assumptions:** Your personal rules, codes, and attitudes.
- **Consequence:** The result or outcome of an event of some kind. In this book, we mainly refer to behavior and emotional consequences (basically the kind of results produced by ways of acting or from specific emotions).

- **Emotion:** CBT can help people with emotional problems like anxiety, depression, shame, guilt, disgust, anger, jealousy, and envy.
- **Experiment:** No, we're not talking about test tubes and chemistry. What we mean are exercises that you devise and try out to see what sort of effect they have on your emotional problems.
- **Exposure:** Action on your part to expose yourself to feared or avoided situations in order to help yourself recover from your problems. Note that we're not referring to the kind of exposure that could get you arrested!
- **Healthy:** Refers to appropriate and constructive behavior, thoughts, or emotions.
- **Unhealthy:** Refers to extreme and destructive behavior, thoughts, or emotions.

REMEMBER

It has long been a challenge to find the right language for helpful versus unhelpful thinking. The psychological literature is full of terms like *dysfunctional assumptions, irrational beliefs,* and *negative automatic thoughts.* The purpose of labeling extreme meanings or inflexible thinking about yourself, the world, and others is to help you step back and perhaps consider whether there may be a more helpful alternative perspective or meaning. Choose term you prefer — the purpose is aimed at supporting growth, health, and healing, not judgment.

Linking thinking and feeling

You may generally conclude that if something happens to you, such as your car breaking down, it's the actual event that makes you feel angry or anxious. Makes sense, right? Well, not entirely. According to CBT, what determines the quality and intensity of the emotion you experience are your *thoughts* about the event.

So, although events contribute to your emotional and behavioral reactions (sometimes significantly), the meaning you give to events can greatly influence the way you feel.

REMEMBER

The more negative the event, the more distressed you probably feel. So, if you lose your job, get mugged, or are involved in a serious accident, you're very likely to feel intensely distressed. Intense distressed feelings in response to very negative events are still considered healthy because they're appropriate to the experience. Keeping your thinking and behavior patterns healthy helps you cope with even the most challenging life situations without developing extreme protracted and disturbing emotional problems.

Attaching meaning to events

Positive events normally lead to positive emotions and negative events to negative emotions. But the personal meanings you assign to events in your life sometimes may lead to unhealthy and problematic emotional reactions. Sometimes your thinking can lead you to attach extreme meanings to relatively minor events. For example, you may decide that your partner working late means that they're about to leave you for someone else. Some of the meanings that you give to events may be unrealistic, inaccurate, and fundamentally unhelpful.

When you attach a faulty meaning to an event, you're very likely to experience an unhealthy negative emotion, such as extreme guilt, as Coral does in the following example. However, when Coral attaches a fair and accurate meaning to the event, she experiences the healthy negative emotion of intense disappointment.

We also use the words *distressed* and *disturbed* to refer to healthy and unhealthy negative emotions.

- **Unhealthy:** Inaccurate or rigid ways of thinking about events that lead you to experience extreme unhealthy negative emotions
- **Healthy:** Accurate and balanced ways of thinking about events that lead you to experience appropriate healthy negative emotions

The difference between distress and disturbance is in the *quality* of the emotion you experience. This is an important concept that we go over more fully in Chapter 7:

EXAMPLE

Coral was putting her young children to bed, but they just wouldn't settle down. After several minutes of trying to get them to sleep, she lost her temper, shouted, and threw a stuffed animal across the room. Table 1-1 shows the unhealthy meaning that Coral gave the event.

TABLE 1-1 Coral's Unhealthy Personal Meaning Page

Event:	Losing my temper with my children
Personal meaning:	I should never get that angry around the kids. This means that I'm a terrible mother
Emotion:	Guilt

The extreme meaning Coral attaches to her loss of temper leads her to feel guilty. Guilt is likely to feed further *self-downing* (extreme self-criticism or putting yourself down on the basis of your actions) and is unlikely to help Coral make it up to her kids. Table 1-2 shows a healthier evaluation.

REMEMBER

In Chapter 14, we discuss the healthy alternative to self-downing, which is self-acceptance.

TABLE 1-2 Coral's Healthy Personal Meaning Page

Event:	Losing my temper with my children
Personal meaning:	I wish I hadn't gotten so angry with the kids. This means that I did a bad thing, but I'm still a pretty good mom overall
Emotion:	Disappointment

Because Coral attaches an appropriate and fair meaning to her temper tantrum, she experiences a healthy negative emotion. Disappointment helps Coral to condemn her *behavior* but not *herself* as a mother. She may now look more closely at her beliefs that led her to become so angry in the first place and make some changes.

Take a recent event from your own life in which you got yourself into a unhealthy emotional state. Use the Personal Meaning Page in Worksheet 1-1 to reassign a different meaning to the event and see if you can end up feeling a healthier emotion. Try to think differently about the event. Perhaps the personal meaning you're giving the event is overly negative and extreme. Try taking a more compassionate and objective view of yourself within the context of the negative event.

TIP

You may find it useful to use these questions as a guide to filling out the worksheet:

- What happened? What did you or someone else do? Record this as the event.
- What does the event mean about you? About other people? The world or life conditions? This is your personal meaning.
- How do you feel inside? Record your emotion.
- Is your personal meaning accurate, fair, and balanced? Or is it inaccurate, biased, and rigid?
- In order to be distressed about the event instead of disturbed, what new meaning could you give to the event?

You can use two pages as we did in Coral's case if you want to see a clear distinction between your personal meanings. If you're having trouble coming up with words for your feelings, take a look at Chapter 6, which covers emotions in depth.

WORKSHEET 1-1 My Personal Meaning Page

Event:	
Personal meaning:	
Emotion:	

Checking How CBT Can Work for You

CBT is growing in popularity as an effective treatment for a host of common psychological problems. A lot of research into CBT has focused on its use for the treatment of anxiety and depression in particular, and the results are encouraging. More and more doctors are recommending CBT because research shows that it helps people to stay well longer.

CBT is used to treat a wide range of psychological problems. Chances are, whatever emotional or behavioral problem you're experiencing, this workbook can help get you going in the right direction. Worksheet 1-2 offers a checklist of some of the problems you may experience that CBT can help you to overcome.

REMEMBER

Even if you think that your problems are too severe for a self-help book like this one to be enough, CBT may still work for you. You may benefit most from seeing a therapist who can offer additional support and guidance. Chapter 19 offers lots of advice on working with a therapist.

WORKSHEET 1-2 Problem Clarification Checklist

❑ Anger problems
❑ Anorexia
❑ Binge eating or overeating
❑ Body dysmorphic disorder (BDD)
❑ Bulimia
❑ Chronic fatigue syndrome (CFS)
❑ Chronic pain
❑ Depression
❑ Excessive use of nonprescription drugs and/or alcohol
❑ Feelings of low self-worth
❑ Gambling
❑ Obsessive-compulsive disorder (OCD)
❑ Ongoing feelings of guilt or shame
❑ Panic attacks
❑ Post-traumatic stress disorder (PTSD)
❑ Procrastination
❑ Social anxiety disorder (social phobia)
❑ Specific phobias
❑ Spending excessive amounts of money
❑ Worrying all the time

REMEMBER

Don't be alarmed if you've checked two, three, or more items on the list; problems often overlap. In fact, having more than one problem at a time is the norm, not the exception. An example of problem overlap is depression and anxiety — people frequently experience both at the same time. You can also make yourself feel guilty about your depression or ashamed about your social phobia, depending on what meanings you give to your original problems. CBT calls this overlap of two or more problems a *meta-emotional problem* or a *secondary emotional problem.* Luckily, the strategies that you use to work on your primary problem usually work on your secondary ones, too. So take heart.

Ranking your problems

Taking stock of the areas of your life you want to target for change before you get started can be useful. Your doctor may have given you a diagnosis, or you may not be clear about what your problem actually is.

Putting your problems down on paper can help you see how they may be interacting with each other. Writing them down also gives you a clearer starting point for overcoming them. Sometimes problems don't fall into neat and tidy categories or they overlap somewhat. You can use the Problem Clarification Checklist in Worksheet 1-3 to help you put your finger on your problems.

Consider what problems you have and how they impact on different areas of your life. Work, home life, relationships, physical health, and school are some areas your problems may impact. Review your list and look for any overlapping symptoms. An example of problems overlapping may be decreased ability to concentrate at work due to sleep disturbance.

EXAMPLE

Mike has arthritis and is very rarely pain-free. Some days are better than others, but the pain is getting him down. Lately, Mike has been drinking more in the evening to help him sleep. Table 1-3 shows how Mike ranks his problems.

TABLE 1-3 Mike's Problem Ranking Worksheet

Rank: Problem	Description of Effects
First-ranking problem: Chronic pain from arthritis	Aches in elbows, wrists, and knees. I'm not able to do activities that I used to really enjoy. My sleep is disturbed because pain often wakes me up. My mood is poor.
Second-ranking problem: Depression	I don't feel like seeing friends or spending time with my family. I find housework and daily shopping overwhelming. I spend too much time dwelling on my thoughts and feelings. I drink alcohol to numb my pain and depressed feelings.
Third-ranking problem: Alcohol use	Sometimes a lot of alcohol can help me sleep, but I wake up feeling worse. I don't like the idea of needing to rely on alcohol to cope. I've read that alcohol is a depressant, so I guess it may be worsening my depression.

In Mike's example, you see that his feelings of depression stem from chronic pain but that his use of alcohol is actually making his depression worse. By examining his Problem Ranking Worksheet, Mike can choose to intervene at several points. Now use Worksheet 1-3 to rank your own problems.

WORKSHEET 1-3 My Problem Ranking Worksheet

Rank: Problem	Description of Effects
First-ranking problem:	
Second-ranking problem:	
Third-ranking problem:	

TIP

You may want to continue the worksheet to include a fourth- or fifth-ranking problem. However, be careful not to make things seem worse than they are! Try to stick to ranking your *main* problems and realize that a lot of other feelings you may be having, such as irritation or loneliness, are often problem *effects* (or in CBT terms, *emotional consequences*).

Breaking down your behaviors

Disturbed emotions tend to lead to destructive and self-destructive behaviors. Destructive behavior rarely aids effective problem-solving. On the contrary, it often creates further problems or worsens existing ones. Worksheet 1-4 is yet another checklist to help you identify different types of big, bad, and ugly behaviors that you may sometimes recognize yourself doing.

WORKSHEET 1-4 Checklist of "Bad Behaviors"

Self-destructive behaviors:
❑ Drinking excessively
❑ Eating poorly (too much or too little)
❑ Engaging in high-risk sexual activities
❑ Gambling
❑ Lashing out verbally or physically
❑ Spending money compulsively or recklessly
❑ Sulking
❑ Taking risks when angry (such as driving recklessly)
❑ Using illegal drugs
Mood-lowering behaviors:
❑ Isolating yourself from friends and family
❑ Letting daily chores mount up
❑ Neglecting your hygiene
❑ Not asking others for help or support
❑ Not engaging in activities you usually enjoy
❑ Repeatedly calling in sick at work
❑ Sleeping too much or too little
❑ Staying in bed all day
❑ Staying indoors most of the time
❑ Stopping taking your medication
Avoidance behaviors:
❑ Avoiding exercise
❑ Doing other unrelated tasks rather than doing what actually needs to be done (such as tidying your desk rather than writing an essay)
❑ Engaging in superstitious behavior in an attempt to ward off feared events
❑ Not answering the phone
❑ Not opening the mail (such as bills)
❑ Not speaking much in social gatherings
❑ Putting off tasks
❑ Staying away from situations that you find threatening (elevators, busy places, parties, and so on)
❑ Using rituals to help quell anxious thoughts and feelings

Because they're human, many people exhibit some of the types of behaviors in this list from time to time. However, these types of behavior are very frequently linked to psychological problems. The more items you've checked off, the more probable it is that you're experiencing emotional disturbance. In turn, your "bad" behaviors are almost certainly making things worse.

EXAMPLE

Stevie has social phobia and feels very anxious in social settings. Table 1-4 shows Stevie's top five unhelpful behaviors.

TABLE 1-4 Stevie's Top Five "Unhealthy Behaviors"

1. Keeping quiet in social settings until I'm absolutely certain what I want to say
2. Avoiding going to parties where I don't know everybody
3. Eating lunch on my own at work
4. Spending too much time indoors
5. Only going to the mall during quiet periods

Stevie's big five fall under the Avoidance Behaviors category on the checklist in Worksheet 1-4. She may feel better in the short term because she's trying so hard to avoid situations in which she feels anxious. In the long term, however, Stevie is keeping her anxiety alive because she doesn't give herself the chance to discover that she can survive social awkwardness.

The big checklist of bad behaviors in Worksheet 1-4 can serve as a guideline for identifying your top five behaviors that may be perpetuating your problems. We offer space to identify your own bad behaviors in Worksheet 1-5.

WORKSHEET 1-5 My Top Five Unhealthy Behaviors

1.

2.

3.

4.

5.

Connecting Emotion, Thinking, and Behavior

To put together everything from this chapter, start by selecting an emotion to investigate. This is your target emotion. In Tables 1-5 and 1-6 Margot chose depression as her target emotion and Tom selected anxiety. You get to choose your target emotion in Worksheet 1-6.

Next consider how your target emotion is affecting your thoughts. Margot's depression-based thinking includes ideas that socializing is pointless and she puts herself down for being a "Debbie Downer." Tom's anxiety-based thinking leads him to conclude that he's helpless in the face of his fears and unable to cope with the discomfort of anxiety.

Now examine how your target emotion and feeling-based thinking are leading you to act. Think about what your target emotion makes you feel like doing. You can include past, present, or even potential future actions. Margot's depressed thoughts lead her to isolate herself, and Tom's anxious thinking tells him to continue avoiding public transport.

Finally, examine how your feeling-based behavior is effecting your target emotion. By isolating herself from her friends, Margot actually makes her depression worse. Tom eases his anxiety in the short term by refusing to get on the bus, but his avoidance makes him even more fearful of using public transport.

TABLE 1-5 Margot's Behavior Effect Analysis

Target emotion:	Depression
Feeling-based thinking:	Going to see a film with my friends is pointless. I don't enjoy socializing anymore, and nobody wants to be around a Debbie Downer like me anyway.
Feeling-based behavior:	Declining invitation to go to see a movie. Staying indoors and avoiding phone calls from friends.
Effect of behavior on target emotion:	I end up lonely and isolated. I give myself a hard time for neglecting my friends. I seem to end up feeling even more depressed.

TABLE 1-6 Tom's Behavior Effect Analysis

Target emotion:	Anxiety
Feeling-based thinking:	Using public transport is too uncomfortable and scary. I'll only panic if I try to use the subway. It's just too painful to even try going on the bus.
Feeling-based behavior:	Walking instead of using public transport. Only going to places I can drive to.
Effect of behavior on target emotion:	The longer I avoid going on subways and buses, the more anxious I feel about it. Lately, I feel anxious if I even go near a subway station or bus stop. Ultimately, I feel my anxiety increasing.

After completing your own Behavior Effect Analysis, you may realize that some of your actions are perpetuating your problems, even though they seem to make sense based on your feelings. We look more closely at this concept (and ways to overcome it!) in Chapters 7, 9, and 10.

WORKSHEET 1-6 My Behavior Effect Analysis

Target emotion:	
Feeling-based thinking:	
Feeling-based behavior:	
Effect of behavior on target emotion:	

Picturing Your Problems as a Simple A-B-C

By this stage you can see that:

- Your thoughts, beliefs, personal meanings, and behavior affect how you feel.
- Your feelings affect how you behave.

Also note that your emotional state can further affect how you think and how you view the world around you. For example, if you're depressed, you tend to have more depressed thoughts and the world may seem bleak, dangerous, and joyless. You may notice bad things in the news and focus much more on negative aspects of your own life. If you're not depressed, the world looks much brighter, even though very little in your personal circumstances has actually changed.

The diagram in Figure 1-1 shows how life events, thoughts, emotions, and behaviors interact and potentially influence one another. We include this figure here as a visual recap of what we've introduced in this chapter. In the figure:

- **Events** include all your past and present experiences, as well as things that may happen in the future. Events can be global or personal or involve other people in your life.
- **Thoughts** include anything that goes on in your mind. Philosophies you live by, personal standards and morals, as well as the way you think about yourself, others, and the world all fall into the *Thoughts* category.
- **Emotions** include feelings of anger, guilt, sadness, and so on. In Chapter 6, we show you the difference between functional distressed feelings and unhelpful disturbed feelings.
- **Behavior** basically includes anything that you do. Your actions and deliberate inaction are both types of behavior. As with emotions, it's possible to have both constructive and destructive behavioral responses to events.

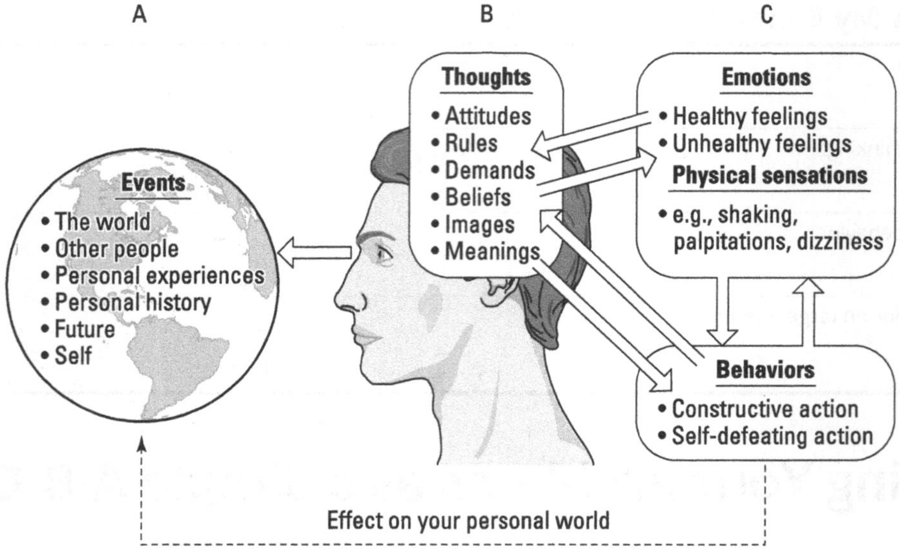

FIGURE 1-1: A visual reminder that how you interpret the world affects your thoughts, feelings, and behavior, which affect how you interpret the world.

TIP

The A-B-C format is the main method CBT uses to formulate or chart problems. We go into the A-B-C format in much more detail in Chapter 3, but Table 1-7 shows basically how it works.

TABLE 1-7 Simple A-B-C Chart

A (Activating Event)	B (Belief/Thought)	C (Emotional and Behavioral Consequences)
Failing an important test	I'm a total idiot for failing.	Emotional: Depression
	I should not have failed!	Behavioral: Decide that retaking the exam is pointless

In essence, the Simple A-B-C Chart is very similar to Worksheet 1-1. However, Worksheet 1-7 shows the format you most often see used in CBT books like this one.

REMEMBER

One of the key benefits of the ABC sequence is that can serve as a reminder that how you feel about experiences is influenced by the meaning you bring to them. Practicing your ABCs can help you identify these meanings and work on changing them if they're unhelpful.

WORKSHEET 1-7 My Simple A-B-C Chart

A (Activating Event)	B (Belief/Thought)	C (Emotional and Behavioral Consequences)
		Emotional:
		Behavioral:

IN THIS CHAPTER

» Making thinking mistakes and thinking corrections

» Getting intimate with your thinking errors

Chapter 2 Recognizing Problematic Thinking Patterns

We all jump to conclusions, make a crisis out of nothing, or take events personally from time to time. Thinking in unhelpful ways is a pretty normal human thing to do. In fact, thinking errors are *so* common that clinicians and researchers have been able to sort them into clear categories. But *common* doesn't mean "harmless." As we discuss in Chapter 1, the way you think has a definite impact on how you end up feeling. So, if you often think in unhealthy ways, you're more likely to experience emotional problems. A central technique of cognitive behavioral therapy (CBT) is helping you recognize more readily when you're thinking in a skewed way. In this chapter, we help you do just that, as well as show you ways to question and readjust your thinking.

Coming to Grips with Common Thinking Errors

In this section, we outline some of the most common thinking mistakes human beings tend to make. You probably don't regularly make all of these thinking errors, but to help you better understand them, we invite you to imagine thinking in the ways described in the examples here. If you identify with a particular thinking error, you'll probably benefit from doing the corresponding worksheet. So, there's no need for you to complete *every* worksheet unless you think it applies to you.

Catastrophizing

Catastrophizing is when you take a relatively minor event and imagine all sorts of terrors and nightmare scenarios resulting from it. Another way of describing this thinking error is "making a mountain out of a molehill."

EXAMPLE

Imagine that you say something to offend your future mother-in-law. From this, you conclude that she'll turn your fiancé against you, the wedding will be off, your parents will be mortified, and nobody will ever want to go out with you again.

You can use the set of questions in Worksheet 2-1 to view your catastrophic thoughts more critically.

WORKSHEET 2-1 De-catastrophizing Your Thoughts

What, if any, hard evidence supports my conclusions?	
What, if any, hard evidence disproves my conclusions?	
Can I adopt a more accurate perspective on the event?	
What are some less terrible conclusions I can make about the event?	
What practical steps can I take to deal with the situation?	

WARNING

For some problems, such as obsessive-compulsive disorder (OCD), getting stuck in challenging catastrophic thoughts can be part of the problem. So, if you have an obsessional or "worry" type of problem, it can be worth switching to focusing on tolerating uncertainty more, and letting catastrophic thoughts pass without engaging with them.

All-or-nothing thinking

All-or-nothing thinking — also called *black-or-white thinking* — involves assuming that a situation is either entirely good or entirely bad, leaving no in-between or gray areas.

EXAMPLE

Say you went to a job interview and answered one question poorly. If you're thinking in an all-or-nothing manner, you may decide that the entire interview was a complete waste based on your one hiccup.

Find a point between the extremes by asking yourself the questions in Worksheet 2-2.

WORKSHEET 2-2 Thinking between Extremes

Am I focusing on only one aspect of the overall event?	
Am I giving one aspect of the event too much importance?	
What is a fair and accurate rating to give this aspect of the event on a scale of one to ten?	
What are some other aspects of the event that can help me to view things more realistically?	
Taking all aspects of the event into account, what is a more balanced rating to give the event?	

Making demands

Making demands is a *big* thinking error. Albert Ellis, who founded one of the very first cognitive behavioral therapies, puts an individual's demands at the very core of emotional and psychological problems.

When you *make demands*, you're expecting yourself, others, and the world to follow your rules and never break them. We all hold attitudes, values, standards, ideals, and beliefs about how the world and everyone in it ideally should act. And holding those opinions is fine as long as we can be flexible and allow room for error and deviation. But if you start *demanding* that everyone follow your rules, you'll be emotionally disturbed when things don't go your way.

EXAMPLE

Imagine that you *prefer* to be treated politely. So, you tell yourself something like, "I want to be treated politely, but I don't absolutely *have* to be treated this way. I can stand a bit of impolite behavior." Now imagine that you turn this *preference* into a *demand*. So, you tell yourself something like, "I must be treated politely, and I can't stand it if I am not!" Can you see how the *preference* allows you to deal with impolite behavior from others without leading to unhealthy anger? Can you see how the *demand* may give rise to unhealthy anger and other negative emotions?

Make your life better by being more flexible in your thinking; Worksheet 2-3 shows you how.

WORKSHEET 2-3 **Thinking Flexibly**

What kind of language am I using in my head? Am I using terms such as *must* or *have to?*	
Do I accept that other people have their own rules and use their own free will?	
Is it possible for me to have my own standards but to *also* allow myself and others to fall short of these standards?	
Is my demand realistic?	
Is my demand ultimately helping me?	
How can I keep my standards and ideals but turn my demands into *preferences?*	

Fortune-telling

With *fortune-telling,* you make predictions about the future and firmly believe that your prophetic visions are correct. The trouble is that many of your predictions are likely to be negative and may stop you from taking goal-directed action.

EXAMPLE

Say you want to approach your boss for a pay raise, but you predict that he'll say "no" and be unpleasant about it. If you listen to your fortune-telling thoughts, you may never take your chances and ask!

Challenge your predictions for the future by submitting them to some empirical tests and answering the questions in Worksheet 2-4.

Mind reading

Oh, how we do love to guess what others are thinking! But, when you *mind-read,* you often assume that others are thinking in judgmental and disapproving ways about you. These assumptions can lead to all sorts of difficulties, such as social anxiety and relationship ruptures.

EXAMPLE

Imagine that you go to a party with a friend and you don't know anyone there. Some people talk to you but then move on to talk to other people they seem to know. You're on your own for a time and notice other people glancing at you. You assume that they're thinking, "Who is *she?* Who invited *her?* What in the world is *she* doing here?"

Try questioning your mind-reading before letting your thoughts run riot; Worksheet 2-5 can help.

WORKSHEET 2-4 **Avoiding Fortune-Telling**

My prediction:	
What might be an alternative prediction?	
How can I test out my prediction?	
What can I gain by risking taking action despite my negative prediction?	
What events from my past may be influencing the way I expect this future event to unfold?	
What action can I take to help myself adjust to a poor outcome? What steps can I take to try to resolve potential problems?	

WORKSHEET 2-5 **Resisting Mind Reading**

What are some alternative explanations to my assumptions?	
Is it possible that my mind reading may be wrong?	
What can I do to test out my mind reading and gather more information?	

Emotional reasoning

Emotional reasoning **is when you decide that your strong feelings are a true reflection of what is actually going on in reality. Because you *feel* a certain way, you decide that your feelings must be correct. You may then fail to take in other information that contradicts your feelings.**

EXAMPLE

Say you feel very jealous of your partner's attention to another person. Because you *feel* so jealous, you may assume that your partner is having an affair. Or if you wake up in the morning *feeling* very anxious, you may assume that there must be something to be afraid of and look for a reason to be worried.

If emotional reasoning is one of your personal thinking errors, practice looking beyond your feelings. Consciously and deliberately put your feelings to one side and use your observation skills to take in the reality of the situation. Your feelings are more likely to reflect your thoughts about what an event *means* to you than to reliably describe what is *actually* going on. Separate fact from feeling by being more skeptical; using Worksheet 2-6 can help.

WORKSHEET 2-6 Favoring Facts over Feelings

What is the event or situation?	
What emotion am I experiencing?	
How might my feelings be leading me to distort the facts?	
What facts may I be ignoring because of my strong feelings?	
If I give myself time for my feelings to subside *before* drawing conclusions, how do I view the situation when I'm feeling calmer?	

Over-generalizing

Do you find yourself thinking in terms of "never" or "always," As in, "Things *never* go my way" or "I *always* screw up important meetings"? Or perhaps you think in global terms like "People can't be trusted" or "The world is unfair." Or maybe you conclude that you're a totally bad parent, partner, employee, or whatever based on one or more of your actions. If so, you're probably *over-generalizing* and making widespread judgments about yourself, others, or the world on the strength of one or two particular features.

This tendency is also called *making the part/hole error* — that is, you judge the whole on the basis of one or more of its parts. Doing so can lead you to make some pretty rash and harsh judgments and to hold a pretty unforgiving attitude.

It's easy to allow a few bad things to cloud your judgment about an overall event or situation. Instead of deciding that something is all bad because of a few hiccups, try reminding yourself to keep the good stuff in sight.

EXAMPLE

Imagine you've recently started a new job. On your third day at work, your boss presents you with a list of objectives, some of which you think are a bit unrealistic. You try to run the list past a few of your colleagues for some feedback, but they're all too busy to talk. You find yourself thinking that you *always* end up with totally unreasonable bosses, the job is *terrible*, and *everyone* you work with is unsupportive. You *never* get the good jobs.

Sort out overgeneralizing by being highly specific about the negative aspects of a particular situation, as Worksheet 2-7 helps demonstrate.

WORKSHEET 2-7 Specific Thinking

What is the *specific* thing I'm basing my judgments on?	
Am I making a *total* judgment of myself, others, or a situation based on this one *specific* aspect?	
What other aspects of myself, others, or the situation am I ignoring?	
Can I suspend *total* judgment and instead judge only the *specific* aspect of myself, others, or the situation?	
How might I benefit from being more specific in my judgments?	

Labeling and rating

So, you call yourself, other people, and the world nasty names, do you? Well, you're in the *labeling and rating* club — and it's an ugly place to be. If you call yourself "useless" every time you screw up, or the world "cruel" every time it deals you a blow, or others "no good" when you're treated impolitely, then you're in danger of feeling a lot of really toxic emotions.

EXAMPLE

Say your friend has recently lost their dad. You don't go to visit her on Friday night because you have prior plans. When you next speak to her, she sounds very low and a bit annoyed with you for not visiting. You then label yourself a totally selfish person and a bad friend because you didn't put your friend's needs first on Friday night.

Try giving up the rating game. Use the questions in Worksheet 2-8 to see yourself and others as more complex than your labels may suggest.

WORKSHEET 2-8 Resisting the Urge to Rate

What is a label I apply to myself or others?	
Am I being fair when I apply this label?	
Am I allowing for varying degrees of goodness or badness in myself, others, or the world?	
What are some other more complex aspects of this person, me, or the situation that I may be overlooking when I apply a label?	
Is it possible for me to label the *specific action* or *event* instead of the whole person, myself, or the world?	

Mental filtering

With *mental filtering*, you let through only the information that fits with what you already believe about yourself, others, or the world. So, if you think of yourself as a failure, you process only information that points to your failing; if you believe that your boss is an ass, you see only evidence that supports that view; and if you think the world is unsafe, you acknowledge only the scary and dangerous news about the world. This filtering process can lead you to have a very biased and negative view of yourself and your environment.

EXAMPLE

Pretend for a moment that you believe that the world is a dangerous and unpleasant place. You pick up the newspaper and focus on the situation in the Middle East, terrorist attacks, and shootings in your city. You fail to take in articles about successful recycling initiatives, crime reduction in major cities, and elderly people being entertained by youth groups.

Tackle this thinking error by letting in additional information that contradicts your viewpoint; Worksheet 2-9 helps you organize your thoughts.

WORKSHEET 2-9 Thinking without Filters

What is my particular filter?	
What information is my filter stopping me from considering?	
How might I think and behave if I were to remove my filter?	

Disqualifying the positive

Disqualifying the positive is very similar to mental filtering. Imagine, for example, that you believe that you're unlikable and socially unacceptable. Your mental filter lets you notice only information that supports your negative self-opinion. If any positive information manages to sneak through your filter, you quickly discredit or disqualify it and throw it back out.

EXAMPLE

Say you believe you're fundamentally unlikable. Someone asks you to go for a drink after work. Instead of seeing the invitation as evidence *against* your idea that you're unlikable, you may think that they're asking you only because nobody else was available or because they feel sorry for you.

The questions in Worksheet 2-10 help you counteract this thinking bias by deliberately and consistently gathering positive data.

WORKSHEET 2-10 Thinking Positively

How do I respond to positive cues from others and my environment?	
Do I acknowledge positive feedback and respond to it?	
What positive information and experiences can I write down? (I can look at my positive data log when I find myself thinking negatively.)	
How can I practice taking a compliment graciously?	
How will acknowledging positive information from others help me?	

Having low frustration tolerance

Having *low frustration tolerance* (LFT) is about deciding that *uncomfortable* equals *unbearable.* Basically, if you have LFT, you're likely to give up striving toward your goals whenever the going gets too tough or painful. The point is to build up your tolerance to discomfort (such as anxiety) when it will help you to push through and overcome or cope better with a problem.

REMEMBER

The adage that anything worth having requires effort and is worth the blood, sweat, and tears really does hold true. A lot of good things in life don't come easily.

EXAMPLE

Imagine you want to improve your health by losing a few pounds and getting fit through exercise. But as soon as you're offered a cream cake, you tell yourself that resisting it is too painful and the deprivation is unbearable. You go to the gym, but as soon as your muscles begin to ache, you decide that you just can't take the discomfort and exercise is too much like hard work, so you go home, order a pizza, and veg out in front of the TV.

Overcome LFT by challenging your attitude toward discomfort and fostering high frustration tolerance; Worksheet 2-11 offers some questions to ask yourself.

WORKSHEET 2-11 Heightening Your Frustration Tolerance

Is what I'm experiencing really intolerable and unbearable? Or is it actually difficult to tolerate but tolerable?	
Is what I'm experiencing really just difficult to tolerate or to bear?	
What are some of the reasons that make bearing this discomfort worthwhile?	
What evidence exists to support the idea that I can tolerate this discomfort?	
What other things worth doing can I push myself to do, even if they're uncomfortable or unpleasant?	

Personalizing

Personalizing involves taking random events and making them personal. If you personalize, you tend to make everything that happens around you *about* you, even if reality indicates otherwise. This tendency can lead you to assume inappropriate responsibility for events and/or to feel unhealthy emotions in response to events that have little or nothing to do with you.

EXAMPLE

Say you plan a barbeque and invite your neighbors. Unfortunately, a freak thunderstorm rolls in just as the burgers are on the grill. Several people rush home because their clothes are soaking wet. One couple starts arguing. In the end, the remaining guests and your family sit down to potato salad in your kitchen while the barbeque pit outside gently smolders. You think that the weather is out to get you, the guests are holding you to blame for their ruined outfits, and clearly your awful barbeque has resulted in the impending divorce of the arguing couple.

Worksheet 2-12 demonstrates that you can remove yourself from the center of the universe and take things less personally by challenging your thoughts.

WORKSHEET 2-12 Thinking More Objectively

What else has contributed to the outcome of the situation other than you?	
Are you taking personal responsibility for things that are not within your control?	
What are some additional reasons that may account for the way people around you are responding?	
Are you really the only person affected by specific events and conditions, or are others affected, too?	
Is what has happened really all about you?	

Listing Your Personal Favorites

All humans occasionally think erroneously. Chances are, you make some thinking mistakes more often than others. If you make a list of the errors described in this chapter that you tend to make most, you can increase your chances of catching yourself in the act. The sooner you notice faulty thinking, the sooner you can strive to correct it. Use Worksheet 2-13 to list your main thinking errors.

WORKSHEET 2-13 My Main Thinking Errors

Knowing Where and When You Think Your Way to Trouble

After looking at the main thinking errors and listing the ones that you tend to make the most often, you can use the examples in Tables 2-1 and 2-2 to fill out Worksheets 2-14 and 2-15 in order to chart and correct those thinking errors.

You'll find that certain situations give rise to your thinking errors. We call these *triggers*. Coming to grips with your personal triggers and your problematic thinking patterns can help you to readjust your thinking and increase your chances of feeling healthy negative emotions.

EXAMPLE

Martha is nominated for employee of the month. She's delighted about the nomination, but it turns out that another worker, Spencer, actually wins the award. Martha gets very unhealthily sad/depressed about not winning. She tells herself that she's a useless employee. She decides that her boss obviously thinks she's inadequate, and she feels hurt that all her hard work was for nothing.

Martha pinpoints four thinking errors she was making about the event of failing to win the work award. She challenges her thinking and changes her unhealthy sadness/depression and hurt to healthy sadness and disappointment. You may not always be making as many thinking errors as Martha did. Sometimes you'll be able to spot only one thinking error. The important thing is to use the worksheets to help you think in a more helpful and balanced way so you can avoid emotional disturbance and act in your own best interests!

TABLE 2-1 Martha's Thought Record

Situation/Event (What happened? When? Where? Who else was involved?)	My Thoughts (What went through your mind at the time?)	Outcome (What was your feeling/emotion? What did you do?)
Spencer won the award instead of me. It happened Friday at work. My boss and supervisor decided who would win the award.	I have to win, or it means I'm not a good worker. My boss and supervisor think I'm bad at my job. I never get recognized for hard work.	I felt depressed and hurt. I pretended to be okay, but I didn't go out to celebrate with Spencer.

WORKSHEET 2-14 My Thought Record

Situation/Event (What happened? When? Where? Who else was involved?)	My Thoughts (What went through your mind at the time?)	Outcome (What was your feeling/emotion? What did you do?)

TABLE 2-2 Martha's Thought Correction Sheet

Thinking Error (List the types of thinking errors you made.)	Thinking Corrections (Record an alternative way of thinking for each error.)	New Outcome (How will you feel and act differently after correcting your thinking?)
Demand making	I was demanding that I win the award, not preferring to win but realizing that winning isn't essential. I can still be a good worker without winning the award.	I still feel sad about losing to Spencer, but not depressed.
All-or-nothing thinking	I decided that the situation was awful on the basis that I didn't win. But it was actually a fun work event, and I could've enjoyed the celebrations even though I lost to Spencer.	I recognize that my work is good and is appreciated by my bosses.
Disqualifying the positive	I ignored the fact that I was nominated in the first place, and this is evidence that my work is adequate.	I feel both disappointed about losing and pleased about being nominated.
Overgeneralizing	It obviously isn't true that I never get recognized for hard work because I was nominated, even if I didn't win.	I will be able to go out next Friday with my friends from work and feel okay.
		I will call Spencer and congratulate him.

WORKSHEET 2-15 My Thought Correction Sheet

Thinking Error (List the types of thinking errors you made.)	Thinking Corrections (Record an alternative way of thinking for each error.)	New Outcome (How will you feel and act differently after correcting your thinking?)

IN THIS CHAPTER

» **Tying negative thoughts to feelings**

» **Using A-B-C forms to target and tackle toxic thoughts**

» **Choosing helpful homework**

Chapter 3
Tackling Toxic Thinking

When you think in more balanced and constructive ways, you reduce emotional and behavioral problems. The way you think about specific events in your life, and the meaning you give to these events, determines how you feel and act in response to them.

This chapter helps you link your thinking to your emotions and behaviors. We introduce you to negative automatic thoughts and show you how to catch yourself thinking in unhelpful ways. A-B-C forms help you break down your problems and change unhealthy thinking in order to change how you feel for the better.

Noticing Your Negative Thinking

Negative automatic thoughts (NATs) are thoughts that seem to just pop into your head without warning or welcome. That's why we refer to these thoughts as "automatic." Frequently, NATs are extreme, distorted, and unhelpful ways of interpreting an event or situation, which is why we refer to them as "negative." NATs can also be examples of common thinking errors. (See Chapter 2 for more on the different types of thinking errors.) However, NATs don't always take the form of typical thinking errors, which means they can be harder to spot. Most people don't notice their negative automatic ways of thinking in response to negative situations. If you do happen to notice your NATs, you may not question the truth and usefulness of them very often.

Noticing your NATs can increase your chances of managing your emotions by allowing you to correct any unhelpful thoughts you may be having about an event. NATs are shortened versions of your beliefs, and noticing them helps you better understand how your beliefs are leading to specific emotions about a given situation. The A-B-C form we introduce later in this chapter helps you change unhelpful beliefs and NATs in order to overcome your emotional problems.

REMEMBER

According to cognitive behavioral therapy (CBT), an event doesn't directly or solely *cause* you to experience an emotion. Instead, the *meaning* that you assign to the event (your thoughts, beliefs, and attitudes about what happened) determines how you ultimately end up feeling and behaving.

The NAT form helps you identify a *trigger situation* (an event that triggers your NATs and leads you to experience a particular negative emotion). It also gives you a chance to record your NATs and link them to how you ended up feeling in the trigger situation.

REMEMBER

A *trigger* can be an actual event, a memory, an image, a past event, a future event, a physical sensation, or your emotions and behaviors.

EXAMPLE

Nick is pretty shy. In fact, you might even say that he's a little socially anxious. He doesn't like to draw attention to himself in public or social situations and often worries about looking foolish. Nick arrives at a bar to meet a few close friends. On his way in, he trips on the doormat and nearly falls over. Table 3-1 shows how Nick used the NAT form.

TABLE 3-1 Nick's NAT Form

NAT Form Questions	Nick's Answers
What was the trigger?	I tripped over at the door of a crowded bar when I was going to meet some friends. A lot of people noticed and a few asked if I was okay.
What were your negative automatic thoughts?	Oh, crap. Everybody saw me trip and they're going to laugh at me. This is just typical of me. I'm such a clumsy idiot. I can't stand the feeling of all these people looking at me and judging me. The whole evening is screwed now. I'll never be able to relax in here after being so clumsy.
What emotions did you experience?	I felt super self-conscious and anxious.

EXAMPLE

Natasha's mother died of a terminal illness two years ago. Unfortunately, her death was sudden and Natasha didn't get a chance to say goodbye. Natasha and her mother argued a few days before her death, so Natasha didn't visit her mother on the day she died. One night Natasha was watching TV and was reminded of her mother by a scene involving a son sitting by his father on his deathbed. Natasha used the NAT form in Table 3-2 to write down her negative automatic thoughts.

TABLE 3-2 Natasha's NAT Form

NAT Form Questions	Natasha's Answers
What was the trigger?	A scene on TV of a father on his deathbed, with his son looking after him. I had a strong memory of arguing with my mom just a few days before she died.
What were your negative automatic thoughts?	I absolutely should not have had an argument with Mom when she was ill. I should have visited her the day she died. I'm a bad daughter and a selfish, horrible person for treating my mom so poorly.
What emotion did you experience?	I felt guilty.

You can see from these two examples that by stopping to think about and record NATs, both Nick and Natasha are more likely to link their thoughts to their extreme and unhelpful emotions.

REMEMBER Triggers aren't limited to actual events that occur in the outside world. They also include internal events, such as dreams, heart palpitations, or feelings like depression. Notice that Nick's troublesome thoughts are triggered by an *actual* event (tripping on a doormat), whereas Natasha's toxic thinking is triggered by an *internal* event (the *memory* of arguing with her mother and being unable to make up before she died).

Try using the NAT form in Worksheet 3-1 to note your immediate thoughts in response to a trigger event. You can also use the form to make sense of a recent or past event when you experienced an extreme negative emotion. Picture the scene in your mind and try to remember how you felt and thought at the time.

If you're having difficulty describing and naming your feelings, turn to Chapter 6, which explains more about healthy and unhealthy emotions.

WORKSHEET 3-1 **My NAT Form**

NAT Form Questions	Your Answers
What was the trigger?	
What were your negative automatic thoughts?	
What emotions did you experience?	

Being Skeptical about Your Negative Automatic Thoughts

Unhealthy thinking very often leads to unhealthy negative emotions, such as depression, guilt, or rage. In other words, thinking distortion leads to emotional disturbance, or thinking badly leads to feeling badly. Additionally, NATs distort the facts, impede problem-solving, and are very often just plain wrong. So, don't believe everything you think! Instead, we encourage you to review your thoughts, put them through a battery of tests (or at least one test!) and decide whether they're fair and accurate reflections of reality. You can formulate a healthier way of thinking if you discover that your NATs are causing you emotional and behavioral problems.

When you think in rigid and extreme ways, you don't leave any room for human error. So, if you believe, for example, that you must not fail at important tasks, you deny the possibility that you may fail at an important task despite your *desire* not to do so. You'll also be very depressed if you *do* fail. A more flexible and balanced way of thinking is to say, "I really don't *want* to fail at important tasks, but the reality exists that I *might* fail." This attitude encourages you to meet your desire to succeed but also allows you to accept the possibility of failing. If you do fail, you're likely to feel appropriately sad instead of depressed.

Chapter 6 is all about healthy and unhealthy negative emotions. Unhealthy feelings like depression stem from rigid and unbalanced thoughts and beliefs. These types of feelings tend to lead to destructive behaviors like avoidance and giving up. Healthy negative emotions like sadness are still uncomfortable, but they tend to lead to constructive behaviors like confronting problems and trying to solve them.

TIP

When deciding whether your thought is true and accurate, ask yourself the following questions:

- Does my thought leave room for error, or does it demand that I always meet certain criteria at all times?
- Does my thought reflect what can actually happen in reality or does it deny reality?
- Would I encourage someone I care about to view the situation this way?
- Does my thought fairly and accurately sum up the situation or is it biased against me?

Have a look at Natasha's cognition correction quiz in Table 3-3, in which she corrects her answers to the NAT form in Table 3-2.

TABLE 3-3 Natasha's Cognition Correction Quiz

My negative automatic thought:	I absolutely should not have had an argument with Mom when she was ill. I should have visited her the day she died. I'm a bad daughter and a selfish, horrible person for treating my mom so poorly.
Can I prove that my thought is true?	Well, it's true that I argued with Mom, but I can't prove that I absolutely shouldn't have. I suppose that if I insist that I shouldn't have argued with Mom, then I'm sort of denying reality. It is true that arguing with a dying person is sort of selfish, but I suppose it isn't true that I'm a totally horrible and selfish person just because of this one act.
Is my thought extreme/rigid or balanced/flexible?	My thought is pretty extreme/rigid because I'm putting a demand on myself to have made up with my mom before she died. I'm also being quite extreme in deciding that I'm horrible and selfish.
Is my thought leading to healthy feelings and behaviors?	I feel really guilty and I keep replaying Mom's last few days in my mind and berating myself. When I feel this guilty, I avoid visiting her grave and I avoid phone calls from my dad because he usually mentions her.
How am I likely to feel and act if I continue thinking in this way?	I'll probably go on feeling guilty about Mom, and I may even get depressed. My guilt means that I avoid people who could offer support. I also spend a lot of time focusing on how bad I feel about not making up with Mom rather than remembering the rest of her life. I don't think I'll allow myself to grieve for Mom properly if I keep thinking in this way.
Would I encourage a friend to think in this way?	No, I wouldn't. I'd try to help a friend to be more compassionate and forgiving with herself.

What evidence can I find against my thought?	Mum was very irritable toward the end of her life, and I suppose she had some responsibility for the argument, too. I did a lot for Mom during her illness and I spent a lot of time with her. I do lots of things for other people in my life, so I suppose that shows that I'm not that horrible and selfish a person. Mom died suddenly, and I had no way of knowing that our argument would be the last time I would see her.
How would I need to change my thought in order to feel better and act more constructively?	I would need to accept that I did argue with Mom just before she died and forgive myself for doing so.
How would thinking in a more balanced/flexible way help me?	Well, I certainly would feel better. I might be able to feel sad about Mom's death without beating myself up so much. I could be more comfortable about spending time with Dad. Maybe I would be able to focus on other things instead of ruminating on Mom's death every time something reminds me of it.
My healthy new thought:	I wish I hadn't argued with Mom before she died, but I did. Arguing with her was unfortunate, and I may have behaved selfishly, but it doesn't make me a horrible daughter.

Try using the cognition correction quiz in Worksheet 3-2 to challenge and change your NATs.

You can look at your NAT form in Worksheet 3-1 again to remind yourself of the negative automatic thoughts you identified. Use the cognition correction quiz in Worksheet 3-2 as many times as you need to until you've challenged all your unhelpful thoughts related to your trigger.

TIP

Turn to Chapter 2 for a comprehensive list of thinking errors and specific questions you can use to challenge each different type of thinking error.

WORKSHEET 3-2 My Cognition Correction Quiz

My negative automatic thought:	
Can I prove that my thought is true?	
Is my thought extreme/rigid or balanced/flexible?	
Is my thought leading to healthy feelings and behaviors?	
How am I likely to feel and act if I continue thinking in this way?	
Would I encourage a friend to think in this way?	
What evidence can I find against my thought?	

(continued)

WORKSHEET 3-2 ***(continued)***

How would I need to change my thought in order to feel better and act more constructively?	
How would thinking in a more balanced/flexible way help me?	
My healthy new thought:	

Working with A-B-C Forms

The A-B-C Form is probably the tool most commonly used by CBT therapists. We've devised two versions of this useful form:

- Form 1 helps you to record trigger events, as well as your thoughts, feelings, and behaviors.
- With Form 2, you can challenge and correct your unhelpful thinking. Using A-B-C Forms can really help you to break down a problem situation. The form can help you identify your thoughts and beliefs that are leading you to feel unhealthy negative emotions and behave in nonconstructive ways.

WARNING

You may encounter many different versions of the A-B-C form, and they may have a different name, like *dysfunctional thought record.* We do our best to provide you with a simple and user-friendly version of the form here. But other versions of the form are okay, too. If you've read other CBT books or been shown a similar form by a CBT therapist, just remember that the same stuff applies to any type of A-B-C form. You can use whatever version of the form you find the most useful.

Filling out Form 1

A-B-C Form 1 helps you see the problem — namely, an activating event or trigger — and your resulting problematic thoughts, feelings, and behaviors. You may want to take note of the following explanations before you start. In A-B-C Form 1:

- **A** is for **activating events,** or triggers, which are situations past, present, or future that trigger your thoughts and beliefs.
- **B** stands for **belief** and represents your thoughts and beliefs. These include the meanings you attach to your trigger and how you think about yourself in relation to the trigger. Your belief determines how you ultimately feel and act in response to your trigger.
- **C** is for **consequences** of your behaviors and emotions. They're what you do and feel in response to your trigger (A) *because* of your thoughts and beliefs (B).

EXAMPLE

Table 3-4 shows Natasha's completed A-B-C Form 1, in which she recorded her activating event, wrote down how she felt and what she did based on those feelings, and identified her negative thoughts.

Because people tend to notice their emotions more readily than the thoughts that produce them, you may find it easier to record your feelings and behaviors (C) prior to recording you thoughts and beliefs (B). For that reason, the A-B-C worksheets ask you to describe consequences (C) before your beliefs (B).

TABLE 3-4 **Natasha's A-B-Cs Catching Up with Her**

Date ___________

Activating Event/Trigger	**Beliefs/Thoughts**	**Thinking Error**
TV programme reminded me of arguing with mum just before she died.	I absolutely should not have argued with mum just before she died and I'm a horrible and selfish daughter/person for doing so.	Demand making Labelling Over-generalising
Consequences		
- I felt guilty and kept replaying our argument in my mind - I avoided answering dad's phone calls in case he mentioned something about mum.		

Use the information you've gathered from the previous tables in this chapter to complete your own Form 1 in Worksheet 3-3.

WORKSHEET 3-3 The A-B-C Form 1

Date ____________

Activating Event/Trigger	**Beliefs/Thoughts**	**Thinking Error**

Consequences

Finishing off with A-B-C Form 2

Now you're ready to use A-B-C Form 2 to help you correct thinking errors, change NATs, and give yourself a chance to feel a healthier negative emotion and act constructively. But before you attempt this next step, here are some explanations for a bit more jargon in case of any confusion:

- **D** stands for *disputing* or questioning the validity of your thoughts, NATs, and beliefs about your trigger and looking for ways to correct your negative thinking.
- **E** stands for the *effect* of challenging and changing your thinking on both your feelings and actions.
- **F** stands for your *functional new thought* or your new way of thinking about the trigger and how it moves you forward.

EXAMPLE

Table 3-5 gives you a peek at Natasha's second A-B-C form.

TABLE 3-5 Natasha's A-B-C Form 2

Dispute	Effect	Functional New Thought
What are some reasons I can generate to question my unhealthy thoughts? My thoughts are too extreme, and I end up feeling very guilty. I'm not solely responsible for the argument with Mom. I wouldn't encourage a friend to be so extreme in their thinking about the same situation.	**How do I feel after challenging my thoughts?** I feel remorseful but not guilty about arguing with Mom prior to her death.	**How can I express my new thought in my own words?** I really wish/prefer that I hadn't argued with Mom before she died, but I did. This may mean that I did a selfish thing, but it doesn't make me a horrible or selfish person overall.
How can I correct my thinking errors? I can prefer but not demand that I hadn't argued with Mom. I can recognize that I'm still an okay person even if I didn't make up with Mom before she died. I can stop labeling myself as horrible and selfish on the basis of this unfortunate and regrettable act.	**How might I act differently as a result of challenging my thoughts?** I am able to focus more on her life rather than on the details of her death. I could probably go to visit her grave. I can answer Dad's phone calls and see him more often because I'm not feeling guilty.	

Try putting your own problem through the paces of A-B-C Form 2, using Worksheet 3-4. The questions in Worksheet 3-2 are designed to help you complete the Dispute section of this form.

WORKSHEET 3-4 My A-B-C Form 2

Dispute	Effect	Functional New Thought
What are some reasons I can generate to question my unhealthy thoughts?	How do I feel after challenging my thoughts?	How can I express my new thought in my own words?
How can I correct my thinking errors?	How might I act differently as a result of challenging my thoughts?	

One of the benefits of the A-B-C forms is that you can carry them with you as handy tools for quickly jotting down the nuts and bolts of any unpleasant triggers and your resulting troublesome emotions. You may find that you're able to do a lot of thought challenging in your head after working through the other worksheets in this chapter. You are then in the position of being able to jot down shorter versions of your questioning in the Dispute section of the second form. The A-B-C forms are also useful because they include nearly all the steps involved in overcoming emotional disturbance.

Trying Out Alternative Thoughts

Disputing your less-than-helpful thoughts and coming up with new, different, and sometimes exciting alternative ways of thinking is a great start. Yes, that's right, we said "start" — there's much more: more fun, more games, and more forms!

If you've been thinking in an unhelpful and slightly skewed manner for a long time, cementing in new and better ways of thinking takes some effort. And one of the best ways to really consolidate your new beliefs and thoughts is to *act on them*. Give them a good test run. Consider your functional new thought from Worksheet 3-4 and ask yourself how you can try out this alternative.

EXAMPLE

Natasha has been making herself feel guilty by thinking in guilt-provoking ways for two years. She wisely understands that changing her guilty thinking will require some practice. Table 3-6 shows some of her ideas for trying out her new alternative functional thoughts.

TABLE 3-6 Natasha's Acting on Alternative Thoughts Form

What is my functional new thought?	I really wish/prefer that I hadn't argued with Mom before she died, but I did. This may mean that I did a selfish thing, but it doesn't make me a horrible or selfish person overall.
How can I put this new thought to the test?	Well, I can try deliberately thinking my new thought every time I'm reminded of Mom's death. I can even try bringing up the memory of arguing with Mom while holding this functional new thought. I can try looking at photos of Mom and practicing this new thought before, after, and during looking at the photos. I can try rehearsing this new thought several times every day, even if I'm not reminded of Mom's death. I can recall memories of Mom's final days and remind myself of all the reasons that my new thought is both accurate and helpful.

Natasha has come up with several good ways of trying out her alternative healthy belief about arguing with her mother in the days before her death. She increases her chances of overcoming her guilt and engaging more with her healthy grief by doing so.

Use Worksheet 3-5 to think of ways to try out your new functional alternative way of thinking about your own trigger event.

WORKSHEET 3-5 My Acting on Alternative Thoughts Form

What is my functional new thought?	
How can I put this new thought to the test?	

Helping Yourself with Homework

In CBT, we encourage people to practice their CBT skills — often called "homework" — as a way of helping them to further their therapeutic gains. *Homework* is often a dreaded word, conjuring up images of teachers and reports. But try not to think of homework in that way now. Instead, think about tasks you can set yourself to help you surmount any emotional or behavioral difficulties you may have. Plus, you can choose your own assignments! You probably know better than anyone else what type of homework you need to do in order to help you formulate better ways of thinking and acting.

EXAMPLE

Natasha is here again to help illustrate the point we're making about homework. She has done her best to try out her new alternative functional thoughts. Now she's taking things one step further by identifying ways of really pushing herself to hold onto her new helpful way of thinking about her mother's death. Check out her efforts in Table 3-7.

TABLE 3-7 Natasha's Homework

What is my functional new thought?	I really wish/prefer that I hadn't argued with Mom before she died, but I did. This may mean that I did a selfish thing, but it doesn't make me a horrible or selfish person overall.
What homework can I give myself to help me enforce this new thought?	I can push myself to tell others about my argument with my mother prior to her death and still think in the new way about it, no matter how they react. I can bring up Mom's death with Dad and think myself out of guilt. I can go to visit Mom's grave and tell her my new way of thinking, or at least rehearse it while I'm there. I can rent movies that have themes or scenes of parents dying and practice thinking my new thought about Mom's death. I can act according to this new thought by refusing to replay the argument but instead choosing to focus on other aspects of Mom's life and death.

Perhaps you can think of other homework assignments Natasha can set herself to help her overcome her guilty thoughts and feelings. Or maybe you can devise some homework for yourself to help you to consolidate your conviction in your new functional way of thinking about your trigger event.

Try setting yourself some healthy belief strengthening homework by using the same worksheet. Remember to build on and make more strenuous those tasks you may have created for yourself in Worksheet 3-6.

WORKSHEET 3-6 My Homework

What is my functional new thought?	
What homework can I give myself to help me enforce this new thought?	

IN THIS CHAPTER

- » Designing and conducting behavioral experiments
- » Gathering evidence to learn more about your thoughts, predictions, or assumptions
- » Doing surveys, collecting data, and storing your results

Chapter 4 Experiencing Experiments

Treating your thoughts, predictions, assumptions, and beliefs as theories or hunches about reality rather than as facts is a cornerstone of cognitive behavioral therapy (CBT). Doing an experiment to examine whether an interpretation or strategy you use is helpful or whether an alternative thought may work better is a key to moving from understanding things in your head to "feeling" them in your gut.

Seeing Things Like a Scientist

When presented with a theory about the world, a scientist asks, "What's the evidence that supports that view?" When presented with the data from an experiment, a scientist goes on to wonder, "Is that a valid conclusion from the data?" and "Could these results be explained in any other way, by another theory?" To further understand the validity of competing theories, a scientist would want to know how to find out more and how to gather more data to see which theory fits the facts best, which would lead to another experiment.

Using CBT resembles being your own personal scientist, trying to see whether your conclusions (your theories) about yourself, the world, or other people, drawn from your personal experiences (your data) are valid or accurate, or whether an alternative conclusion may be more accurate. And just like a scientist, you may need to conduct further experiments to compare two or more theories to see which one best fits the facts.

You can use experiments to help yourself check out many different kinds of thoughts, from an automatic thought that pops into your head to a core belief that you've held for a very long time.

REMEMBER

Some theories are hard to give up, and you may sometimes have to repeat experiments to gather enough data to reduce your conviction in an old theory and build your conviction in a new one.

Executing excellent experiments

Use the checklist in Worksheet 4-1 to help make sure that your behavioral experiments are effective.

WORKSHEET 4-1 Experiment Checklist

❑	Have you identified the thought you want to test in a clear, testable fashion?
❑	Have you formulated an alternative theory or thought?
❑	Have you been specific about how, where, when, or with whom you'll conduct your experiment?
❑	Is your experiment challenging enough to help test your prediction?
❑	Is your experiment realistic and manageable?
❑	Have you considered what may interfere with the results of your experiment (such as safety behaviors, subtle avoidance, escaping from the situation) and planned to overcome them (for example, by purposefully dropping a safety behavior)? (See Chapter 7 for more on safety behaviors and other problematic coping strategies.)
❑	Is your experiment long enough to gather the evidence you need to test out your thoughts? (For example, it would take, at the very least, 20 minutes to discover that your anxiety reduced within a situation.)
❑	Have you considered whether you need to carry out another experiment?

Putting predictions to the test

At the risk of stating the obvious, seeing something for yourself makes it far easier to believe it's true. A behavioral experiment should help you do exactly that — see for yourself whether a prediction comes true. To conduct your own behavioral experiment, follow these steps:

1. **Describe the problem.**

   Whatever your problem, describe it specifically.

   For example, Sheila is afraid that she won't be able to cope with colleagues' questions about why she's been off sick for three months suffering from depression.

2. **Identify the prediction you want to test in your experiment.**

   State your problem as a hypothesis, using the classic if/then structure.

Sheila's hypothesis is "I won't be able to cope if people ask me questions about being off sick. If they do, I'll get too anxious and feel so ashamed that I'll have to run out of the office, and then it will be even harder to get back to work."

3. **Formulate an alternative prediction.**

   Instead of your worst fear, think of milder, less drastic circumstances that are as likely to be realized as your fears.

   In the example, Sheila's alternative may be something like, "I suppose it might not be as bad as I think, and I can give superficial answers and stress that I'm happy to be fit enough to return to work."

4. **Specify how you will test your predictions.**

   Write down the specific actions you can take to prove whether your predictions are correct.

   Sheila can test her predictions by returning to work on Wednesday so her first week back isn't too long. She can plan to greet colleagues she feels will be welcoming first and turn to them for support if she needs it.

5. **Write down the results of your experiment.**

   Record your feelings and reactions, as well as other people's behavior and reactions.

   Sheila's results look like this: "I felt really nervous as I walked into the office, but everyone seemed quite pleased to see me. The office was really busy, and I think they were far more interested in having me back than where I'd been. I got the impression my boss was concerned that I didn't overdo it, but *no one* probed about my illness!"

6. **Analyze the results of your experiment.**

   Look at your predictions from Steps 2 and 3 and evaluate how accurate they were.

   Sheila's analysis is, "I still need to recognize that the way I think is being dragged into negativity a bit, because the way I thought things might go was far worse than reality. But I guess feeling worried about going back to work is pretty normal, which might've made me catastrophize a bit more. I still need to keep putting my negative thoughts to the test!"

TIP

You may want to use the thought record sheet from Chapter 2 (Worksheet 2-14) to help you note and organize some of the negative predictions that tend to enter your mind.

Use Worksheet 4-2 to design experiments to test out your own thoughts.

WORKSHEET 4-2 My Prediction Sheet

Describe the problem:	
Identify the prediction you want to test:	
Formulate an alternative prediction:	

(continued)

WORKSHEET 4-2 *(continued)*

Specify how you will test your prediction:	
Write down the results of your experiment:	
Analyze the results of your experiment:	

You may still have some reservations about whether your old or alternative prediction is most accurate and choose to conduct another experiment in order to learn more.

Finding out which theory works best

Some problems create thoughts that can't be proven or disproven. This outcome is particularly true of obsessive-compulsive disorder (OCD) and anxiety problems. In these instances, you can experiment with treating your problem as if it's a psychological problem, and use CBT to tackle it, even if you're not yet convinced your problems are the product of your thoughts and behaviors. You can then be guided in your next step by how this strategy works. For example, you can treat intrusive thoughts of causing harm as if they are the product of excessive worry rather than the product of your being bad or dangerous.

Moray uses Table 4-1 to record the results of his experiment to determine how it works if he treats his fears of having a heart problem as if they are a worry problem.

TABLE 4-1 Moray's Health Anxiety Prediction Sheet

Describe the problem:	I'm worried that my heart pounding is a sign of a heart problem. Even though I've seen three doctors, I can't be convinced that there's nothing wrong with me.
Identify the prediction you want to test:	Treating my problem as if it's an anxiety problem will make no difference. What I really need is better proof that my heart is okay.
Formulate an alternative prediction:	Treating my problem as if it's an anxiety problem and reducing my self-monitoring and checking will help me become less anxious.
Specify how you will test your prediction:	I'll keep a frequency chart for my checking behaviors and deliberately resist seeking reassurance, checking my body, and monitoring my heart rate. I'll also stop using the internet to search for an answer as to what my problem might be or to reassure myself that there's nothing wrong.
Write down the results of your experiment:	After a week, I've noticed that I have fewer really anxious days and my worries about my heart aren't on my mind quite as much as they were.
Analyze the results of your experiment:	It makes sense to keep reducing my checking, but I'm not yet convinced my problem is "just" anxiety.

TIP

You can sometimes learn even more about the effect of a strategy such as checking, reassurance seeking, trying to control your thoughts, or trying to resist anxiety by comparing a "usual" level of such a strategy against a day of really increasing that strategy. Repeating this experiment a couple of times should give you a clearer understanding of the effect of a coping response. Many people find that when they discover for themselves that a coping strategy actually makes them feel worse, they feel far more determined to abandon that strategy.

Conducting a self-help survey

The people with clipboards seeking your opinion on a new brand of mayonnaise can actually be an inspiration for change! Surveying friends and family members about their experiences can be especially valuable in helping you realize that you are not alone in experiencing a particular kind of thought, feeling, or bodily sensation. This knowledge, in turn, can help you feel more normal and reduce feelings of anxiety and shame. The trick here is to be very clear about the kinds of information you ask for.

TIP

Multiple-choice questions can help because they add clarity about what you're looking for. For example, ask a question such as: "How often do you have unwanted thoughts about hurting someone?" And then provide answer options like: (a) Never, (b) Once or twice a year, (c) About once a month, (d) About once a week, (e) Daily. You can combine multiple-choice questions with more open questions like "Please describe the most upsetting unwanted thought that popped into your head in the last month."

Moray used Table 4-2 to increase his understanding of how anxiety can affect people's bodies by surveying his friends about their bodily sensations when feeling scared.

TABLE 4-2 Moray's Survey Behavioral Experiment

Describe the problem:	I'm worried that my heart pounding is a sign of a heart problem. Even though I've seen three doctors I can't be convinced that there's nothing wrong with me.
Identify the prediction you want to test in your experiment:	Other people don't get such strong feelings of their heart pounding if they feel anxious, which means there must be something physically wrong with me.
Formulate an alternative prediction:	Some people may also have strong bodily sensations when they feel anxious.
Specify how you will test your prediction:	I'll ask ten people about how their body reacted the last time they felt really scared or anxious. I can use a couple of friends, my dad (who used to suffer from anxiety), and some of the people from the anxiety management group I belong to.
Write down the results of your experiment:	I spoke to eight people in total. Seven reported strong bodily sensations — heart pounding, feeling hot, wobbly legs — and one guy from the group described feeling really unreal and distant from his surroundings when anxious.
Analyze the results of your experiment:	I guess when people say it's "just" anxiety, they don't always realize how much of a physical experience it can be. It doesn't prove that there's nothing wrong with me, but it does confirm that very strong and even strange bodily sensations can be caused by anxiety.

WARNING

Use surveys to gather useful new information, rather than as reassurance to try to eliminate any doubts. At best, reassurance brings only very temporary relief. Ultimately it just fuels your worries.

Acting as an observer

Sometimes throwing yourself into the deep end of confronting your fears can prove too difficult. A creative solution to this dilemma is to get someone else to jump in for you! This scenario really can be a meaningful stepping stone in learning that what you're *afraid* will happen may *not* actually come true. By having someone act out the experiment you fear, with you acting as observer, you can see how accurate your predictions about what will happen are.

EXAMPLE

Ray was very afraid that he would have a panic attack in a public place and collapse. He feared doing so would be extremely humiliating and cause a massive inconvenience to the people around him. This fear meant that Ray limited going far from home as much as possible and escaped from any public situation as fast as he could if he felt himself start to feel panicky. Ray enlisted some help to tackle his panic and avoidance, using Table 4-3.

TABLE 4-3 Ray's Pride Paralysis Prediction Sheet

Describe the problem:	Panic attacks.
Identify the prediction you want to test:	If I collapse in a supermarket, everyone will stop and stare, and if there turns out not to be anything seriously wrong with me, the people working in the store will hate me.
Formulate an alternative prediction:	I can't imagine things going any other way.
Specify how you will test your prediction:	My friend Zac has agreed to pretend to collapse in the supermarket, and I'm going to watch and make note of what happens from a few feet away.
Write down the results of your experiment:	When Zac pretended to collapse, a couple of people noticed, and one man stopped to see if he was okay. Most people just carried on shopping. A shop assistant brought him a chair and suggested calling the paramedics, but Zac reassured them he was fine and got up and walked away after a couple of minutes.
Analyze the results of your experiment:	Zac found the whole thing quite funny, and he certainly wasn't freaked out. The people seemed mostly indifferent or nice. It really has made the possibility of collapsing seem a bit less scary.

TIP

You need to see the experiment for yourself because you'll probably discount what someone reports if they just tell you about it later. But keep in mind that observing someone else may not be a substitute for ultimately putting your predictions to the test yourself.

You can also use observation without setting up an experiment. For example, a woman who thought she was being ignored observed how much eye contact people in the street made with each other and found she was really overestimating how often people look at each other.

Writing Down Your Results

To make good use of the data you collect, keeping written records of your experiments is helpful. Doing so can help you to reflect on all your hard work and build a portfolio of evidence to help challenge unhelpful thoughts and build up your conviction in more helpful alternatives. Use Worksheet 4-3 to record the results of your experiment.

WORKSHEET 4-3 My Behavioral Experiment Record Sheet

Date: ____________________

Prediction or Theory	**Experiment**	**Results**	**Conclusion/Comments**
Outline the thought, belief, or theory you are testing. Rate your strength of conviction 1–100%.	Plan what you will do (including where, when, how, with whom), being as specific as you can.	Record what actually happened including relevant thoughts, emotions, physical sensations, and other people's behavior.	Write down what you have learned about your prediction or theory in light of results. Re-rate your strength of conviction 0–100%.

Guidance on carrying out a behavioral experiment: 1. Be clear and specific about the negative and alternative predictions you are testing. Rate your strength of conviction in the prediction or theory you are testing or evaluating. 2. Decide upon your experiment, and be as clear as you can be as to how you will measure your results. 3. Record the results of your experiment, emphasising clear, observable outcomes. 4. Evaluate the results of your experiment. Write down what these results suggest in terms of the accuracy of your predictions, or which theory the evidence supports. 5. Consider whether a further behavioral experiment might be helpful.

REMEMBER

Carrying out behavioral experiments is a no-lose proposition. Whatever the outcome, you'll have more information about the nature of your problem, which you can use to inform your solutions.

IN THIS CHAPTER

- » Finding out where your attention is aimed
- » Getting better at deliberately aiming your attention
- » Using task concentration
- » Getting out of your head
- » Being more mindful

Chapter 5 Controlling Concentration and Reducing Rumination

A large part of cognitive behavioral therapy (CBT) involves dealing with the content of your thoughts, but CBT also recognizes more recent developments in areas such as mindfulness meditation. Basically, sometimes your thoughts are best left alone. Mindfulness and other similar techniques emphasize *accepting* unwelcome thoughts and essentially allowing them to play themselves out without any interruption or intervention on your part. This strategy can be very useful for dealing with unpleasant thoughts, images, or physical sensations. If you're able to accept your thoughts as *just thoughts* rather than interpreting them as *facts,* you can lessen their emotional impact.

In this chapter, we introduce some basic exercises that you can use to better manage troublesome thoughts, irksome images, and fearsome physical feelings.

Aiming Your Attention

Particularly if you suffer from anxiety or depression, you're likely to have a lot of threatening or pessimistic thoughts (or both). Not a lot of fun. Harnessing the ability to *not* pay attention to your thoughts can be very useful in these circumstances. Concentrating on anxious or depressed thinking can further lower your mood or heighten your anxiety. With practice, you can learn to *disattend* to your thinking and focus your attention on the outside world instead.

REMEMBER

Turning your attention *away* from your thoughts and mental images — or *disattending* — is not the same as thought suppression. Suppression involves trying to deny, control, or stop unwelcome mental activity. Thought suppression tends to have a paradoxical effect — the more you try to stop thinking certain things, the more you tend to produce the exact sort of thoughts that you mean to avoid. In essence, suppression is the *opposite* of accepting the presence of unpleasant thoughts and images. You accept your mental activity, however unpleasant, but then *choose* to aim your attention away from it.

TIP

One way to pay less attention to or disattend from depressing and anxious thoughts is by regarding them as background noise. When you put the TV or radio on between channels you tend to get static. Try imagining that your unhelpful negative thoughts are like interference on the radio or the music you hear played in elevators or when you're on hold on the phone. These sounds can be annoying, but we tend to ignore them instead of focusing on them.

The attention analysis worksheet is devised to help you note where you focus most of your attention — on the outside world or on your internal thoughts and feelings. It also aids you in seeing the benefits of changing your focus of attention.

EXAMPLE

Matt has been suffering from an episode of depression for the past few weeks. (See Chapter 10 for more on overcoming depression.) Increasingly, he's staying indoors and withdrawing from other people. Matt often has thoughts about how bad he feels and how bleak the future seems. Because these thoughts feel very intense and important, Matt focuses on them a lot. When he does venture outdoors, Matt feels very uncomfortable and detached from the world around him. He then tends to dwell on how odd and uncomfortable he feels. Matt often appears to be in a bit of a daze because he's so absorbed in his own thoughts and feelings.

Matt used the guidelines in Table 5-1 to better understand and re-aim his attention.

TABLE 5-1 **Matt's Attention Analysis**

Where is my attention mainly focused? On the outside world around me or on my internal thoughts, images, and feelings?	My attention is mainly focused on my internal world. I pay a lot of attention to how low and tired I'm feeling and search for possible reasons for my depression. I also focus on bleak images of the future and how bad I feel compared to other times in my life. I realize that I also spend a lot of time stuck in a cycle of thinking the same sorts of things over and over, normally about my lack of energy and motivation to do daily tasks.
When I do focus my attention on the outside world, what external information do I tend to notice?	When I go out of the house, I focus on how weird and detached I feel. I also look at other people and notice how normal and content they look in comparison to me. Sometimes I focus on how little I enjoy activities that I used to like or how difficult I find everyday tasks such as grocery shopping and going to the bank. I dwell on how I once found these tasks simple and ordinary and how they now seem like such a big deal.
What external things might I focus on to help me stop paying attention to my internal thoughts and feelings?	I could focus more on the task at hand rather than on how difficult I'm finding it. I could also take more time to experience the sounds, smells, and sights around me. I could pay more attention to how other people look and act and try to interact with shopkeepers and other people more often. I could try to focus on what other people are saying and doing instead of comparing myself to them.

What are some additional practical strategies I can use to help me turn my attention away from unhelpful thoughts and feelings?	I can turn on a podcast when I'm getting myself ready in the morning and listen to a soothing or interesting program. I can make a phone call or go out to meet a friend instead of allowing myself to get stuck indoors thinking the same depressing thoughts each day. I can play a computer game, do a puzzle or crossword, or do something physical, such as gardening, housework, or some DIY project — anything that requires some concentration and draws my attention away from my bad feelings and negative thoughts.
What are the effects of refocusing my attention? (Complete this section after at least three days of deliberately aiming your attention away from your internal thoughts and feelings.)	After a few days of deliberately and consistently focusing my attention on tasks and my environment, I noticed a slight lift in my mood. I'm also better able to get on with the day and override my depressed feelings if I don't pay attention to them too much. When I'm out of the house, I notice that by focusing on other people and the world around me, I feel less weird and detached.

TIP

Your anxious or depressed thoughts can be very compelling, so be patient with yourself as you work on breaking free from ruminating. Be prepared for your attention to return to unhelpful negative thoughts and feelings. Simply redirect your attention onto more benign activities every time it wanders into gloomy territory. Gaining greater control over your attention and concentration takes practice.

EXAMPLE

Sue is anxious about lots of things, but in particular she suffers from anxiety in social situations. (See Chapter 9 for more about how to combat anxiety.) She often worries about what people think of her when she's out socially. Sue often plans conversations in her head prior to speaking in the hopes that she'll appear interesting. After Sue returns home from a party or an evening out with friends, she often reviews the evening and looks for any possible social faux pas that she may have committed.

Table 5-2 shows the results when Sue used the attention analysis worksheet to get a better idea of what she was focusing on during social interaction and the effects of changing her attention focus.

TABLE 5-2 Sue's Attention Analysis

Where is my attention mainly focused? On the outside world around me or on my internal thoughts, images, and feelings?	I mainly focus on my anxious feelings and on how I appear to the other people present. I focus a lot on what to say next and wonder how people will react to whatever I say and do. Sometimes I get distracted by my thoughts about not fitting in with other people or about how uncomfortable I feel socially. I also monitor myself for blushing, shaking, or other signs of social awkwardness that others might notice and consider odd.
When I do focus my attention on the outside world, what external information do I tend to notice?	I tend to look for signs of people reacting badly to what I say or looking bored when I'm talking. I monitor other people for subtle signs that they either like or dislike me. I also focus on how much more easily others seem to make social chitchat than I do.
What external things might I focus on to help me stop paying attention to my internal thoughts and feelings?	I could focus on what people are saying rather than on planning what to say next. I could take in the environment more by focusing on the music, atmosphere, decor, and so on.

(continued)

TABLE 5-2 *(continued)*

What are some additional practical strategies I can use to help me turn my attention away from unhelpful thoughts and feelings?	I can resist the urge to replay social interactions and look for social errors that I may have made. Instead, I can focus on the enjoyable aspects of the event. I can also deliberately resist monitoring myself for signs of anxiety, such as blushing and shaking. Instead of focusing my attention on trying to stop my hands from trembling, I can focus on tasks like paying for a drink. I can also switch my attention from looking for signs of whether people like me and focus my attention on what my impressions are of them.
What are the effects of refocusing my attention? (Complete this section after at least three days of deliberately aiming your attention away from your internal thoughts and feelings.)	When I pay more attention to the conversation and stop preparing what to say, things tend to flow more naturally. I feel less anxious and awkward when I focus my attention on the environment but don't monitor others for their reactions to me.

Whether you're having depressed or anxious thoughts and feelings or you're experiencing unwelcome images and unwanted thoughts of a different nature (such as those experienced in obsessive-compulsive disorder; see Chapter 11), redirecting your attention may be helpful. In Chapter 10, we zero in on depression, a problem that frequently responds well to targeting and reducing rumination by redirecting your attention away from dwelling on your negative mood and thoughts.

Worksheet 5-1 gives you the chance to try using the attention analysis worksheet yourself and see if it has a positive effect.

WORKSHEET 5-1 **My Attention Analysis**

Where is my attention mainly focused? On the outside world around me or on my internal thoughts, images, and feelings?	
When I do focus my attention on the outside world, what external information do I tend to notice?	
What external things might I focus on to help me stop paying attention to my internal thoughts and feelings?	
What are some additional practical strategies I can use to help me turn my attention away from unhelpful thoughts and feelings?	
What are the effects of refocusing my attention? (Complete this section after at least three days of deliberately aiming your attention away from your internal thoughts and feelings.)	

Training Yourself in Task Concentration

The purpose of task concentration exercises is to help you get better at *choosing* what you concentrate on instead of allowing your attention to wander. Everyone has the ability to focus their attention and to concentrate on a task while filtering out extraneous stimuli. Some people are better at doing this than others, possibly as a result of practice. Imagine a busy, open-plan office with a lot of people doing different jobs and talking on phones. Although a lot of background noise and activity is happening, the employees learn to concentrate on their tasks and tune out distractions. Or imagine that you're trying to negotiate a tricky driving situation — you probably turn your attention to the task of driving and fail to notice songs on the radio as much.

You can get better at concentrating more on tasks and the environment and less on yourself, your thoughts, and your feelings. If you're suffering from an emotional problem, you're probably spending more time than you realize focusing on unhelpful thoughts and sensations.

Start by making a list of five *nonthreatening situations* (situations in which you experience little or no anxiety or distress). Then make a list of five more *threatening situations* (situations that you may be avoiding because they make you feel anxious or distressed). Start from the least anxiety provoking and progress to the most anxiety-provoking situation. Have a look at how Sue did this in Table 5-3.

TABLE 5-3 **Sue's Situations**

My five nonthreatening situations:
1. Going to the movies with my best friend
2. Having dinner at my parents' house with just the family
3. Traveling on the train during quiet times
4. Going to the local pub with my best friend and her boyfriend
5. Walking my dog in the park
My five threatening situations (from easiest to hardest):
1. Going out for a drink with my coworkers
2. Having something to eat in a busy cafe on my own
3. Traveling on the train during really busy periods
4. Going to a different pub to meet several friends or people I don't know well
5. Going to a party where I know only one or two people

Sue used her five nonthreatening situations as opportunities to practice switching her attention focus back and forth between herself and tasks or the environment. When she felt that she'd mastered this skill, Sue pushed herself into her list of threatening situations and practiced concentrating on tasks and the environment rather than on her anxious thoughts and feelings.

You can use this technique to better monitor the effects of task concentration on your mood and physical sensations. Doing so also gives you a chance to work on strengthening your attention muscles.

Make your own list of situations using Worksheet 5-2.

REMEMBER It's generally easier to disattend from unhelpful thoughts in situations where you're pretty comfortable than in those that provoke anxiety or low mood. By listing both threatening and nonthreatening situations, you can practice deliberately directing your attention where you want it to go in situations where you feel okay and eventually do the same in less comfortable situations.

WORKSHEET 5-2 My Situations

My five nonthreatening situations:
1.
2.
3.
4.
5.

My five threatening situations (from easiest to hardest):
1.
2.
3.
4.
5.

TIP

Try these steps to help you get behind the steering wheel of your attention:

1. **Focus on your internal feelings and thoughts for a few minutes (you can time yourself if you like).**

   Note any unpleasant physical sensations and negative thinking and images.

2. **Interrupt those thoughts and turn your attention to your environment and other people.**

   Keep your attention on the outside world for a few minutes (time yourself if you like) and make mental notes of what you see going on around you.

3. **Switch your attention back and forth between your internal world and the external world.**

   Try keeping your attention on the external environment for longer periods, pulling your attention away from your internal thoughts and feelings if it wanders.

4. **After you've gotten used to turning your attention to what you decide to focus on, try doing the same in situations you typically find threatening.**

5. **Work your way through your threatening situations starting from the easiest to the hardest, like Sue did in Table 5-3.**

WARNING

Don't give up or become disheartened if you find this exercise difficult to master at first. It takes time and practice.

Practice yo-yoing your attention between yourself and the outside world in your nonthreatening situations until you feel you're ready to give the process a go in the more personally threatening situations on your second list.

Worksheet 5-3 provides an opportunity to make a record of your efforts. Use the worksheet to record the details of a specific event in which you deliberately focused your attention and concentration onto the outside world plus particular tasks. Make sure that you clearly record strategies that helped you to reduce negative feelings and thoughts. By recording what you learned through the exercise, you'll better remember the benefits next time round. You can use Worksheet 5-3 as many times as needed.

EXAMPLE

Sue used Table 5-4 to record the results of her task concentration training.

TABLE 5-4 Sue's Task Concentration Record

Where was I?	At a work event held in a banquet hall.
What was I doing?	I was at a manager's going-away party. I was mingling with other guests and serving myself food and drinks.
Who was I with?	About 60 other employees were there. Three women who work in my office were there, but otherwise I didn't really know anyone else.
What methods did I use to keep concentrating on the task and the external environment?	I concentrated on getting some food and ordering a drink. I watched people dancing and tried to make eye contact with other people. Instead of sitting hidden in a corner, I forced myself to stand in a more central position in the room. I made small talk with several people I vaguely knew rather than sticking like glue to the three women from my office. I even danced to a few songs with a group of people, even though I didn't really know them.
What did I learn from this exercise?	At first I felt really self-conscious and anxious, but after about half an hour I started to feel okay. Pulling my attention away from myself and resisting monitoring myself for blushing and shaking took a lot of effort. But it really helped to focus my attention on watching other people and to concentrate on tasks such as eating and getting a drink. I noticed that by making eye contact and standing in the middle of the hall many people approached me to make small talk. I actually managed to enjoy myself.

WARNING

As Sue noted, focusing on the external environment and tasks rather than on herself wasn't easy! This process may sound simple but mastering it takes a lot of persistence and determination. Don't be tempted to give up too quickly. Stick with it!

Recording results of any behavioral changes you make can be useful. You can look back at your records to remind yourself of the benefits of changing aspects of your behavior if you experience a resurgence of your original problems. Keeping a record also allows you to clearly see what specific strategies worked.

Now's your chance to use the task concentration record sheet to record your learning and observations using Worksheet 5-3.

WORKSHEET 5-3 My Task Concentration Record

Where was I?	
What was I doing?	
Who was I with?	
What methods did I use to keep concentrating on the task and the external environment?	
What did I learn from this exercise?	

Finding Your Focus

Hopefully, the exercises in the previous sections have given you a good idea of where you tend to aim your attention and the positive effects of changing your focus to tasks and the environment around you. Using a simple pie chart is another quick and effective way of monitoring the focus of your attention and recording how you divided your attention or concentration in a given situation.

EXAMPLE

Sue used the pie chart method to make a more visual record of her attention focus while at the work party. Sue's chart is shown in Table 5-5.

TABLE 5-5 Sue's Pie Chart

What was the situation?	A going-away party in a banquet hall for a manager who was moving on to another job. About 60 other employees were present, 3 of whom I knew reasonably well.
How was my attention divided during the majority of the time that I remained in the situation?	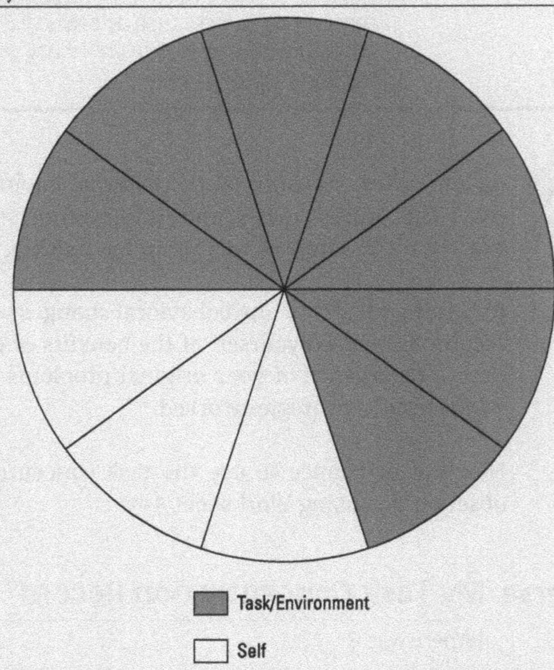

You can see from the pie chart that Sue focused roughly 70 percent of her attention on tasks and other people or the environment. Only about 30 percent of her attention was focused on herself, her thoughts, and her feelings for the majority of the party.

TIP

If you're experiencing anxiety, depression, or other troublesome emotional problems, you're likely to benefit from focusing as much of your attention as possible on others or the environment and concentrating deliberately on tasks. In short, the less attention you pay to yourself and your internal world, the better for you!

Try using the blank pie chart in Worksheet 5-4. Simply record the situation and shade in segments of the pie that represent your attention focus on others or the environment. Leave the segments that represent attention focused on yourself (thoughts, feelings, images, and physical sensations) unshaded.

WORKSHEET 5-4 My Pie Chart

What was the situation?

How was my attention divided for the majority of the time that I remained in the situation?

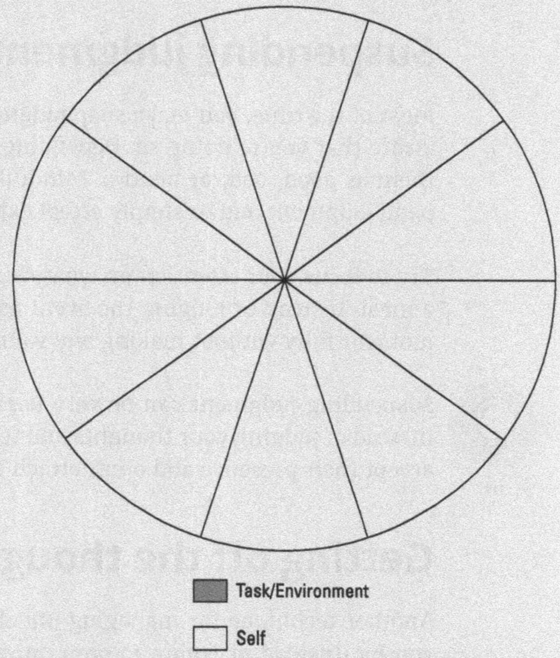

Making Your Mind More Mindful

Mindfulness meditation is gaining in popularity because this approach helps people manage stress, depression, and other conditions such as chronic pain. We can't completely explain meditation in this section, but we offer you a quick look.

The whole experience of mindfulness resembles looking at the world with fresh eyes, free from judgment or comment. The idea is to hold your attention in the present moment and to focus as much as possible on the here and now.

WARNING The techniques described in the following sections may sound very simple or even easy. In practice, though, these techniques for managing your thoughts are very difficult to master. People spend years practicing various forms of meditation, so be prepared to find the process difficult at first.

Living in the present

This technique is similar to concentrating on tasks. Instead of allowing your mind to wander into worry territory or planning your next move, focus as much as you can on whatever you're currently doing.

Even if you're brushing your teeth or sitting in a chair near a window, focus your attention on the *actual experience* of brushing your teeth or on what you can *see* out the window and how your body *feels* in the chair.

Suspending judgment

Most of the time, you make snap judgments about your experiences without even being wholly aware that you're doing so. Depending on the value you assign to your experiences, you label them as good, bad, or neutral. Mindfulness meditation is about becoming better able to suspend judgment and to simply *accept* experiences.

Try to focus your attention on whatever you're *doing,* be it gardening, waiting in line, or eating a meal. Instead of judging the event as good, bad, boring, or satisfying, try to experience the moment fully without making any value judgments about it.

TIP

Suspending judgment can be very useful for dealing with unwelcome thoughts and feelings. Instead of judging your thoughts and feelings as bad or as indications that you're unwell, try to accept their presence and don't attach any value or meaning to them.

Getting off the thought train

Another technique for managing unhelpful thoughts involves allowing your thoughts to pass you by. Instead of trying to stop unwelcome thoughts or getting involved in thinking more *about* unwelcome thoughts, just *observe* them.

TIP

Imagine your thoughts and feelings as cars on a train. Instead of engaging with your thoughts, watch them pass through the station and continue on down the track. Resist the urge to jump on the thought train and instead just let it chug on by.

Knowing when to ignore yourself

Many of the negative thoughts you experience when you're having emotional problems are likely to be inaccurate, biased, and distorted perceptions of reality (see Chapter 2 for more about thinking errors). So, in addition to challenging and changing your thinking (which we talk about in Chapter 3), ignoring or disregarding many of the thoughts you generate when you're emotionally disturbed is best.

EXAMPLE

Matt became aware of recurring themes to his thinking when he was feeling very depressed. He made a note of these themes and decided to regard these thoughts as symptoms of his depression rather than as factual, true, or accurate. Table 5-6 shows the results.

TABLE 5-6 Matt's Thematic Toxic Thoughts

What is my main emotional problem?	Depression.
What are some of the typical thoughts I have when I feel this way?	I'll never be normal again. What's the point of life anyway? How did I get this depressed? Everything is difficult and nothing is enjoyable. I'm a real disappointment to everyone in my life and to myself. The world is a terrible place.
What good reasons exist for disregarding these thoughts?	These are just typical things I tend to think when my mood is low. If I were feeling better, I'd see things more positively and very differently. These thoughts are just a by-product of depressed feelings and don't accurately represent my future or reality.
What effect does ignoring/disregarding these thoughts have on my mood?	If I really make an effort to consider these thoughts as just an unpleasant part of depression, I tend to feel a bit better. I can choose to turn my attention away from this type of thinking, and then I notice that the thoughts often fade away.

You can use Worksheet 5-5 to help identify troublesome themes to your thinking. See if you can pinpoint when you're better off ignoring yourself!

WORKSHEET 5-5 My Thematic Toxic Thoughts

What is my main emotional problem?	
What are some of the typical thoughts I have when I feel this way?	
What good reasons exist for disregarding these thoughts?	
What effect does ignoring/disregarding these thoughts have on my mood?	

Mindfully mundane

All the little things that you do as part of your everyday routine you can probably start doing more mindfully if you put your mind to it. Consider this approach another way of strengthening your attention muscles and increasing your control over your concentration. Often people hurry through various tasks in an attempt to get them over and done with. Instead, you can take a little time to focus on the subtle aspects of each of your daily duties. For example, focus on the feel of the water when you're washing the dishes, the taste of the glue from the back of a stamp you've just licked, the whirring of the washing machine that you've just turned on, and the taste and feel of the toothpaste on your tongue as you brush your teeth.

Use Worksheet 5-6 to make a list of daily tasks that you can do more mindfully in a deliberate effort to practice controlling and redirecting your attention.

WORKSHEET 5-6 My List of Daily Duties

What are some everyday tasks that I can do more mindfully?	

2 Defining Your Problems and Setting Goals

IN THIS PART . . .

This part covers healthy and unhealthy negative emotions and gives you the chance to assess your own emotional responses. We also show you how some of the ways in which you try to cope with problems may be problematic. Finally, we focus on setting goals for tackling your problems.

IN THIS CHAPTER

» Naming your feelings

» Understanding what your emotions are made of

» Discerning the difference between the two types of emotions

» Spotlighting your problematic emotions

Chapter 6 Getting Emotional

Many therapists specializing in cognitive behavioral therapy (CBT) make a distinction between two types of negative feeling states or emotions: healthy and unhealthy. *Healthy emotions* are those feelings you have in response to negative events that are appropriate to the event, lead to constructive action, and don't significantly interfere with the rest of your life. *Unhealthy emotions* are feelings you have that are out of proportion to the event in question, tend to lead to self-destructive behaviors, and cause problems in other areas of your life. One of the goals of this workbook is to help you experience healthy negative emotions more often.

In this chapter, we introduce you to different ways of identifying your feelings in the first place, show you ways of discerning between the two types of negative emotions, and help you identify your problematic emotions.

Expanding Your Emotional Vocabulary

So, you know that you're feeling *something.* Yes, an emotion's definitely going on in there, but what on earth *is* it? And what should you call this churning internal experience?

Naming your feelings isn't always easy. Psychologists can use lots of different words to describe subtly different emotions because they deal with that kind of thing all the time. But you may be more accustomed to using vague terms to articulate how you feel inside. Perhaps you use words such as *upset, worked up,* or *bad.* These words give an indication that you're in a negative emotional state, but they don't really provide much more information than that.

Applying a specific label or name to your feelings has some advantages. Label feelings:

- Makes it easier for others (and even for yourself) to understand the precise nature of what you're feeling.
- Has been shown to improve a person's ability to process uncomfortable emotions.
- Makes it easier for you to work out whether what you're feeling is a healthy or unhealthy negative emotion.
- Makes it easier for you to select an alternative healthy negative emotion as a goal.

One way of giving a name to your feelings is to begin by noting what triggered your feelings. A *trigger* is the event, potential event, or thought that starts your emotional juices flowing.

After you've identified the trigger, look closely at your *action tendencies* (how your emotion leads you to act, or want to act — whether you actually do so or not). Your *actual behavior* includes what your actions are in response to your emotion. Your *emotional guess* is your attempt to unravel what you're feeling and to decide on what label or name to give to your emotional experience. The name you decide best describes your internal feelings is your *emotional label*. Following are examples of what we mean.

EXAMPLE

Horace's wife of ten years moved out of the family home and asked him for a divorce. His wife's decision was unexpected and seemed to come from out of the blue. Horace knows that he feels very upset, but he's having trouble describing what he's feeling. Table 6-1 shows how Horace uncovers his basic emotion.

TABLE 6-1 Horace's Feeling Fact File

Trigger:	My wife has left me.
Actual behavior:	Crying a lot. Avoiding people who may ask questions about my wife and our marriage. Searching my mind for possible ways this could have been avoided. Eating less. Looking at pictures of my wife and crying.
Action tendencies:	I want to stay in bed all day, although I do drag myself to work. I don't want to talk to anyone about what has happened in my marriage. I don't want to look after myself or my home anymore.
Emotional guess:	Looking at what I've been doing and feeling like doing, I think I may be feeling very sad and possibly depressed. If I saw a friend of mine responding this way to the same event, I'd probably say that they were feeling depressed.
Emotional label:	Depressed.

EXAMPLE

Lois has a friend who repeatedly cancels their dates to meet. Sometimes her friend has a plausible excuse for breaking their arrangements, but more often she seems to have found another option that is more attractive to her. This scenario often leaves Lois with no alternative plans for the evening. On this occasion, Lois's friend has canceled a long-standing agreement to attend a concert. Lois is now left with a spare ticket and no companion. Lois's efforts to get to her real feelings about this situation are shown in Table 6-2.

TABLE 6-2 Lois's Feeling Fact File

Trigger:	My friend canceled our plans to go to the concert at the last minute.
Actual behavior:	I didn't say much to her on the phone but was quite sulky. I tore up both tickets and put them in the trash. I thought about how badly she treats me and what a good friend I am to her.
Action tendencies:	I will not call her again and will wait for her to call me. I will not make any attempt to go out with her and will try to make her apologize for treating me so badly.
Emotional guess:	I feel angry with my friend for letting me down again. I can't believe the way she treats me. Doesn't she realize that I'm now left all on my own? I guess that I'm angry with her, but more than that, I'm very upset that she's let me down so many times. I just don't deserve that kind of treatment. I guess my feelings are more hurt than angry.
Emotional label:	Hurt.

Both Horace and Lois are able to give names to their emotional experience by looking more closely at what their behaviors actually are and how they feel like behaving or plan to behave in the future. See if you can give a name to your emotion by using the same method and completing Worksheet 6-1.

WORKSHEET 6-1 My Feeling Fact File

Actual behavior:	
Action tendencies:	
Emotional guess:	
Emotional label:	

Hopefully, you find Worksheet 6-1 useful in helping you identify your basic emotion. But if you still find the process difficult, don't worry. Sometimes what you need are more feeling words at your fingertips.

TIP

Here's a list of common human emotions. You can use this list as a springboard to finding other words that describe variations on the same basic feelings. Then you'll have more feeling labels to choose from and use to describe emotions. You can use a thesaurus or dictionary to find more feeling words.

- Anger
- Anxiety
- Concern
- Depression
- Disappointment
- Embarrassment
- Envy
- Fear
- Grief
- Guilt
- Hurt
- Jealousy
- Regret
- Remorse
- Sadness
- Shame

REMEMBER

Keep in mind that this list is by no means exhaustive. Feel free to add as many emotion words as you like. In the rest of this chapter, we show you ways of determining whether your emotions are in the healthy or unhealthy camp, whatever you choose to call them.

Understanding the Anatomy of Emotions

Feelings don't exist in a self-contained bubble. Human emotions exist in *context.* Confused? Fear not. Horace and Lois in the previous section show how behaviors are a fundamental aspect of emotions. All human emotions — whether positive or negative, healthy or unhealthy — are composed of four dimensions. These dimensions interact and reinforce one another. Figure 6-1 shows this relationship.

Noting what is going on in the four dimensions of your emotion offers important clues to the type of emotion you're experiencing — healthy or unhealthy. See how Horace does this with Table 6-3.

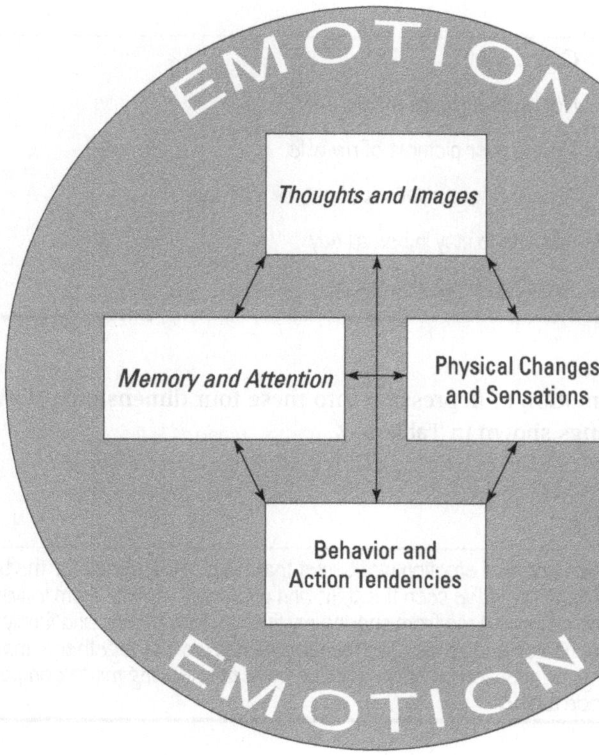

FIGURE 6-1: The dimension of emotions.

TABLE 6-3 **Horace's Four-Dimensional Emotion**

Emotion:	Depression
Thoughts and images:	I keep thinking about what I might have done to drive my wife away. I have thoughts about how miserable and hopeless my future is going to be. I have images of my wife in the arms of another man. I imagine myself being alone as I get older.
Physical sensations and changes:	I have a gnawing pain in the pit of my stomach almost all the time. I burst into tears easily. My appetite has disappeared and I'm losing weight.
Memory and attention:	I've been searching my memory for clues that my wife was planning to leave me, things that I should've picked up on. I keep remembering how in love we were when we were first married. I keep noticing couples in the street looking happy. I keep hearing love songs on the radio and noticing romantic films on TV.

(continued)

TABLE 6-3 *(continued)*

Behavior and action tendencies:	Crying a lot. Not making myself meals. Poring over pictures of my wife. Avoiding conversations about my marriage. Wanting to stay in bed all day. Avoiding friends and family.

Having broken down his emotion of depression into these four dimensions, Horace makes the realizations about his feelings shown in Table 6-4.

TABLE 6-4 **Horace's Realizations**

I can see by analyzing my four-dimensional emotion worksheet that I'm blaming myself for the breakdown of my marriage and telling myself that I should've seen the signs and prevented my wife from leaving. I can also see that my avoidance behavior is stopping me from sharing my feelings with friends and family who may be able to offer support. Looking at photos and dwelling on the happy times we had together is making my depression worse. Also, focusing my attention on happy-looking couples is leading me to compare my situation with theirs and lowering my mood further.

Use Worksheet 6-2 to break down your identified emotion into the four dimensions.

WORKSHEET 6-2 **My Four-Dimensional Emotion**

Emotion:	
Thoughts and images:	
Physical sensations and changes:	
Memory and attention:	
Behavior and action tendencies:	

Now you can use the space in Worksheet 6-3 to record any realizations you've had about your emotional experience.

WORKSHEET 6-3 My Realizations

____

____

____

____

____

Figuring Out Whether Your Feelings Are Healthy or Unhealthy

As you may already realize, your thoughts, attention, focus, behavior, and even some of your physical sensations are ways of determining whether you're in the grip of an unhealthy or healthy emotional experience. These aspects or dimensions of emotional experience are different depending on the type of feeling you're having. For example, the action tendencies associated with healthy sadness tend to be constructive. They help you to accept and adjust to a negative event or situation. On the other hand, the action tendencies associated with unhealthy depression tend to be destructive because they prevent you from accepting the negative event and moving forward.

In general, healthy negative emotions are less intensely uncomfortable than their unhealthy counterparts. Even if you're extremely sad, you're likely to feel less intense discomfort or emotional pain than if you're unhealthily depressed.

Taking note of your thinking

Rigid thinking is a surefire sign that you're feeling something unhealthy. *Rigid thinking* involves demanding that you, others, and the world play by certain rules — your rules. This attitude is troublesome because you leave no room for deviation or error. So, when your demands aren't met (and they frequently won't be), you're likely to become emotionally disturbed.

The alternative to rigid/demand-based thinking is *flexible/preference-based thinking.* Here, you hold preferences, standards, and ideals for how you, others, and the world perform. But — and the *but* is crucial — you also accept the possibility of your preferences not being met. So, when you fail to live up to your personal standards, others behave in undesirable ways, or the world refuses to follow your plans, you may feel emotionally distressed, but not unduly disturbed.

When you hold demands that aren't met, you're also at risk of putting down yourself or others harshly. Doing so can lead to more emotional pain and more practical problems, too.

TIP

Look out for words and phrases such as *should, must, it's essential, have to, got to,* and *ought to* in your thinking and self-talk. These words are often signals that you're thinking rigidly.

EXAMPLE

Samantha is very sensitive to criticism from others. She often senses that she's being criticized when someone makes even a slightly negative comment. Samantha's husband sat down for dinner and mentioned that the pasta was overcooked and that he didn't much like the meal she'd prepared. Samantha was very angry about her husband's comments and threw a tantrum, screaming at him for being so ungrateful and smashing things around in the kitchen. She and her husband went to bed without speaking.

You can use a thought test to see if your thinking about a given event or situation is rigid/demand-based or flexible/preference-based. The outcome is the acid test for knowing whether your emotion is healthy or unhealthy. Take a look at Samantha's thought test in Table 6-5.

TABLE 6-5 Samantha's Thought Test

Thought:	My husband must not criticize my cooking, and he's totally ungrateful for doing so.
Is my thought flexible/ preference-based?	No, it isn't. I guess if I say that he must not criticize my cooking, then I'm not leaving room for the possibility that he may do so.
Is my thought true? Does it fit with reality?	I guess if it were true that he must not criticize my cooking, then it must mean that he's lacking free will. The reality is that he did say that the pasta was overcooked and that he didn't like the meal I'd prepared. So, I guess this just goes to show that there's no reason that he must not be critical about the meal I prepared.
Is my thought helpful?	Well, I did get pretty angry and say a lot of vicious things. I also smashed a lot of china while freaking out at him. We went to bed without speaking and the evening was pretty unpleasant. So, I guess my thought wasn't very helpful all in all.
Is my thought leading me to put myself down?	Not at first. But I feel pretty down on myself now for getting so angry with my husband.
Is my thought leading me to put down other people?	Oh, yes. And how I think he's despicable for being so ungrateful.
Based on all this, is my thought leading to a healthy or unhealthy emotion?	Unhealthy.

Samantha's example shows that her rigid thinking led her to become unhealthily angry with her husband. If she had held a flexible preference such as "I really prefer that my husband not criticize my cooking, but there's no reason why he must not do so," she may have felt healthily angry or annoyed about his unflattering remarks.

Now it's your turn. Recall a recent event when you may have been experiencing an unhealthy emotion, but you're not completely sure. Use the thought test in Worksheet 6-4 to find out whether your thinking at the time was flexible or rigid and your emotion healthy or unhealthy.

If you find, like Samantha did, that your thought is resulting in an unhealthy negative emotion, you can try replacing it with a more flexible preference. Chapters 1, 2, and 3 discuss in greater detail how your thinking can influence how you feel and behave.

WORKSHEET 6-4 My Thought Test

Thought:	
Is my thought flexible/preference-based?	
Is my thought true? Does it fit with reality?	
Is my thought helpful?	
Is my thought leading me to put myself down?	
Is my thought leading me to put down other people?	
Based on all this, is my thought leading to a healthy or unhealthy emotion?	

Being aware of your behavior

Your emotions dictate your behavior to a large extent. By acknowledging the ways you act when you're emotionally charged up, you can further determine the relative health of your feelings. Table 6-6 shows some of the typical behaviors that tend to go hand in hand with healthy and unhealthy emotions.

REMEMBER

We also call behaviors *action tendencies* because you may feel like you want to act in a certain way but not actually do it.

TABLE 6-6 Action Tendencies of Healthy and Unhealthy Feelings

Unhealthy Emotion	Action Tendencies	Healthy Emotion	Action Tendencies
Anger, rage	Shouting, being violent and abusive, putting the other person down, insisting that you're right	Annoyance, anger	Asserting yourself in a respectful but firm manner, not becoming abusive or violent, being willing to consider the other person's point of view
Anxiety	Avoiding threat, seeking excessive reassurance	Concern	Facing up to threats, seeking a reasonable amount of reassurance
Depression	Withdrawing from social reinforcements and meaningful or enjoyed activities, self-isolating	Sadness	After a period of mourning and reflection, reinvesting in the company of others, carrying on with meaningful or enjoyed activities
Acidic envy	Spoiling another person's enjoyment of what you want but don't have, sour grapes, pretending you don't really want what they have	Benign envy	Striving to gain what another person has that you desire but don't have, allowing others to enjoy what they have without trying to spoil it for them, admitting that you want what they have

(continued)

TABLE 6-6 *(continued)*

Unhealthy Emotion	Action Tendencies	Healthy Emotion	Action Tendencies
Guilt	Begging for forgiveness from or avoiding facing the person you've wronged, taking too much responsibility for the wrongdoing	Remorse	Asking for forgiveness and facing up to the person you've wronged, taking the correct amount of responsibility for the wrongdoing
Hurt	Sulking, trying to hint at what the other person has done wrong so they have to make the first move	Disappointment	Voicing your feelings, giving the other person a chance to explain or apologize, being willing to make the first move
Acidic jealousy	Spying or checking up on another person, questioning them and setting tests for them, being suspicious	Benign jealousy	Asking honest and straightforward questions, being open-minded
Shame	Avoiding the gaze of others, hiding away and withdrawing	Regret	Maintaining eye contact with others, holding your head up and keeping in contact with others

TIP

Keep in mind that you can use any word you like to describe your actual emotion. You don't need to use the labels in Table 6-6. Just make sure that you use a different term for your healthy emotion and the unhealthy alternative. Samantha, for example, may use the term *rage* to describe her unhealthy emotion and the term *ticked off* to describe her healthy emotion.

Using the terms from Table 6-6, you can now do a quick behavior test to see what type of emotion you're experiencing. We use the example of Samantha again in Table 6-7 to show you how it's done.

TABLE 6-7 **Samantha's Behavior Test**

Event:	My husband criticized the meal I prepared.
What did I actually do?	I shouted at him for being so ungrateful. I called him a lot of bad names. I stormed around the kitchen and broke some china. I refused to speak to him for the rest of the evening.
What did I feel like doing?	I really wanted to hit or punch him when he said the pasta was overcooked. I was tempted to kick him out of the house and demand a divorce.
Does my behavior fit with a healthy emotion?	No.
My emotional label:	Unhealthy rage.

Based on her behavior test, Samantha can see that she was in the grip of an unhealthy emotion from dinnertime onward.

Now it's your turn. Recall a recent event in your life when you think you experienced an unhealthy emotion and use the information in Table 6-6 and the space in Worksheet 6-5 to help you determine if your emotion was unhealthy.

WORKSHEET 6-5 My Behavior Test

Event:	
What did I actually do?	
What did I feel like doing?	
Does my behavior fit with a healthy emotion?	
My emotional label:	

Finding out what you focus on

Another way of pinning down whether you're engulfed by the turbulent seas of an unhealthy emotional reaction or surfing the cresting waves of a healthy alternative is by noticing where your attention is focused. This tactic involves analyzing the direction your thoughts take, what you're picking up within your environment, which memories you may dredge up, or how you're viewing your future.

Your emotions have an effect on your focus. For example, when you're depressed, you tend to focus on other painful losses in the past and view the future as bleak. If you're angry with someone, your attention is likely to home in on additional reasons to be angry with them. When you're hurt, you may find your thoughts tuning into ways that others and the world have done you wrong. Table 6-8 outlines common areas of focus for both healthy and unhealthy negative emotions.

TABLE 6-8 Attention Focus of Healthy and Unhealthy Feelings

Unhealthy Emotion	Attention Focus	Healthy Emotion	Attention Focus
Anger, rage	You focus on any evidence of malicious intent from others. You focus on additional reasons to be angry with people.	Annoyance, anger	You don't look for malicious intent in the actions of others unnecessarily. You don't focus on additional reasons to support your anger.
Anxiety	You overestimate the degree of risk or threat. You underestimate your personal ability to cope with the risk or threat.	Concern	You view the degree of risk or threat realistically, fully acknowledging your ability to cope with or overcome the risk or threat.

(continued)

TABLE 6-8 ***(continued)***

Unhealthy Emotion	Attention Focus	Healthy Emotion	Attention Focus
Depression	You focus on past loss or failure. You see the future as hopeless or painful.	Sadness	You're able to imagine yourself feeling happier in the future. You don't dwell on past losses or failures.
Acidic envy	You focus on reasons to put down the desired possession or situation of another person that you lack. You think about how to deprive the other person of the desired possession.	Benign envy	You focus on how you might reasonably obtain the desired possession or situation of another person that you lack. You're able to focus on being pleased for the other person.
Guilt	You blame yourself entirely for the wrongdoing. You expect and look for punishment. You look for evidence that others are blaming you for the wrongdoing.	Remorse	You take appropriate responsibility for the wrongdoing and take into account other factors. You don't expect to be punished but rather are willing to make amends. You're able to recognize forgiveness from others and to accept their forgiveness.
Hurt	You focus on how badly you've been treated and on how undeserving you are of such treatment. You dredge up past hurts. You look for proof that the other person is uncaring and indifferent.	Disappointment	You're able to see the event in perspective without dwelling on past hurts. You don't focus on how unjustly you've been treated. You're able to see evidence that the other person cares.
Acidic jealousy	You focus on threats to your relationship where they may not actually exist.	Benign jealousy	You're able to see the difference between a real and present danger to your relationship and mere hunches or suspicions.
Shame	You see disapproval from others where it doesn't exist. You overestimate the unacceptability of what has happened or been revealed about you.	Regret	You're able to respond to attempts from others to accept you. You view yourself with some compassion.

Take the attention focus test as yet another way of determining the type of emotion you're experiencing in response to a negative event. Table 6-9 is an example of how Samantha did it.

It's your turn again. Use Table 6-8 and Worksheet 6-6 to do your own attention focus test.

Congratulations! You're now well equipped to take any emotion you experience and put it through these tests to see whether it's healthy or unhealthy.

TABLE 6-9 Samantha's Attention Focus Test

Event:	My husband criticized the meal I prepared.
What direction did my attention take?	I focused on how wrong he was to say what he did about the pasta and on how ungrateful he was. I assumed that he was being deliberately mean-spirited and unkind. I remembered lots of little incidents over the last few weeks when he had been uncomplimentary.
Does my attention focus fit with a healthy emotion?	No.
My emotional label:	Unhealthy rage.

WORKSHEET 6-6 My Attention Focus Test

Event:	
What direction did my attention take?	
Does my attention focus fit with a healthy emotion?	
My emotional label:	

Avoiding being fooled by physical feelings

Many (or most) emotions, both healthy and unhealthy, are accompanied by physical sensations, or *symptoms*. As a general rule, the symptoms you have when you're feeling healthy distress aren't as uncomfortable or debilitating as those associated with unhealthy disturbance. Physical symptoms of healthy distress also tend to reduce or disappear more quickly.

REMEMBER

We use the word *distressed* to refer to healthy negative emotions and the word *disturbed* to describe unhealthy ones.

You can measure your physical feelings or symptoms in terms of intensity and duration.

EXAMPLE

Simon has a big presentation to give before the board at work. Simon usually puts a lot of pressure on himself to achieve highly and to not make mistakes. As a result, he feels very anxious before giving a presentation. Happily for Simon, he has used this workbook and paid close attention to Chapters 1, 2, 3, and 6. He now can think more flexibly about the possibility of making a mistake and of not reaching his personal standard of achievement. So, Simon can now feel healthily concerned before any future presentations.

Take a look at Simon's symptom synopsis in Tables 6-10 and 6-11.

TABLE 6-10 Simon's Disturbed Symptom Synopsis

Unhealthy emotion:	Anxiety
Symptom description:	Sleep disturbance, sweating, shaking, churning feeling in stomach
Intensity (on a scale where 1 is mild and 10 is severe):	9
Duration:	My sleep is disturbed for about four nights prior to the presentation. I wake up and worry about messing it up. That churning feeling in my stomach is there almost constantly from about a week before the presentation. My hands shake and I sweat throughout the entire presentation, although I do my best to hide it.

TABLE 6-11 Simon's Distressed Symptom Synopsis

Healthy emotion:	Concern
Symptom description:	Minor sleep disturbance, some sweating, trembling in hands, churning feeling in stomach
Intensity (on a scale where 1 is mild and 10 is severe):	4
Duration:	My sleep is a bit disturbed the night before the presentation, but I worry only slightly about messing it up. The churning feeling in my stomach happens only fleetingly, when I'm reminded about the upcoming presentation, and it goes away almost instantly. My hands tremble and I sweat more at the start of the presentation, but that stops when I get into it.

You can probably see from the example of Simon that his physical symptoms are similar for both anxiety and concern, but in the latter case they're less intense and don't go on as long. You can use the same method to compare the intensity and duration of any physical feelings you have in conjunction with your emotion using Worksheets 6-7 and 6-8.

WORKSHEET 6-7 My Disturbed Symptom Synopsis

Unhealthy emotion:	
Symptom description:	
Intensity (on a scale where 1 is mild and 10 is severe):	
Duration:	

WORKSHEET 6-8 My Distressed Symptom Synopsis

Healthy emotion:	
Symptom description:	
Intensity (on a scale where 1 is mild and 10 is severe):	
Duration:	

The intensity and duration of any physical sensations that go along with your emotional experience can indicate which type of emotion you're feeling. But a degree of overlap exists in this area with both types of emotions.

TIP

Many of the physical reactions and sensations that you experience are similar for both types of emotions. For example, you may be tearful and lose your appetite whether you're sad or depressed. For this reason, using your thoughts, behaviors, and attention focus as reliable indicators of what type of emotion you're dealing with is best.

Charting Your Problem Emotions

After you've identified your emotions as either healthy or unhealthy, your next step is to decide which unhealthy emotions you want to target for change. These emotions are probably the ones you experience the most often or those that interfere most significantly with the smooth running of your life. You can use Tables 6-6 and 6-8 to list your problem emotions in Worksheet 6-9.

WORKSHEET 6-9 My Problem Emotions

Identifying themes and triggers

Although your behavior, thinking style, and attention focus are different for healthy and unhealthy negative emotions, the *theme* (key aspects of a broad situation that give rise to a particular emotion) is the same. Getting familiar with the themes that accompany different emotional experiences can help you to accurately pinpoint the nature of your feelings. You're then in a better position to figure out whether your emotion is healthy or unhealthy.

Table 6-12 lists the themes attached to each emotional pairing.

TABLE 6-12 **Feeling Themes**

Unhealthy Emotion	Healthy Emotion	Theme
Anxiety	Concern	Perceived threat, risk, or danger.
Depression	Sadness	Loss or failure.
Acidic envy	Benign envy	Another person has something desirable that you lack.
Guilt	Remorse	Broken moral code by doing something wrong or by failing to do something (sin of commission or omission).
Hurt	Disappointment	You are treated badly and are undeserving.
Acidic jealousy	Benign jealousy	Threat to your relationship.
Rage	Annoyance	Personal rule is broken and/or self-esteem is threatened.
Shame	Regret	Undesirable or unacceptable personal information has been publicly revealed by yourself or others.

By noting any recurrent themes in your life, you can begin to notice triggers or specific events that start you off on an unhealthily emotional roller coaster.

Note how Samantha used the theme and trigger tracker to identify her problem emotions more specifically in Table 6-13.

TABLE 6-13 **Samantha's Theme and Trigger Tracker**

Theme:	Personal rule is broken and/or self-esteem is threatened.
Unhealthy emotion:	Rage.
Triggers:	My husband criticizes my cooking.
	My boss is unhappy with a report.
	Someone steals my parking space.
	A friend turns up an hour late for coffee.

It's your turn now. Try your hand at Worksheet 6-10.

You may have more than one problem emotion and, hence, more than one theme and a throng of potential triggers. So, feel free to use Worksheet 6-10 again — once for each problem emotion.

WORKSHEET 6-10 My Theme and Trigger Tracker

Theme:	
Unhealthy emotion:	
Triggers:	

Making a problem statement

Here's the good news: Having possibly realized that you have lots of unhealthy negative emotional responses to life events, you can do something about it! But first you need to make a problem statement. Have a look at Samantha's in Table 6-14.

TABLE 6-14 Samantha's Problem Statement

Feeling rage about my husband's critical remarks, leading me to call him names, break plates, and give him the cold shoulder.
Goal: To be ticked off instead of raging.

Samantha's problem statement includes her unhealthy emotion, the trigger, and her unhealthy behavior. This statement provides a lot of information about where she can intervene to change her rage to healthy anger or annoyance, or as she calls it being ticked off.

Fill in Worksheet 6-11.

WORKSHEET 6-11 My Problem Statement

Feeling ________________ about ________________ leading me to ________________.
Goal:

You can write as many problem statements as you need to, depending on how many problem emotions you have. Several chapters in this book can help you overcome your emotional problems now that you're so good at identifying them. And if you do your best to *behave* in accordance with your healthy emotional goal, turn your *attention* to the things that fit with a healthy negative emotion, and, above all, strive to *think* in a flexible, preference-based way, then you're on the road to emotional well-being!

IN THIS CHAPTER

- **Recognizing when your solution becomes the problem**
- **Tolerating short-term pain for long-term gain**
- **Visualizing a vicious flower**

Chapter 7

Targeting Troublesome Tactics

If you feel emotionally disturbed, doing whatever reduces your emotional discomfort seems sensible. You may be doing what you think is best to help you cope with your psychological problems. Unfortunately, some of the strategies you're using to make yourself feel temporarily better may well be maintaining your problem in the long run. You probably aren't aware of perpetuating your problems with some of your coping behaviors. Most people don't know exactly how to best help themselves overcome problems such as depression or anxiety. In this chapter, we deal with some common self-defeating coping strategies.

Identifying Self-Defeating Strategies

The first step in identifying self-defeating strategies is recognizing which of your tactics are maintaining your problems or even making them worse. Here are some examples of what we mean by *problematic strategies:*

- Avoiding situations that you fear or that provoke anxiety.
- Using some strategies to increase "safety" within an anxiety-provoking situation (called *safety-seeking behaviors* or *safety behaviors*), such as holding on tightly to a handle on the train because of a fear of falling.
- Taking drugs or using alcohol to block out uncomfortable emotions.

- Hiding aspects of yourself that you feel ashamed about.
- Putting off dealing with practical problems and tasks that you find unpleasant.
- Withdrawing from your usual routine.
- Isolating yourself from friends and family.
- Worrying. Many people think that by worrying about potential negative events, they'll prevent bad things from happening or prepare themselves to deal with such events. Although worrying may *seem* like a way of solving or preventing future problems, it actually becomes a problem itself because it promotes anxiety.
- Performing rituals. People who suffer with anxiety disorders like obsessive-compulsive disorder (OCD; see Chapter 11) often insist that they perform everyday tasks like dressing or cleaning themselves in a very rigid, ordered pattern. They often worry that if they fail to execute tasks in a precise way, something bad will happen to themselves or others. If the pattern is interrupted, these people become very anxious and often make themselves begin the ritual all over again and may spend hours trying to get their rituals done exactly right.
- Checking things over and over. It's normal to check that you've locked the door or that you've got your keys in your bag once or twice. But people with anxiety problems often check things like this so many times that they find it very difficult to leave the house and arrive at work or appointments on time.

Obviously, you may be using many more possible troublesome tactics in addition to the ones listed here. The types of coping strategies you choose depend on what type of problem you're experiencing. We cover anxiety, depression, and OCD in more detail in Chapters 9, 10, and 11, respectively.

REMEMBER

The old adage that sometimes you have to feel worse before you feel better is often true. In CBT, we encourage you to drop your troublesome coping tactics in favor of healthier behaviors that ultimately will help you overcome your problems. This approach can mean doing things that cause you short-term anxiety or discomfort in the spirit of getting well.

Demanding control and insisting on certainty

If you suffer from an anxiety problem such as post-traumatic stress disorder (PTSD), OCD, or panic attacks, you probably like to be in control. No doubt you also try to be as certain as possible about situations before you enter them. You may have the same demands for control and certainty if you have an anger or jealousy problem.

The trouble is, if you're trying hard to control things that are beyond your control (such as certain physical sensations, other people's thoughts, or even your own thoughts), it can be pretty disheartening. The same goes for certainty. Many things exist in life that you simply can't be 100 percent certain about, no matter how hard you try.

If you continue to try (in vain) to be in a state of absolute control and utter certainty at all times, you're likely to become even more anxious, angry, jealous, or depressed. Learning to accept limitations to your personal power and to live with uncertainty can really make a positive difference in how you feel.

Trying to control how others behave and what they think about you is common. But it's a fruitless endeavor because other people are outside your sphere of control. You can't control what other people do or think most of the time. You may be able to *influence* others to behave and think the way you'd like, or *request* that they behave and think the way you'd like, but it's ultimately up to them to decide on their own thoughts and actions. Try giving other people permission to make their own decisions and form their own opinions.

Also keep in mind that you can't — and don't *need* to — control your physical sensations, such as blushing, breathing, swallowing, or your heart beating. Try letting your body get on with the physical symptoms of anxiety (see Chapter 9) and allow them to subside on their own. Trying to control a physical side effect of anxiety usually leads to further anxiety or panic. Also, allow your body to get on with the business of operating without your guidance or intervention. Breathing is so automatic that you can do it when you're asleep or even in a coma! Try trusting your body to do its job — even when you're feeling anxious.

The same goes for life events. Life is often unpredictable, uncertain, and even unfair. If you insist that you need certainty about what life is about to deal you at all times, then you're very likely to have a lot of anxiety. No one can control random life events, and trying too hard to do so will only generate worry and anxiety. Often people assume that because something negative happened to them once, they're more vulnerable to the same sort of bad event happening to them again. Although this is rarely the case, people may go to great lengths to try to get a guarantee that nothing bad will happen. This behavior is understandable but ultimately problematic. Instead, try to have some faith in your ability to cope with adverse events if and when they occur. Also, work on accepting the idea that life is uncertain and always has been. Living with uncertainty is part of being human, so it's something you do every day — even though you may not realize it.

The worksheet in this section helps you clearly identify specific situations in which you may be trying too hard to gain control or certainty. It also helps you understand how your attempts to be *totally* in control and certain are maintaining problems like anxiety and depression.

EXAMPLE

Connie was involved in a serious traffic accident 18 months ago. She recovered from her physical injuries but is still suffering psychologically. Connie was riding in the back seat of the car that crashed. Since the accident, she has avoided driving on the highway and will only go in a vehicle if she can drive. If she begins to feel anxious when driving, she tries very hard to control her breathing. She monitors how fast she is breathing and tries to make her breathing deep and regular. Unfortunately, this means that Connie becomes *over-aware* of her breathing. Because breathing is an automatic bodily function, Connie doesn't need to focus on her breath. If she leaves it alone, her breathing will take care of itself. Connie also reads the weather reports before she travels in order to be certain that the conditions are favorable for driving. If anyone else is in the car with Connie, she insists that they don't speak to her or distract her in any way.

Connie is trying to be absolutely certain that she won't be involved in another accident. She used Table 7-1 to help understand her demands for certainty and control and to monitor their effects.

Use Worksheet 7-1 to help you figure out when to relinquish control and accept uncertainty.

TABLE 7-1 Connie's Control and Certainty Checkup

What is my main emotional problem?	Anxiety (PTSD).
In what ways am I demanding control?	Trying to control my breathing when I feel anxious, refusing to be a passenger so that I can be in control of the car, telling others how to behave when I'm driving, controlling where I drive and avoiding motorways.
In what ways am I insisting on certainty?	Checking the weather forecast so I can be certain that it won't rain or be stormy when I'm in the car, telling people to be quiet in the car so that I can be certain I won't be distracted, planning all journeys so that I can be certain to avoid the motorway.
How are my control demands affecting my main emotional problem?	Demanding control keeps me feeling on edge when driving. Trying to control my breathing and anxiety symptoms doesn't work — it just makes me panicky. Then I think of myself as weak for having a panic episode. I think of the accident a lot when I'm trying to control things related to driving. I feel more anxious and unsafe because of my control demands.
How is my insistence on certainty affecting my main emotional problem?	Going to such lengths to try to make certain that I stay safe and don't have an accident means that I'm always expecting something bad to happen when I'm in the car. I feel anxious just at the thought of car travel because of my certainty demands. The more I try to control my thoughts/images about the accident, the more distressing I find them.

WORKSHEET 7-1 My Control and Certainty Checkup

What is my main emotional problem?	
In what ways am I demanding control?	
In what ways am I insisting on certainty?	
How are my control demands affecting my main emotional problem?	
How is my insistence on certainty affecting my main emotional problem?	

Adding up avoidance and getting yourself down

Avoidance is a very common unhelpful coping strategy. If you're afraid of something or feel anxious in certain situations, you're better off avoiding these things, right? Wrong. The more you avoid whatever frightens you and provokes your anxiety, the more you reinforce the idea that a real threat exists. Continued avoidance keeps you anxious and can diminish your overall functioning. Likewise, putting off tasks that you find distasteful or don't feel like doing can lead to practical problems and worsen depression. Sometimes, facing your fears and doing things you don't want to do is worth it. Grinning and bearing it is often in your best interest.

In Chapter 9, we provide more worksheets devised to help you construct exposure exercises for confronting avoidance and overcoming fears. Chapter 10 has useful information and worksheets to help you schedule daily activities and re-engage with previously enjoyed practices. Here, we offer a few pointers to help you avoid avoidance and get on with neglected activities *now:*

1. **Make a list of the situations you're currently avoiding or neglecting due to your emotional problems of anxiety or depression.**
2. **Rank these situations in order of least frightening to most frightening or least anxiety-producing to most anxiety-producing.**

   Basically, rank the situations according to how badly you want to avoid them.
3. **Put yourself into your feared situation regularly, long enough to help build your tolerance.**

   Try your hardest to push yourself into your anxiety-provoking situations. Doing so helps you adjust to the situation and begin to take it in stride.

   Also, give yourself credit for being able to cope with uncomfortable feelings in these situations.
4. **Work your way up your list.**

If you're depressed and you don't find pleasure in activities you once enjoyed or feel like hiding away from people because of your low mood, urge yourself to do the opposite! Doing the things you like to do and being around other people may lift your mood, provide you with understanding and support, or even just help you to feel more like yourself again. Self-isolation is a big feature of depression and reinforces loneliness. It's often worth going out with other people just for the sake of it, whether you really enjoy it or not. You may not have the great time that you used to have, but being with others is very likely to stop you from feeling worse.

EXAMPLE

Mark has been depressed for a few months. He was under a lot of pressure at work and at one stage worried that he would lose his job if he didn't work late to meet deadlines. His depression may have been partly triggered by protracted stress. Mark feels demotivated at work and has often called in sick. He has also stopped going to the gym because he just feels too tired. His friends invite him out, but he doesn't enjoy socializing as much as he used to, so he often declines. Mark spends much of the day in bed watching TV or dozing. The stack of mail is mounting up, but Mark can't face opening it, so bills are going unpaid. Mark knows that he should visit his doctor to talk about his depression, but he feels hopeless.

Mark listed the activities his depression led him to avoid, his reasons for avoiding them, and the results of his avoidance in Table 7-2.

Worksheet 7-2 provides you with space to list the things you avoid, why you avoid them, and the price you pay for ignoring them.

In Table 7-3, Mark noted how his behavior was reinforcing his depression.

Whether you're feeling depressed, anxious, unhealthily angry, or jealous (to name but a few; see Chapter 6 for more emotions), now is an opportunity for you to underline whatever you may be doing to try to cope with and alleviate your emotional problem.

TABLE 7-2 Mark's Avoidance List

My primary emotional problem: Feeling depressed		
Things I'm Avoiding	**Reason for Avoidance**	**Effects of Avoidance**
Opening the mail	Can't face it.	Bills mounting up.
Going to work	Too stressful and overwhelming.	My boss keeps calling. I worry about sick days mounting up. I get anxious and filled with dread at the thought of going back to work.
Talking to my boss about reducing my workload	He won't understand and will think I'm incompetent.	Stress remains, and I don't get a chance to assert myself or find out what my boss would actually suggest.
Going to doctor	It's hopeless. He can't help.	I don't have a doctor's note. I'm not getting advice or help. I'm not on medication.

WORKSHEET 7-2 My Avoidance List

My primary emotional problem:		
Things I'm Avoiding	**Reason for Avoidance**	**Effects of Avoidance**

TABLE 7-3 Mark's Unhelpful Behaviors

Unhelpful Behaviors	Reason for Behavior	Effect of Behavior
Staying in bed all day.	Feel unable to face the world.	More depression and fear. Sleep disturbance.
Not socializing.	I don't want to see anyone or let them see how messed up I am.	I am isolated from my friends, feel very alone, and think too much.
Not going to the gym.	I'm too tired and weak.	My fitness is diminishing and I feel less healthy and strong generally. I have no social interaction and more depressed thoughts.

REMEMBER

What helps you feel better in the immediate present often keeps your problem going into the future. Avoiding things like work, talking to others, and answering the phone are typical examples of unhelpful avoidance. Also, consider the things you may be doing to dull your unpleasant feelings — things like drinking too much, using drugs, shopping, eating or watching TV to distract yourself. Reversing these types of behaviors is often a key first step to overcoming your emotional problems. Use Worksheet 7-3 to list your unhelpful behaviors.

WORKSHEET 7-3 My Unhelpful Behaviors

Unhelpful Behaviors	Reason for Behavior	Effect of Behavior

REMEMBER

Very often, doing the exact opposite of what your mood dictates, or encourages you to do, is the best thing for you in the long run. So, if you feel like avoiding work or socializing, often you'll do yourself a world of good by thrusting yourself into social situations and confronting work issues head-on. Likewise, if immersing yourself in drugs and alcohol or mindless TV watching helps take your mind off your feelings in the present, resisting these behaviors may well aid you in confronting your problems and give you the chance to come up with possible solutions for them.

By allocating a time slot for constructive action, you make it more probable that you'll carry it out. It's very easy to have good intentions but let them slide because you've not given yourself a definite time slot to carry them out. Get good at giving yourself time frames for doing things that are in your best interest, whatever they may be. Cleaning the house, talking to your boss, working out, socializing, paying bills, returning phone calls, and so on are all examples of tasks that you can allocate specific times to completing.

EXAMPLE

Mark used Table 7-4 to record healthier ways of dealing with his symptoms of depression and to allocate specific times to perform his neglected duties.

TABLE 7-4 Mark's Alternative Behaviors

Healthy Alternative Coping Strategies	Potential Benefits of Healthy Coping Strategies	Allocated Time Slot
Doing the opposite of what my depression dictates!	If I act against my depressed thoughts and actions, I may stop my mood from getting even worse.	
Sticking to a daily schedule and forcing myself to get up at the same time every day. Avoiding naps.	If I get up at the same time every day and don't nap, I may get my sleep routine back on track.	Get out of bed at 8 a.m. every day.
Going back to the gym.	Going to the gym may give me a much-needed endorphin rush.	Monday, Wednesday, and Friday at 3 p.m.

(continued)

TABLE 7-4 *(continued)*

Healthy Alternative Coping Strategies	Potential Benefits of Healthy Coping Strategies	Allocated Time Slot
Opening the post and paying the bills.	I'll feel more on top of things and less hopeless if I pay the bills.	10 a.m. every morning.
Contacting work about my illness.	If I inform work of my depression, at least they'll know what's going on. I won't need to hide under the covers avoiding the ringing phone.	Monday at 9 a.m.
Visiting the doctor.	My doctor may be able to refer me to a therapist or give me some antidepressants, or both. A note from my doctor will help secure my job.	Tuesday at 1 p.m.
Keeping in touch with friends and family.	Seeing friends and family may help me feel more "normal" again. They might even be supportive and understanding. The more time I spend with others, the less isolated I'll be. Keeping busy gives me less time to focus on my depressed thoughts and lack of energy.	Thursday evenings and weekends.

Chapter 10 covers depression and how to use an activity schedule. Scheduling your activities (both leisure and work-related) can really help you get things done despite low energy and motivation.

Use Worksheet 7-4 to identify more healthy behaviors and assign a set time to carry out the tasks you've been putting off.

WORKSHEET 7-4 **My Alternative Behaviors**

Healthy Alternative Coping Strategies	Potential Benefits of Healthy Coping Strategies	Allocated Time Slot

REMEMBER

Some tasks seem far more off-putting when you just think about them than when you actually start doing them. Doing tasks in the absence of energy and motivation can serve to increase both. If you're depressed, you may not initially get your usual level of enjoyment from pleasurable activities, because depression can interfere with your ability to enjoy things. But be assured that doing something is better than doing nothing. Feelings of achievement, satisfaction, and enjoyment will return in time. Be patient with yourself.

Worrying yourself sick

A bit of worry is entirely normal. Note we said "a bit." It's normal for problems or responsibilities to enter your mind and for you to try to think of how best to sort them out. But many people make worrying a full-time occupation. Excessive worrying is a nonproductive bad habit. If you're someone who worries all the time about the tiniest everyday things, you no doubt find it exhausting.

The most fervent worriers frequently worry about events that haven't yet happened, that may never happen, or over which they have no control. It's like trying to solve an unsolvable problem. Here are the two main reasons you may be trapped in a cycle of excessive and undue worry:

- You may believe that worrying somehow protects you from negative life events — as though worrying somehow better equips you to deal with bad things.
- You may also believe that worrying will magically prevent bad things from happening to you — as though worrying will somehow provide clues and insight into a bad thing before it happens.

You may think that the best way to deal with your practical or psychological problems is to worry them out. Not so. Life just isn't governable like that. You can worry until the cows come home, and you still won't be able to control random events. Worry is *not* the same as problem-solving thought and action. It's a recipe for further anxiety and feelings of helplessness.

Think of your worry as a bad habit or a problematic process that needs to be interrupted. Don't let yourself dwell on the *content* of your worries; instead, recognize that worry *itself* is your main problem. Chapter 5 offers some helpful hints on learning to accept and ignore your thoughts.

WARNING

If you're one of those people who believes that if only you can work through *every* conceivable worry, you'll be able to relax and enjoy life, lots of luck! It'll never happen. You'll always find another thing to worry about, and you'll never learn to give your brain a break. You may even end up worrying that worrying so much is harmful. Actually, it isn't — but it *is* fruitless and very uncomfortable.

Worksheet 7-5 provides you with an opportunity to interrupt your worry process.

WORKSHEET 7-5 **My Worry Workout**

1. Am I currently worrying about something that hasn't yet happened? (Answer Yes or No only.)

2. Is this current worry a real-life problem that I can work on resolving? (Answer Yes or No only.)

If Yes, what do I need to put into action to solve the problem? List specific actions you can take.

(continued)

WORKSHEET 7-5 *(continued)*

If No, what can I do to interrupt the worry process? List specific activities that will absorb your attention.
3. Am I worrying in an attempt to prevent this negative thing from happening? (Answer Yes or No only.)
4. Am I worrying in an attempt to protect myself from this negative event should it happen? (Answer Yes or No only.)
5. Being as objective as possible, is this current worry just another example of my overall worry problem? (Answer Yes or No only.)
If Yes (as it probably will be!), revisit your "If No" answer under Step 2 and turn your attention to more interesting and productive things! List them here.

WARNING

When you first begin to resist the worry process, you'll feel very uncomfortable and even unsafe or irresponsible. These feelings are simply because you're going against the grain of your tendency — you're worrying about not worrying! Expect to feel odd and drawn back to your worries as you begin the quest for a worry-free life. Stick with your resistance and, over time, you'll retrain your brain to let worries pass and to focus on more productive aspects of your life.

When Feeling Better Stops You from Getting Better

We all like to take the edge off our uncomfortable feelings, which is very understandable but not always helpful in the long run. Often, attempts to make yourself feel better only bring about the kind of results you most want to avoid. So, if you desperately try not to be socially awkward, you may well end up being so self-conscious that you say something odd or behave in an aloof manner. That scenario is just one example of how trying to feel better in the "here and now" can actually make you worse in the "there and later." We expand on this concept a bit more in the following sections.

Stopping yourself from self-medicating your mood

Perhaps a little alcohol will take the sting out of your guilt, anxiety, or depression. Maybe a little extra dose of a sleeping pill will quiet your anxious mind, stop the flashbacks, or quell intrusive images. Yep, can't argue with that. Drugs and alcohol are pretty effective mood-altering substances — in the short term. But be warned: These immediate interventions have long-term ramifications. You may end up addicted to sleeping pills or dependent on alcohol. Or you may just feel more depressed and anxious the next day when you wake up with a hangover. Not fun.

Self-medicating habits can extend to normally innocuous activities such as shopping, watching TV, or scrolling endlessly on your phone. Basically, anything you do to distract yourself or deal indirectly with a core problem is termed *self-medicating* in psychotherapy.

EXAMPLE

Verity has a problem with low self-worth. She feels very depressed and hates herself if she fails to achieve highly at work or falters in her personal life as a mother and partner. Verity often sees *total* failure in very minor things, such as being late to work or not having dinner on the table at a certain time. She drinks wine in the evenings to calm her anxiety and relieve her sense of guilt. On the weekends, Verity takes her kids out and buys them toys that the family can't afford to try to make up for her perceived shortcomings as a mother.

Verity used Table 7-5 to highlight her self-medicating behaviors and to see how they're becoming problems themselves.

TABLE 7-5 Verity's Mood Self-Medication Morass

My problematic unhealthy emotions: Depression and guilt	
How do I self-medicate my mood?	By drinking wine in the evenings (sometimes a lot) and by shopping for treats for the kids (and sometimes for myself).
How does this affect my mood in the short term?	When I'm actually drinking the wine, I get a feeling of relief and happiness. I feel great after I've bought something for the kids, and I get a real buzz out of buying something for myself.
How does this affect my mood in the long term?	If I've drunk a lot the night before, I feel ill, tired, and guilty the next morning when I wake up. I feel like a bad mother and a useless employee, and this feeling can last for several hours or sometimes days. When I make myself feel better through shopping, I often experience a real mood crash after the initial euphoria wears off. This can happen an hour or a day after the spree. Then I get credit card bills and feel overwhelmed and guilty about spending money so freely.
What other effects does self-medicating have on my life?	I'm sinking deeper into debt. I often drink too much when I'm out, and I feel that I've been a bit inappropriate, which I then berate myself over. I think that I'm becoming dependent on alcohol to make myself feel okay and to feel I can cope with social situations and everyday life.

REMEMBER

Self-medicating behaviors can include anything that you do for immediate relief or gratification. Usually, anything that you're doing too much of can be classed as such a behavior. Shopping, drinking, eating, sleeping, watching TV, or even innocuous activities such as sex and reading can become problematic solutions if done too much or in lieu of other more productive behaviors. So, as honestly as possible, check out your motivation for whatever you're doing.

Use Worksheet 7-6 to assess your self-medicating behaviors and their short- and long-term effects.

Requesting reassurance and seeking safety

Looking for ways to secure your safety and asking others to reassure you that the worst won't happen are two other common self-defeating strategies for dealing with problems. People who suffer anxiety or jealousy problems often employ these tactics.

WORKSHEET 7-6 My Mood Self-Medication Morass

My problematic unhealthy emotions:	
How do I self-medicate my mood?	
How does this affect my mood in the short term?	
How does this affect my mood in the long term?	
What other effects does self-medicating have on my life?	

Why don't these strategies work? Well, the reality is that your problem is insecurity — not a real danger or threat to your relationship. So, if your partner reassures you that they aren't about to leave you, you'll feel better — but only for a very short time because you can't be reassured. If you're told that the plane won't crash or your job is safe, you'll believe it for about ten minutes before you start obsessing and worrying again. Nothing sinks in for terribly long. You can't be convinced that you're safe. The more you look for reassurance and seek safety, the more anxious and unsafe you'll feel in the long term.

The answer to this conundrum is to accept the possibility that your partner could one day leave you (even if that situation isn't terribly likely) or that your safety will be compromised and you'll either survive or not. Stop seeking safety and reassurance from others who can't actually give you any guarantees! Instead, start stopping your tongue and letting your fears subside on their own. They will, if you let them.

Listing the people who you most often approach for reassurance helps you recognize your self-defeating habits. As a rule, you tend to wrestle reassurance from the people you're most comfortable with, like partners, close friends, and family. Resisting this helps you to learn to give yourself reasonable reassurance and may improve your relationships with those close to you. Try refocusing your attention on how the people you care about most are feeling and what's going on in their lives rather than using them solely to quell your fears and anxieties.

Use Worksheet 7-7 to help you stop the unhelpful reassurance seeking and self-defeating safety seeking.

WORKSHEET 7-7 My Reassurance and Safety-Seeking Checklist

My primary emotional/psychological problem:	
Who do I go to for bouts of reassurance? List the names of specific people.	
Does this reassurance last for more than a few hours or days? (Answer Yes or No only.)	
How do I try to safeguard my safety? List specific actions.	

My primary emotional/psychological problem:	
Who do I ask to try to guarantee my safety? List names of specific people.	
Do I feel safe for more than a few minutes or hours? (Answer Yes or No only.)	
Do I end up going through the same safety and reassurance processes over and over again? (Answer Yes or No only.)	
What does this tell me about my attempts to make myself feel safe and reassured in the long term?	
Is it a long-term solution? (Answer Yes or No only.)	
How might resisting the urge to seek safety and ask for reassurance benefit me in the long term?	

Putting Petals on Your Vicious Flower

You've probably heard of a vicious circle. We now present the vicious flower. This flower involves all the principles embodied in the worksheets throughout this chapter and provides a more visual image of how you may be perpetuating your own problems without even realizing that you're doing so! Some people respond better to visual aids than to written ones. Or maybe you want to use both, which is also fine.

Use these steps for filling out your vicious flower:

1. **In the trigger box, record an event that leads you to feel an unhealthy emotion such as guilt, depression, anxiety, or shame.**

   See Chapter 6 for more about healthy and unhealthy emotions.

2. **In the middle circle, write down any thoughts or meanings you give to the trigger.**
3. **In the top petal, record what aspects of the experience you focus on most when you're triggered.**
4. **In the corresponding petals, record your emotions, behaviors, and physical sensations in response to the trigger event.**

EXAMPLE

Jon has panic attacks. When in the grips of an attack, he feels that he's about to collapse. He tries to sit down or hold onto something solid. Jon thinks that drinking water will stop the panic. He also tries to stop or abate physical sensations such as dizziness, heart racing, and sweating. He thinks that people will mock him about his attacks and behavior. Table 7-6 shows how Jon filled in the petals on his vicious flower.

Now think about your own psychological or emotional problem and fill in the vicious flower in Worksheet 7-8 for a visual view of your self-defeating coping strategies.

TABLE 7-6 **Jon's Vicious Flower**

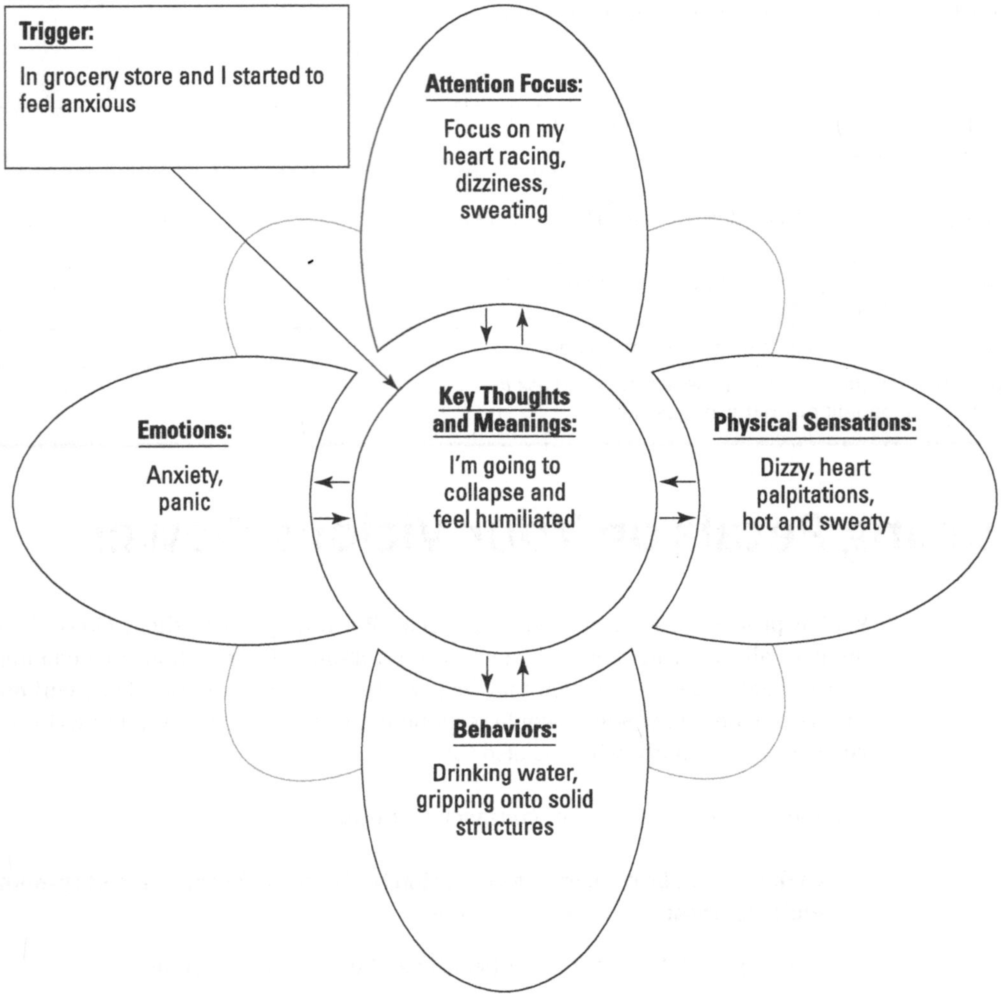

Uprooting your vicious flower

Now you need to tear out the roots of your vicious, flaming, fretful, and ferocious flower! And doing so is pretty straightforward in theory, if sometimes not in practice. Hopefully, filling in the fearsome flower will bring to light how you're keeping the nasty thing growing.

EXAMPLE

Poor sweet Jon, as shown in Table 7-6, tries to stop his panic symptoms by telling himself that he should be able to control his wobbly legs, racing heart, and sweating by sitting down or grabbing onto any available solid structure. But in actual fact, he only ends up increasing his feelings of anxiety and panic. Jon used Table 7-7 to uproot his poisonous petunia.

Now have a go at uprooting your own vicious flower in Worksheet 7-9.

WORKSHEET 7-8 Your Vicious Flower

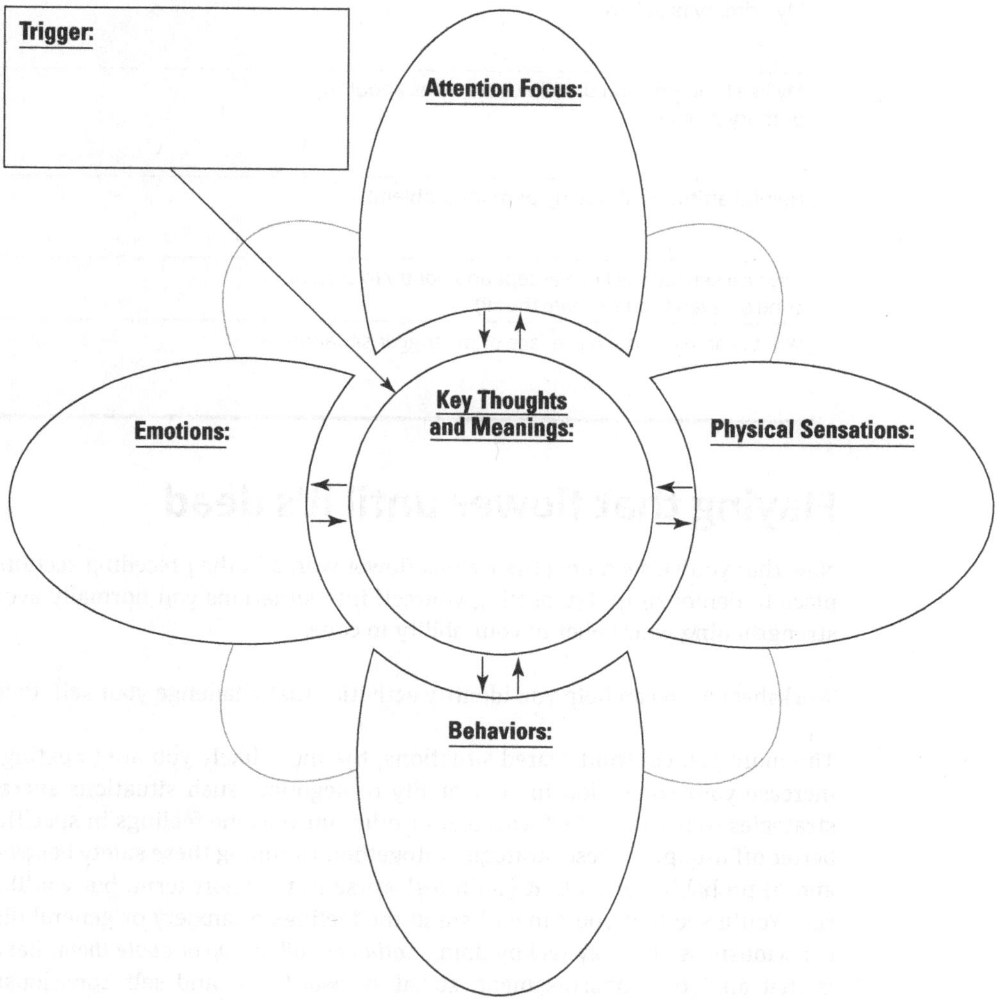

TABLE 7-7 Jon's Uprooting the Vicious Flower Format

My primary problem: Panic attacks	
My key thoughts and unhelpful attitudes about my primary problem:	I'll collapse if I don't stop my dizzy sensations! My legs are already wobbly and will give way from under me. This will be so humiliating. Everyone will laugh at me and ridicule me!
Helpful attitudes about my primary problem:	If I collapse, so be it. Even if people laugh at me, I can take it. Chances are, someone will try to help me rather than ridicule me. I can still respect myself as a person despite my panic attacks.
Physical sensations I can accept and not try to stop or control (even though I hate them!):	Dizziness, wobbly legs, racing heart
What I can try to do in the face of my trigger situation:	Don't sit down. Ride out the panic until it subsides. Stop carrying a bottle of water with me everywhere. Stop grabbing on to objects that may provide physical support.

WORKSHEET 7-9 My Uprooting the Vicious Flower Format

My primary problem:	
My key thoughts and unhelpful attitudes about my primary problem:	
Helpful attitudes about my primary problem:	
Physical sensations I can accept and *not* try to stop or control (even though I *hate* them!):	
What I can try to do in the face of my trigger situation:	

Flaying that flower until it's dead

Now that you've seen how the vicious flower works in the preceding sections, you're in a good place to demolish it! Try putting yourself into situations you normally avoid with the goal of strengthening your belief in your ability to cope.

Worksheet 7-10 can help you identify activities that challenge your self-defeating beliefs.

The more you confront feared situations, the more likely you are to extinguish your fear and increase your conviction in your ability to negotiate such situations successfully. If you use strategies to help you deal with fear or other unwelcome feelings in specific situations, you're better off dropping these strategies altogether. Dropping these safety behaviors (see Chapters 7 and 9) probably means that you'll feel worse in the short term, but you'll benefit in the long run. You'll see that you can withstand the feelings of anxiety or general discomfort and self-consciousness you may feel by doing *nothing at all to stop or abate them.* Basically, the message is that anxiety, embarrassment, social awkwardness, and self-consciousness are distinctly unpleasant but they won't — under any circumstances — kill you.

WORKSHEET 7-10 Your Flower-Flaying Fact File

My primary emotional/psychological problem:	
Situations I avoid to stop my problem from being triggered:	
If I face these situations, how will it ultimately benefit me?	
Which safety-seeking behaviors can I strive to drop?	
How might dropping these safety behaviors help me to overcome my primary problem?	
What ultimate beneficial effect might flaying my flower have on my primary problem?	

IN THIS CHAPTER

- » Using SPORT to score goals
- » Increasing your motivation to change
- » Making a goal statement
- » Paying attention to your progress

Chapter 8 Getting Goal-Directed

Unless you know where you're going, getting somewhere is difficult. Sometimes you may know that you're unhappy, emotionally distraught, or caught up in a cycle of self-destructive behaviors. What you may be less clear on is how exactly you want things to be different. Many people have difficulty breaking out of destructive patterns and overcoming emotional problems because they're too vague about their goals. Often we hear people say, "I just want to feel better" or "I want my life to improve." We have no doubt that these desires are sincere, but they aren't specific enough to act on.

In order to get the most out of any self-help, cognitive behavioral therapy (CBT), or other therapeutic treatment, you need to be clear about what your problems are and what your goals are in relation to these problems. This chapter helps you make clear problem statements and establish specific goals. Think of it like satellite navigation: Where you are and a clear destination are the essential starting points for your recovery or personal-growth journey.

Giving Goals a SPORT-ing Chance

The acronym *SPORT* stands for *specific, positive, observable, realistic,* and *timed.* We'd like you to carefully consider these five aspects of your goals:

- » **Specific:** Be precise about when, where, and with whom you want to feel and/or behave more constructively.
- » **Positive:** State your goals in positive terms. What do you want to achieve or work toward? What do you want to strive to gain in your personal life?

- **Observable:** Consider how an objective individual could note that you've changed. What positive changes might you notice in your own thinking and actions?
- **Realistic:** Make your goals clear, concrete, and within your scope of achievement. Focus on goals that involve changing your personal reactions to life events instead of on changing others or life events over which you have very little power.
- **Timed:** Setting a time frame to help you keep your goals in sight. Think about setting yourself clear times to carry out identified tasks. Doing a task list with spotlighted times to do each task can help you actually get on with what you need to do.

Feeling different

Choosing appropriate healthy negative emotions as goals in response to a negative life event is very important. You may be tempted to choose a goal of indifference. Denying reality may work for a short time, but eventually your true feelings will catch up with you. For example, if you're going through a divorce, you may want to not care about the divorce and to have no real feelings about it at all. This attitude is understandable but highly unrealistic.

If you really care about something happening to you, it's only normal and right that you should feel negatively about that situation. In order to not care about a divorce, you'd have to not care about your spouse or your marriage and this is clearly not the case. Going for a goal of indifference requires that you to lie to yourself about your feelings. So, you're wise to choose healthy sadness and healthy anger as emotional goals.

We strenuously recommend that you review Chapter 6 before doing the next two worksheets. Doing so will help you choose the right emotional and behavioral goals for your situation.

REMEMBER

The idea is not to avoid feeling any negative emotions but rather to experience healthy emotional distress instead of unhealthy emotional disturbance.

Give some serious thought to the situation/problem about which you're setting goals. Consider how you're currently feeling about the situation and what would be an appropriate and healthy emotion to feel instead. Then complete Worksheet 8-1.

WORKSHEET 8-1 My Emotional Goal

What is my problem situation?	
What is my unhealthy negative emotion?	
How is this emotion causing me further problems?	
What healthy negative emotion would I like to feel instead?	

How will I need to change my thinking in order to achieve this emotional goal?	
How will achieving my emotional goal be helpful to me?	

Acting different

The way you feel has great bearing on the way you act. Clear distinctions exist between behaviors associated with healthy and unhealthy negative emotions. Healthy negative emotions allow you to adapt to circumstances and behave in constructive ways to better your situation where possible. Unhealthy negative emotions generally impede adaptation and potential problem-solving (see Chapter 6). So, when setting your emotional goals, including behavioral goals can be very helpful.

Completing Worksheet 8-2 can help you to clarify your goals further.

WORKSHEET 8-2 My Behavioral Goals

What is my problem situation?	
What is my healthy negative emotional goal?	
What sorts of actions are typical of this healthy negative emotion?	
What *specific* actions can I adopt that fit with my emotional goal?	
How will carrying out these actions be helpful to me?	

Structuring your goal statements

Your goal statement puts together the results from your completed worksheets and includes:

- Your problem situation or *trigger*
- Your emotional goal
- Your behavioral goal

EXAMPLE

Tom is currently going through a divorce. After two years of marriage, his wife decided that she was no longer in love with him and initiated divorce proceedings. Tom is very angry with his wife. He finds it difficult to remain civil when they're discussing the sale of their house and other financial arrangements. Tom hasn't given his wife access to their home so that she can collect her belongings. The situation is getting messy and, because lawyers are involved, expensive. Tom's performance at work is suffering because he is drinking to calm his enraged feelings and is often hung over or absent from work. He has stopped going out socially and spends most evenings at home brooding about how unfairly his wife has treated him. When he does speak to friends or family about the impending divorce, he either talks trash about his wife or talks about how he might be able to get revenge. Tom knows that he's not handling this negative event very well and decides to set some goals to deal with it more constructively. His goal statement is shown in Table 8-1.

TABLE 8-1 Tom's Goal Statement

My goal is to feel healthy anger and sadness (emotional goal)
about my wife divorcing me (problem or situation)
and to act with civility toward my wife (behavioral goal).

Make your own goal statement using the same template in Worksheet 8-3.

WORKSHEET 8-3 My Goal Statement

My goal is to feel ____________________ (emotional goal)
about ____________________ (problem or situation)
and to act ____________________ (behavioral goal).

Being a complete SPORT

Now you're ready to make a concise problem and goal statement. Take your work from these sections to your CBT therapist if you're seeing one. If not, keep your work and review your goals regularly to help keep you on track. Try not to lose sight of the reward!

Table 8-2 shows how Tom created his SPORT page and serves as an example of how to ask yourself the right kind of questions in order to set good goals.

TABLE 8-2 Tom's SPORT Page

Specific: Where, when, and with whom do I want to feel/act differently?	
Where?	At work and at home.
When?	When I'm at work, I want to be clear-headed. I want to attend work regularly. I want to act differently when dealing with the divorce.
With whom?	My boss and work colleagues. My soon-to-be ex-wife.
How do I want to feel?	I want to feel healthy anger rather than rage.
How do I want to behave?	I want to behave in a civil and controlled manner with my wife. I want to be responsible and focused at work.

Positive: How can I state my goal in a positive way?	
What do I want to work toward feeling?	Healthy anger/annoyance.
What do I want to work toward doing?	Sorting out the divorce with a minimum of cost and disruption.
Observable: What changes will I notice when I'm getting closer to my goal?	
How will I feel differently?	I'll feel sad about the end of my relationship and angry about my wife's decision but without the desire for revenge.
What will I be doing differently?	I won't drink to numb my feelings of outrage. I'll go to work regularly and without a hangover. I'll stop snapping at my colleagues and boss. I'll be able to talk to my wife calmly and coolly about arrangements for selling the house. I'll be paying less to the lawyers because my wife and I will be able to agree on the details of the divorce without excessive legal mediation.
What changes might other people in my life notice?	People will see that I'm at work and properly prepared to do my job. I'll be less volatile with others. My wife may notice that I'm calmer and no longer hurling abuse at her every time we speak. I'll go out more socially and talk about things other than ways to take revenge on my wife. I'll agree on a time with my wife for her to collect her belongings from the house.
Realistic: Is my goal concrete and within my reach?	
How hard will I need to work to achieve my goal?	Very hard at first, but with practice and time, I'll come to accept her decision even if I don't like it.
Do I have the skills and resources that are necessary to reach my goal?	Yes. I'm not usually aggressive, and I'm capable of keeping a level head in other types of highly emotional situations.
Can I visualize/imagine myself reaching my goal?	Yes. I can imagine completing the divorce and moving on with my life in time.
Timed: What is a reasonable time frame to set for achieving my goal?	
When can I get started with goal-directed behavior?	I can start changing my angry behavior today. The divorce should be complete within six months. I'll give myself until the actual divorce comes through to accept my wife's decision.
What days and times can I devote to carrying out goal-related tasks?	I can practice thinking in a healthy way about the divorce every day. I can also practice healthy anger tomorrow when I speak to my lawyer. I'll try to be cool and controlled when I speak to my wife on Friday about the house, and I'll let her come and get her stuff. I'll only drink on the weekends, and I'll abstain on weeknights.
When and how often will I review my progress?	I'll sit down and review my progress every Sunday evening at around 8 p.m., after dinner.

You can see that Tom keeps his goals focused on things that are within his sphere of control. Although he can't make his wife love him again, Tom can choose how to feel about and respond to the upcoming divorce.

Use the SPORT page in Worksheet 8-4 to help you really home in on how you feel, act, and think differently.

WARNING

Aside from not setting SPORT-ing goals, another common error that people make with regard to goal setting is reaching too far and expecting too much, too soon. Your goals need to be realistic and achievable. If you set your sights too high, you may get discouraged.

WORKSHEET 8-4 My SPORT Page

Specific: Where, when, and with whom do I want to feel/act differently?	
Where?	
When?	
With whom?	
How do I want to feel?	
How do I want to behave?	
Positive: How can I state my goal in a positive way?	
What do I want to work toward feeling?	
What do I want to work toward doing?	
Observable: What changes will I notice when I'm getting closer to my goal?	
How will I feel differently?	
What will I be doing differently?	
What changes might other people in my life notice?	
Realistic: Is my goal concrete and within my reach?	
How hard will I need to work to achieve my goal?	
Do I have the skills and resources that are necessary to reach my goal?	
Can I visualize/imagine myself reaching my goal?	
Timed: What is a reasonable time frame to set for achieving my goal?	
When can I get started with goal-directed behavior?	
What days and times can I devote to carrying out goal-related tasks?	
When and how often will I review my progress?	

Some disorders and problems can take longer than others to overcome, so try to be flexible about the time you allow yourself to reach your given goals. Avoid making your goals too easy to achieve, though. You may decide that your goals are trivial and that reaching them isn't helping you if you fail to make them challenging enough. Ideally, strike a balance between too easy and too hard.

Manufacturing More Motivation

Sometimes you may be very motivated to pursue your goals and other times you may be less enthusiastic or downright apathetic. Don't make the mistake of waiting too long for motivation to come before you get started on goal-directed action. Motivation isn't to be waited for, it's to be gone after with a club. After all, change requires effort and involves discomfort, so why would you expect to always feel utterly gung-ho about pursuing your goals?

You're not the only person on the planet who finds making positive change difficult and daunting at times — quite the opposite, in fact. Luckily, you can use the techniques we offer in these sections to maximize your existing motivation and to get moving in the absence of motivation.

Writing up reasons for change

Inspiration and *benefit* are two watchwords here. Who or what inspires you to change your ways and why? What are the short-, medium-, and long-term benefits of change? Thinking of sources of inspiration and recounting the benefits of continuing your goal pursuit can be really helpful.

Use Worksheet 8-5 to ignite your inspiration!

WORKSHEET 8-5 **My Sources of Inspiration**

Who are some role models who display characteristics I would like to adopt? (Include people you know personally or famous people and/or fictional characters.)	
What characteristics do these people display that I'd like to adopt?	
How do these characteristics relate to my defined goals? (Include both emotional goals and behavioral goals.)	
What are some inspirational stories I've heard that I can draw on?	
What lessons can I take from these stories about people overcoming adversity?	

(continued)

WORKSHEET 8-5 ***(continued)***

How can I apply these lessons to my own life and my goal pursuit?	
What images or metaphors help me to visualize myself reaching my goals?	
What proverbs, quotes, song lyrics, or icons inspire me to carry on with goal-directed action?	

Carrying out a cost-benefit analysis

You can use the cost-benefit analysis form to review the benefits and the costs of your emotional and behavioral goals. Costs are inherent to giving up an unhealthy emotion or behavior, although they very often are outweighed by the benefits of reaching your healthy emotional and behavioral goals. For example, one of the costs of giving up the unhealthy rage that Tom identifies is not impressing upon his wife and friends how badly he thinks he's been treated. Although this situation may be a short-term cost, in the long term, it's small change in comparison to getting on with his life. Doing a cost-benefit analysis can help you to evaluate accurately what going for your goals *costs* you and what it ultimately *pays* you.

Short-term benefits are those that you may feel immediately, like pain relief, reassurance, fleeting relief from anxiety or fear or reduced anger and/or jealousy. Short-term benefits for others may mean that you stop badgering your loved ones for specific answers or that you engage in family life instead of testing everyone.

Long-term benefits relate to how you'll feel tomorrow, the next day, or in the weeks that follow. They also include how others close to you may be affected by your behavior in the long term. Think about whether your actions are making your relationships more secure and positive or less secure and potentially negative.

Don't forget to factor in the costs and benefits to your loved ones — close friends and family — and work associates who are affected by your destructive behavior.

REMEMBER

The more reasons you can come up with that support the benefit of positive change and emphasize the downside of staying the same, the more motivation you'll garner.

Complete Worksheet 8-6 to see if you can identify any costs of striving for your goals and any benefits of doing so. Ideally, the benefits will by far outshine the costs, but remember to think *both* short and long term. Sometimes short-term pain is really a necessary step toward long-term gain!

WORKSHEET 8-6 My CBA Form

My emotional/behavioral goal:
Costs of obtaining my goal in the short term For myself: For others:
Benefits of obtaining my goal in the short term For myself: For others:
Costs of obtaining my goal in the long term For myself: For others:
Benefits of obtaining my goal in the long term For myself: For others:

(continued)

WORKSHEET 8-6 *(continued)*

Do the benefits of obtaining my emotional and behavioral goals ultimately outweigh the costs in the long term? For myself: For others:
Why and how will I benefit most from obtaining my goals?

Tracking Your Progress

Keeping a watchful eye on your progress toward achieving your identified goals can really help to bolster motivation. Ignoring or overlooking your achievements, especially small ones, is easy. Even inching toward your goals is better than standing still. So, take some time to review your progress, give yourself credit for effort, and note positive effects regularly.

Worksheet 8-7 provides some helpful questions to aid you in checking out your progress toward your goals. Use this report on a weekly or biweekly basis to not only help you recognize changes but also inspire you if you're flagging.

WORKSHEET 8-7 My Progress Report

What problem/situation have I been tackling?	
What is my emotional goal?	
What is my behavioral goal?	
How long have I been working toward this goal? (Be specific about days, weeks, or months.)	
How intense is my emotional problem now? (Use a scale of 0–10 where 0 is no problem at all and 10 is the worst imaginable and impossible to cope with.)	
How intense are my behavioral problems now? (Use a scale of 0–10 where 0 is no problem at all and 10 is the worst imaginable and impossible to cope with.)	

Has the intensity of these two problems reduced since I began working toward my identified goals?	
What changes (however small) have I made for the better?	
Is there anything that I could be doing to further my progress toward my goals?	
Is there anything I can be thinking to further my progress toward my goals?	
How close am I to reaching my emotional and behavioral goals? (Use a scale of 1–10, where 1 is no progress at all and 10 is your goal being achieved.)	

REMEMBER

Be compassionate with yourself! Change is extremely hard work. If you haven't made as much headway as you'd like, be encouraging to yourself rather than being abusive or punishing. Kicking yourself when you're down is totally pointless. Instead, pick yourself up, shake yourself off, and give yourself an encouraging pat along.

WARNING

Change is often not predictable or linear. So, by all means use Worksheet 8-7 to track your progress, but also be aware that you may sometimes slip back into unhealthy ways of feeling and acting. *Setbacks are not a disaster.* They're very normal. In fact, it's often a sign that you've changed something significant. Try to keep yourself on the straight and narrow, but also forgive yourself if you stumble along the way. Taking two steps forward and one step backward on the road to permanent change is only to be expected. Checking your progress weekly or biweekly (but not more often!) can help you to see that you *can* recover and move forward from a difficult week. Good luck going for your own personal gold!

3

Putting CBT into Practice

IN THIS PART . . .

This part is all about putting CBT into practice on specific problems like anxiety, depression, obsessive-compulsive disorder (OCD), low self-esteem, and relationship problems.

IN THIS CHAPTER

» Tolerating and accepting the unpleasant physical effects of anxiety

» Facing your fears and defeating them

» Forming fear-defusing philosophies

» Figuring out what to do if you're a worrier

Chapter 9 Taking an Axe to Anxiety

Anxiety is what you feel in response to a threatening situation. You may experience anxiety as extreme fear (in the case of phobias), overwhelming physical feelings (in the case of panic disorder), or a relatively constant feeling of unease and agitation. Anxiety comes in many different forms and can affect just about anyone from any walk of life. Anxiety can be extremely unpleasant and uncomfortable. Severe anxiety can interfere with your ability to live a satisfying life. At its worst, you may find that anxiety restricts you from socializing, prevents you from doing your job, or stops you from leaving your house. Some people become anxious following a specific identifiable traumatic event. More often, however, anxiety slowly builds up without your being able to put your finger on a definite cause.

In this chapter, we show you how to confront anxiety and overcome it. No matter what form your anxiety takes, the techniques in this chapter are very likely to be useful to you.

Your doctor or psychiatrist may have diagnosed you with an anxiety disorder or you may recognize symptoms within yourself. It can be helpful to have a clear diagnosis of your particular type of anxiety problem, but you can use this chapter to overcome your anxiety whether you've been given a formal diagnosis or not. See the nearby sidebar for a breakdown of common anxiety disorders.

COMMON ANXIETY DISORDERS

Here are some of the more common anxiety disorders:

- **Generalized anxiety disorder (GAD)** is a condition characterized by persistent and excessive worry about everyday events.

  Obsessive-compulsive disorder (OCD) can take many different forms (see Chapter 11 for a comprehensive definition), but it's characterized by unwelcome intrusive thoughts and a compulsion to carry out elaborate rituals in an unrealistic effort to prevent feared events from happening.

- **Panic attacks** often lead people to believe that they're having a heart attack or about to pass out or even die because the physical sensations are so strong. Panic attacks may occur in specific situations, or they can just seem to come out of the blue.

  Phobias are specific fears of everyday things or situations. Phobias are called *irrational fears* because the degree of fear experienced is out of proportion to the actual threat involved. People can develop phobias of nearly anything, but more common ones include *agoraphobia* (a phobia of crowded places and/or being away from familiar areas where you feel safe), *claustrophobia* (fear of being in a confined space), *emetophobia* (fear of vomiting), *acrophobia* (fear of heights), *trypanophobia* (fear of needles and injections), and *zoophobia* (fear of animals).

- **Post-traumatic stress disorder (PTSD)** is a state of anxiety resulting from a traumatic event that was life-threatening or that significantly threatened a person's physical integrity. People can develop PTSD from witnessing an event that leads them to feel extreme fear and horror. Possible examples of traumatic events leading to PTSD may include traffic accidents, robberies, natural disasters, assault, and war.

Philosophies that Fend Off Fear

Anxiety can be pretty unpleasant, to say the least. We in no way want to invalidate your physical symptoms, disturbing thoughts, or personal experiences, but we do want to encourage you to try adopting some anti-anxiety attitudes. Think of your anxious feelings as bullies trying to convince you that they're bigger, tougher, and more dangerous than they actually are. More bark than bite, all talk and no trousers, full of hot air — you get the picture. You need to put an end to the intimidation!

Anxiety typically involves the following ways of thinking:

- Overestimating the probability of a threat or negative event occurring
- Overestimating how bad it would be if the threat or negative event did occur
- Underestimating your ability to cope with or surmount the threat or negative event

TIP

Axe your anxiety by using the following ways of thinking as weapons:

- Be realistic about the probability of the threat or negative event occurring: "It could happen, but it's not as likely as I imagine."
- Put the badness of the threat or negative event into perspective. We call this tactic *anti-awfulizing*: "It's bad but not terrible, unfortunate but not awful, difficult but not disastrous, hard but not horrible."
- Give yourself some credit for your coping abilities. Hold a high-tolerance philosophy: "It's uncomfortable, but I can stand it," "It's difficult to cope with, but I can cope," "It's hard to bear, but it's still bearable."

The following sections give you opportunities to put these fear-defusing philosophies into practice with your specific anxiety problems and symptoms.

Surfing bodily sensations

Anxiety comes with a host of physical and mental sensations. These sensations can be intense and frightening. If you suffer from panic attacks, you're probably no stranger to many of the symptoms shown in Figure 9-1.

Misinterpreting your physical sensations as dangerous or as serious signs of ill health can be all too easy. If you don't recognize your physical and mental sensations as part and parcel of anxiety, you may mistakenly think that you're going crazy, unable to breathe, about to pass out, having a heart attack, or even dying.

REMEMBER

The types of symptoms shown in Figure 9-1 are very common. Though they can be deeply uncomfortable, they're not dangerous.

It's understandable that you may want to stop your symptoms and control them. Unfortunately, attempts to fight against the physical feelings of anxiety almost always have a paradoxical effect. You actually end up panicking about your anxious feelings and, by trying to eliminate or control them, you actually worsen and perpetuate them. Your attempts to avoid, stop, or reduce physical sensations are also known as *safety behaviors.*

WARNING

See your doctor if you have real health concerns worthy of medical investigation. Getting a clean bill of health prior to launching yourself into exposure exercises (more about these in the following sections and in Chapter 4) may help you to normalize your uncomfortable physical symptoms of anxiety. If you suffer from health anxiety, however (and worry that you may have a serious disease or illness despite evidence to the contrary), *resisting* seeing the doctor for frequent reassurance that you're not in ill health is probably in your best interest.

EXAMPLE

Stan suffers from agoraphobia and panic attacks. He finds it almost impossible to imagine going further than a few streets from his house. If Stan can avoid public places such as shops or public transport, he does. He often has a panic attack when he finds himself in unfamiliar surroundings or in the middle of a crowd. Usually, Stan notices a hot feeling in his limbs first; then his chest tightens, and he feels as though he's fighting to get enough air in his lungs. Stan tries desperately to stop the warm feeling in his arms and legs; he also frantically gasps for air.

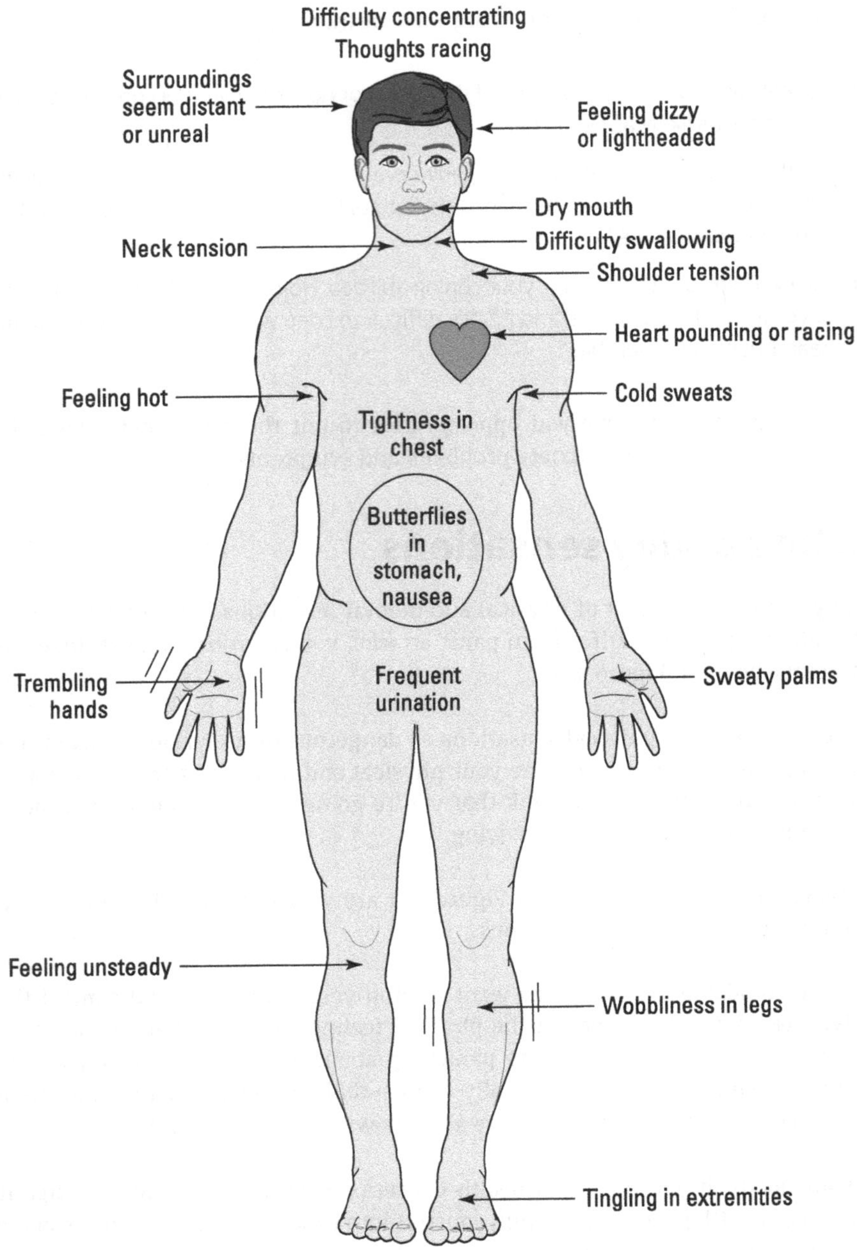

FIGURE 9-1: Common physical sensations of anxiety.

Stan used Table 9-1 to accept his physical symptoms and allow them to subside on their own.

Now that you've seen how Stan used the bodily sensations worksheet, you can use Worksheet 9-1 yourself.

TABLE 9-1 Stan's Surfing Bodily Sensations Worksheet

What are the main bodily sensations I experience when I'm anxious? (Refer to Figure 9-1.)	Hot tingling feelings in my arms and legs. Tightening in my chest. Dizziness. I feel like I can't breathe normally or get enough oxygen. My jaw clenches, and I grit my teeth.
What "awfulizing" and "I can't stand it" type of thoughts do I typically have about my physical symptoms of anxiety?	As soon as I notice a physical anxiety symptom (such as heat in my limbs), I tend to think: "Oh, no, here comes another panic attack! Panic attacks are the most horrible thing in the world, and I can't cope with having them anymore." Before I knew what a panic attack was, I used to think, "Oh, no, what's happening to me? I'm going to suffocate!" I also often have thoughts such as, "I've got to prevent another panic attack" and "I can't stand these feeling in my limbs and chest."
What do I usually do to try to stop or control my physical symptoms of anxiety?	I try to cool myself down by sipping water or fanning myself and loosening my clothing. If I'm out in public, I'll flee the situation as soon as possible and return home to safety. I try to do breathing exercises and get as much air into my lungs as possible. I grab onto something or sit down if possible. I look for places I can "hide away" in case other people notice my behavior and think I'm odd.
What effects do my attempts to stop or control my symptoms tend to have?	I used to think that gasping for air prevented me from suffocating, but it actually just makes normal breathing harder. Every time I flee a situation, it reinforces my belief that I can't go out without panicking. By trying to stop my anxiety symptoms, I actually focus on them more and end up making them worse. My attempts to sit down or hide from others reinforce my belief that panic attacks make me "weird" and that other people will ridicule me rather than try to help me. Because I try so hard to stop a panic attack from happening, I deprive myself of the opportunity to see that I can actually survive them. All my attempts to control my anxiety symptoms lead me to panic about having a panic attack!
What are some helpful "high-tolerance"/"anti-awfulizing" beliefs I can hold to help me allow these unpleasant symptoms to subside naturally?	As uncomfortable as these symptoms are, they are a natural result of anxiety and aren't dangerous. Having these symptoms may be extremely unpleasant, but I can tolerate and cope with them. Panic attacks are bad, but there are worse things that could happen. If I just let these physical sensations happen and carry on with my task, they'll eventually pass by themselves. Anxiety doesn't make me a "weird" or "odd" person. I'm just a normal person who happens to have a problem with panic attacks. Other people may be more concerned about me and compassionate toward me than I imagine.

WORKSHEET 9-1 My Surfing Bodily Sensations Worksheet

What are the main bodily sensations I experience when anxious? (Refer to Figure 9-1.)	
What "awfulizing" and "I can't stand it" type of thoughts do I typically have about my physical symptoms of anxiety?	
What do I usually do to try to stop or control my physical symptoms of anxiety?	
What effects do my attempts to stop or control my symptoms tend to have?	
What are some helpful "high tolerance"/"anti-awfulizing" beliefs I can hold to help me allow these unpleasant symptoms to subside naturally?	

TIP

After you adopt a few of your own fear-defusing philosophies and demonstrate to yourself the negative effects of working too hard to quell your anxiety symptoms, do your best to just leave them alone! Instead of fighting against the waves of anxiety, surf them. Imagine your unpleasant physical or mental sensations as a rough, choppy sea. Just let yourself ride with the waves until the storm has passed. Chapter 5 offers techniques for dealing with troublesome thoughts; you can also use these techniques to help yourself accept and tolerate unpleasant physical sensations.

Being realistic about the probability of bad events

When you have an anxiety problem, you fear bad things happening *and* tend to assume that they're very likely to happen. Whether you worry about becoming ill, harm coming to yourself or your loved ones, being socially rejected, or having a panic attack, you overestimate the likelihood of these bad things happening.

REMEMBER

Anxiety can influence how you think to a significant degree. You may find it useful to complete the next two worksheets *during* a bout of anxiety and again when you're *not* anxious. Doing so can help illustrate how greatly your emotional state can impede your ability to think rationally and problem-solve.

EXAMPLE

Stan expects that if he walks downtown (about 3 miles from his home), he'll have a severe panic attack. He assumes that he'll be completely incapacitated and unable to get home again. Stan also thinks that anyone who notices his anguish will refuse to help him. He imagines being stranded far from home, with no one coming to his aid, and finally being found by the police. Stan used Table 9-2 to readjust his ideas about the probability of bad things happening.

Of course, absolutely guaranteeing that the events you're imagining *won't* happen isn't feasible — many things are *possible.* But where anxiety is concerned, most of the events you predict will happen are extremely improbable.

Try being more realistic about the likelihood of your feared event occurring by using Worksheet 9-2.

TABLE 9-2 Stan's Probability Page

What is the bad event I'm imagining or predicting will happen?	Being totally incapacitated by panic downtown. I'm unable to move and people look at me like I'm a freak. Hours later, the police pick me up.

In reality, how likely is it that this bad event will happen?

0	1	2	(3)	4	5	6	7	8	9	10
No probability at all		Highly unlikely to happen			Equal probability that it will or will not happen		Very likely to happen		Almost certain to happen	

WORKSHEET 9-2 My Probability Page

What is the bad event I'm imagining or predicting will happen?	

In reality, how likely is it that this bad event will happen?

0	1	2	3	4	5	6	7	8	9	10
No probability at all		Highly unlikely to happen			Equal probability that it will or will not happen		Very likely to happen		Almost certain to happen	

Bringing bad events back into perspective

Anxiety frequently leads you to make a feared event more terrible in your own mind than it actually is in real life. When you're riddled with anxiety, you tend to inflate bad or negative events out of proportion and decide that they're awful, world ending, and unbearable. The good news is, events rarely are this bad. Most of the time, you would be able to cope with your feared event no matter how uncomfortable and difficult it may be.

Anti-anxiety ways of thinking involve increasing your belief in your ability to cope with unpleasant sensations and events. Try telling yourself that you can and will cope with your anxiety — even though it's not easy to do so. Remind yourself that you've come through episodes of fear and panic before, and despite finding it intensely uncomfortable, you've survived. You can also try to develop healthier attitudes about the possibility of other people judging you negatively. Attaching too much importance to what others may be thinking of you will cause you to feel even more anxious. Instead take the attitude that "it's unfortunate if others think badly of me, but it's not terrible or unbearable." Keep in mind that no matter how embarrassing you find your symptoms of anxiety, other people may be more compassionate and understanding than you expect.

EXAMPLE

Let's take Stan's fear of having a panic attack downtown and see how he used Table 9-3 to put his panic predictions back into perspective. Stan tried to think rationally and objectively about his ability to cope with his panic sensations and other people's possible reactions to him.

TABLE 9-3 Stan's Perspective Page

What is the bad event I'm imagining or predicting will happen?	Being totally incapacitated by panic downtown. I'm unable to move and people look at me like I'm a freak. Hours later, the police pick me up.

In reality, how bad would it be if this event actually happened?

0	1	2	3	4	5	6	(7)	8	9	10
Not bad at all		Minimally bad but fairly easy to cope with			Moderately bad but many worse things could happen. I'd still manage to cope		Very bad and extremely difficult to cope with		Worst possible thing ever	

What thoughts or beliefs would help me to successfully cope with this bad event if it actually happened?	I'm having symptoms of anxiety, and they will pass in time. I can tolerate these intensely unpleasant feelings, and they will diminish of their own accord. If people think I'm a freak, they're wrong. I'm just having a panic attack!
What practical action could I take to resolve or adjust to the event if it actually happened?	I could try to redirect my attention away from my physical symptoms and onto a task such as shopping. I could allow my symptoms to subside and then make my way back home on foot as planned. I could ask for help if I really needed to. If I really was stranded, I could call a friend to pick me up.

Now try to really give yourself some credit for your coping skills as you fill in Worksheet 9-3.

WORKSHEET 9-3 My Perspective Page

What is the bad event I'm imagining or predicting will happen?	

In reality, how bad would it be if this event actually happened?

0	1	2	3	4	5	6	7	8	9	10
Not bad at all		Minimally bad but fairly easy to cope with			Moderately bad but many worse things could happen. I'd still manage to cope		Very bad and extremely difficult to cope with		Worst possible thing ever	

What thoughts or beliefs would help me to successfully cope with this bad event if it actually happened?	
What practical action could I take to resolve or adjust to the event if it actually happened?	

Exposing Yourself

Exposure exercises involve identifying your fears and making plans to face up to them. Facing your fears in a planned and deliberate way is the best way we know to overcome anxiety problems. Although facing your fears isn't fun, it is effective. Think about how fed up you are with your anxiety problem. Have you had enough of living your life through a veil of fear? Do you think the short-term pain of doing exposure work is worth it for the long-term gain of beating anxiety? We hope so.

Following is a list of tips for executing effective exposures:

REMEMBER

- Make your exposures challenging enough to be pretty uncomfortable but not so overwhelming that you're unlikely to stick with the technique.
- Keep exposing yourself to feared situations regularly and make them progressively more challenging each time.

  Once is not enough. As a rule, you need to keep exposing yourself to your fears regularly until you become habituated or desensitized to them.
- Make your exposure sessions long enough for them to work.
- Remind yourself that, in CBT, the acronym FEAR stands for: Face Everything And Recover!
- Hold the belief that you can accept, tolerate, and withstand the discomfort of anxiety. You don't have to *like* it, but you can *survive* it.
- Keep a record of your exposure work to track your progress.

In the following sections, we include worksheets to enable you to put these points into practice.

Challenging yourself to a duel

REMEMBER

The idea is not to fight your symptoms of anxiety but rather to fight the avoidance and safety-seeking behaviors that fuel your anxiety.

The next worksheet involves two simple steps:

1. **In the first column, make a list of five to ten situations in which you typically experience anxiety.**
2. **In the second column, give each situation a rating from 0 to 10, where 0 means no anxiety at all, 5 means moderate anxiety, and 10 means extreme anxiety (as bad as it gets based on the degree of anxiety you anticipate experiencing).**

Table 9-4 shows panic-attack prone Stan's list.

Now make your own list of challenges using Worksheet 9-4. You don't need to list them in order of difficulty at this stage. Just record them as they come to your mind and then give them an anxiety rating from 0 to 10.

TABLE 9-4 Stan's List of Challenges

Anxiety-Provoking Situation	Anticipated Degree of Anxiety
Going to the corner shop	3
Phoning work about my sick leave	9
Walking downtown	10
Shopping for groceries	8
Going to the local bar	6
Going to work	10
Taking the bus	7
Sitting in my garden	1
Answering the phone	2
Going to my friend's house	5

WORKSHEET 9-4 Your List of Challenges

Anxiety-Provoking Situation	Anticipated Degree of Anxiety

TIP

Include situations that you've been avoiding due to your anxious feelings. If you've been anxious and avoidant for a long time, you may forget to include activities that you once did. Really thoroughly investigate aspects of your life that you've neglected due to anxiety.

Refer to Worksheet 9-4 and the ratings you allocated to feared situations. Next list your rated situations from mildest (minimal anxiety) to most severe (major anxiety) in Worksheet 9-5. The final column of the worksheet can be used to rate how high your anxiety actually was when you confronted a specific situation. Often, this rating will be lower than your anticipated rating. This is because the anticipation of doing something you fear is often worse than actually doing it. The idea is to fill in this column *after* your exposure work.

And there you have it, your fear-facing hierarchy. Now you can plan when and where to face your anxiety-provoking situations, from baby steps to giant steps. Your hierarchy gives you a sensible order of anxieties to confront and overcome, and the next section helps you devise a plan to do just that.

WORKSHEET 9-5 My Graded Hierarchy

Anxiety-Provoking Situation	Anticipated Anxiety Level (0–10)	Actual Anxiety Level (0–10)

Preparing your exposure plan

Now you need to transform intention into action. Most people are unlikely to get started with exposures unless they allocate the time to do so. Frankly, exposing yourself to your fears isn't a barrel of laughs, so putting it off is easier than getting on with it. But putting off exposure work in the present means putting up with anxiety in the future. Chapter 8 shows you how to conduct a cost-benefit analysis (CBA) that can help elicit personal commitment to a goal. You may want to turn to that chapter if your commitment to exposure work is waning.

REMEMBER

Exposing yourself to your fears often isn't as bad as you think it will be. The more often you do exposure work, the more quickly you'll overcome your anxiety problem.

Using your results from Worksheet 9-5, list your least anxiety-provoking situations and the anxiety rating you gave to each. Stan, for example, recorded sitting in his garden, answering the phone, and going to the corner shop as his first three exposure activities. These become your first targets of specific exposure activities to confront. Now decide exactly which day and at what time you'll do your first exposure session. Committing yourself to a definite time helps you to actually do it. Also, allocate times to repeat the *same* exposure because repetition is the key to overcoming your anxieties. Don't leave more than a day between repetitions if at all possible. The more often you do exposure work, the better. Stan decided to sit in his garden for half an hour three times a day for the whole week. He also decided to answer his phone every time it rang and to go to the corner shop once on Monday, twice on Tuesday, and three times on Wednesday.

TIP

Exposure needs to last long enough to help you build up tolerance to your fear. We've helped people with exposure sessions that have lasted as little as 20 minutes to as long as half a day. In the past, the guidelines was to remain in the situation until your anxiety diminishes by about 50 percent. However, we now know that many people make good progress with exposure over time, even if they don't really experience a drop in anxiety within the exposure session. You don't need to stick slavishly to approaching your fear in graded steps. You can move around your hierarchy, treating it like a menu of triggers. The key is that you're overcoming avoidance, dropping safety-seeking behaviors, and putting in prolonged and regular practice to build up that tolerance and gather evidence that helps correct any unhelpful thoughts.

Use Worksheet 9-6 to help you prepare your exposure plan.

WORKSHEET 9-6 My Exposure Plan

Specific Exposure Activity	Hierarchy Grading	Day and Time Allocated to First Exposure Session	Days and Times Allocated to Repeat Exposures

TIP

Progressing through your graded hierarchy ensures that you challenge yourself without becoming overwhelmed. However, don't go too slow! Think about whether you'd be able to manage going up the tiers of your hierarchy two at a time. Jump in at the deep end if you think you can manage it.

Keeping good records

A record of your efforts helps you see the progress you've made. Maintaining a record also helps you to see whether you're staying in the situation long enough for your anxiety to come down *naturally*. The length of time you need to stick with an exposure session in order for it to be effective varies. Sometimes 20 minutes may be long enough, but in other situations you may need to tough out your discomfort for an hour or even longer. Rating your anxiety at the beginning, middle, and end of an exposure session can be a useful tool.

Use Worksheet 9-7 to record your exposure work. Again 0 means no anxiety at all, 5 means moderate anxiety, and 10 means severe anxiety.

WORKSHEET 9-7 My Exposure Activity Account

Description of Exposure Activity	Total Length of Exposure Session	Initial Anxiety Rating (0–10)	Middle Anxiety Rating (0–10)	End Anxiety Rating (0–10)

Description of Exposure Activity	Total Length of Exposure Session	Initial Anxiety Rating (0–10)	Middle Anxiety Rating (0–10)	End Anxiety Rating (0–10)

Searching Out Your Safety Behaviors

Chapter 7 is all about solutions that are ultimately self-defeating. These so-called "solutions" may give you some short-term relief, but they end up keeping your problems going or even making them worse. Sometimes your anxiety may remain high during an exposure. If this situation occurs, you may be using a safety behavior without realizing it. Searching out all your safety behaviors and making a note of them is crucial for just this reason. Doing so gives you a much better chance of dropping them.

REMEMBER

A safety behavior is anything you do to try to minimize your anxious feelings, prevent others from noticing your anxiety, or keep yourself safe from imagined events like collapsing during a panic attack. The list of possible safety behaviors is pretty much endless, but Stan provides an example of some of the more common safety behaviors people use to deal with panic.

To uncover your own safety behaviors, take careful note of what you do in anxiety-provoking situations, however minor, because you think it will help you to cope.

EXAMPLE

Stan realized that he was using a lot of different behaviors because he thought they'd either stave off panic or curtail his panic sensations. Stan recorded his self-sabotaging strategies for dealing with his panic attacks and agoraphobia in Table 9-5. Have a look at a few examples.

TABLE 9-5 Stan's Safety Behaviors

Feared Situation	Typical Safety Behaviors
Riding the bus	Sitting by the door
	Listening to music on my phone
	Avoiding eye contact with others
	Monitoring my breathing
Going to the corner shop	Going when it's quiet
	Having the correct change in advance
	Paying quickly and rushing home

(continued)

TABLE 9-5 *(continued)*

Feared Situation	Typical Safety Behaviors
Going to the local bar	Facing away from others
	Dressing in light clothes to stop feeling hot
	Planning when I can leave and go home
	Avoiding alcohol in case I get dizzy
	Fiddling with my keys and phone to hide my shaking hands
	Monitoring myself for symptoms of panic

Now look at your graded hierarchy in Worksheet 9-5 and think about anything you do in those situations to try to stop, minimize, or control your anxious feelings and physical sensations. List them in Worksheet 9-8.

WORKSHEET 9-8 My Safety Behaviors

Feared Situation	Typical Safety Behaviors

Ways out of Wearisome Worry

If you have an anxiety problem of one kind or another, chances are, you worry. Sure, everyone worries from time to time. In order to avoid worry altogether, you'd have to not care about anything. But there's a big difference between healthy concern and unhealthy anxiety. The latter involves unproductive worry. (Refer to Chapter 6 for further information about the differences between healthy and unhealthy negative emotions.) Worry takes up a lot of time and energy, is unproductive, and feeds anxiety.

You can use Worksheet 9-9 to figure out whether you're a full-blown worrier.

If you notice that your current most pressing worries tend to recur time and again albeit in slightly different forms, you have some definite worry themes. This means that you probably tend to worry about these areas of your life too much, even when nothing is going wrong. Common worry themes often include finances, health, relationships, and other people's opinions of you. This worksheet is devised to help you understand that you may have a worry problem more than you have *actual* problems. In other words, the process of worrying is what's causing you the most trouble.

WORKSHEET 9-9 My Worrier Worksheet

What are my top three current worries?
1.
2.
3.

Do my worries have common themes? Do I tend to worry about the same types of things over and over? Record themes here.
Theme 1:
Theme 2:
Theme 3:

Is worrying disrupting my sleep, dampening my enjoyment of life, damaging my relationships, or impairing my ability to concentrate or function? List specific examples of how your worry is problematic.			
Do you tend to believe that you're unable to effectively cope with your identified worry themes?			
❑ Almost never	❑ Sometimes	❑ Often	❑ Almost always
After you resolve one worry, do you soon find yourself focusing on a new worry?			
❑ Almost never	❑ Sometimes	❑ Often	❑ Almost always
Do you think that if only you could resolve all your worries, you'd finally be able to relax?			
❑ Almost never	❑ Sometimes	❑ Often	❑ Almost always
Do you frequently worry about possible negative events that haven't even happened?			
❑ Almost never	❑ Sometimes	❑ Often	❑ Almost always
Do you try to solve every potential problem before it happens?			
❑ Almost never	❑ Sometimes	❑ Often	❑ Almost always
Do you believe that worrying will either prepare you for bad events or prevent bad things from happening?			
❑ Almost never	❑ Sometimes	❑ Often	❑ Almost always

If you checked lots of "almost always" and "often" boxes in Worksheet 9-9, you probably worry to an unhealthy degree.

If you've been worrying for a long time, you may not understand that you can train yourself to let go of worrying thoughts. Worrying is like a bad habit — with persistence, you can break it. Doing so takes a lot of hard work but the result is *so* worth it. You may feel strange and even vulnerable when you first start resisting your worry habit, but with time, you'll get used to the sweet relief of no longer being a constant worrier.

TIP

Don't give yourself too much time to worry. Absorb yourself in activities and become skilled at redirecting your attention away from worrying thoughts. Chapter 5 has more advice on how to redirect your thoughts. Choose activities that require concentration, like solving puzzle, playing a computer game, or listening to others. Exercise is also good for you in so many ways and can really help you to "sweat out" your worries.

When worry takes hold, try using Worksheet 9-10 to break its grip.

WORKSHEET 9-10 My Worry Whacker Worksheet

My current worry:	
Is this worry an actual problem that I can work to solve today?	
If yes, what practical actions can I take to solve the problem?	
Step 1:	
Step 2:	
Step 3:	
Step 4:	
Step 5:	
If not, what activities can I turn my attention to instead of focusing on my worrying thoughts?	
1.	
2.	

3.	
4.	
5.	

REMEMBER

Worry is a stubborn customer. Don't be fooled by niggling feelings that you should be worrying about something. Remind yourself that worrying does nothing to prevent or solve problems. You can negotiate life just fine without the worry habit.

IN THIS CHAPTER

» Checking for signs of depression

» Understanding how avoidance and blocking out maintain depression

» Realizing the worst about ruminating

» Activating yourself for more rewarding living

Chapter 10
Dealing a Blow to Depression

Depression is a painful and common emotional problem. It can range from feeling down for a few weeks and often improving of its own accord, to being severe enough to require hospital treatment. Fortunately, cognitive behavioral therapy (CBT) is a scientifically proven treatment for depression supported by hundreds of research trials. CBT can work with or without antidepressant medication and is proven to reduce relapse rates.

Almost by definition, a depressed mind will say, "Trying anything is pointless, nothing can be done to help me." As we hope you'll discover, this belief is very far from the truth. It's part of the negative self-talk that can keep a person depressed.

This chapter focuses on the *behavioral* part of CBT and shows you that gradually facing up to things you're avoiding, increasingly engaging in activities you find rewarding, and constructively dealing with any difficulties you have can have a profound effect on your low mood. We also outline how *ruminating* (going over and over things in your mind) can sometimes appear to be a way of solving problems but, in fact, may well be driving down your mood. Spotting and interrupting rumination is another powerful tool for overcoming depression.

Discerning Whether You're Depressed

Identifying common symptoms of depression has a number of advantages. It can give you a clearer idea of whether you're suffering from "ups and downs" or "the blues" or whether you have symptoms of a recognized illness. Use Worksheet 10-1 to identify any symptoms of depression you experience. You can then show this checklist to your doctor and discuss possible treatment options. You can also use the checklist as a reference point to come back to as you work to overcome your depression and see how your symptoms are improving.

WORKSHEET 10-1 My Symptoms of Depression Checklist

❑	I constantly feel sad, down, depressed, or empty.
❑	I have a general lack of interest in what's going on around me.
❑	I've noticed a big increase or decrease in my appetite and weight.
❑	I have difficulty sleeping. I am unable to fall asleep and/or wake up early, and I'm unable to get back to sleep.
❑	I feel slow and lacking in motivation.
❑	I feel guilty or worthless.
❑	I find concentrating and making decisions difficult.
❑	I feel that I might be better off dead.

WARNING

If you check off the first or second question, as well as four others, and you've felt that way for at least two weeks, there's a good chance that you're suffering from depression. The principles outlined in this book will probably help you, but you may also consider seeking professional help from a doctor or therapist. See Chapter 19 for more on working with a healthcare professional.

Assessing Your Avoidance

As we point out in more depth in Chapter 7, the strategies human beings use to try to help themselves feel better often make emotional problems worse. Avoiding daily tasks and social interaction is part of depression. It can be very tempting to give in to your depressed feelings and hide away from other people and your responsibilities. However, such avoidance can often lead to a life that is less rewarding, leave you less in control of your life, lead to mounting financial problems, reduce your ability to problem-solve, and decrease the support you get from other people.

Consider what you may be avoiding doing (including hobbies and chores) and what you may be doing to try to block out painful thoughts and feelings. The effect of some activities varies according to what function they serve. Enjoying a favorite TV program, for example, may be rewarding and part of a mood-lifting plan, but watching endless hours of TV to block out the world will maintain your depression.

Blocking-out behaviors tend to be things you do instead of tackling tasks that are in your best interest to address. So, watching TV instead of opening the mail or answering the phone may be an example of a blocking-out behavior and an avoidance behavior. Often you'll engage in blocking-out behaviors because your mood is so low that everything seems pointless and overwhelming. Unfortunately, the more you let things pile up, the more depressed you're likely to feel.

Blocking-out behaviors can also include things like using drugs, alcohol, or food to help numb your depressed feelings. These things may work in the short term, but they usually lead to worsened depression the next day.

Table 10-1 shows common types of avoidance and blocking-out behaviors that feature in depression. Use the table to help you identify your own depression-maintaining behaviors. You can then target these behaviors for change and replace them with more constructive behaviors.

TABLE 10-1 Avoidance and Blocking-Out Behaviors

Activities You Avoid	Blocking-Out Behaviors
Seeing friends in social situations	Trying not to think about problems
Answering the phone or email	Watching TV or movies
Opening and dealing with the mail	Drinking alcohol or using other substances to escape
Taking care of your home (paying bills, doing household chores, and so on)	Staying in bed or going back to bed during the day
Taking care of yourself (showering, eating properly, and so on)	Using sex or pornography excessively
Getting out of bed in the morning	Playing computer games
Speaking to people about your problems	Comfort eating
Communicating with people close to you	Surfing the web and using chatrooms
Taking part in your hobbies and interests	Exercising excessively

EXAMPLE

Rashid has been feeling depressed since he missed a promotion at work. He lives alone, has been off work for six weeks, and has become quite isolated. Table 10-2 shows how he assessed his avoidance and blocking-out behaviors.

TABLE 10-2 Rashid's Avoidance and Blocking-Out Assessment

What are you avoiding?	Picking up the phone and responding to emails. I keep making excuses so I don't have to see my friends. I'm not really cleaning up after myself.
What are the undesirable or unhelpful effects of this avoidance?	I feel lonely much of the day and really stuck in a rut. The flat is becoming shamefully messy.
What are you doing to try to block out painful thoughts or feelings?	Watching TV and old DVDs most of the day. Drinking wine and eating junk food at night.
What are the undesirable or unhelpful effects of these strategies?	Feeling fat and unhealthy. I'm not really dealing with anything, so I just end up feeling helpless.

Use Worksheet 10-2 to identify things you're avoiding and strategies you're using to try to block things out.

WORKSHEET 10-2 My Avoidance and Blocking-Out Assessment

What are you avoiding?	
What is the undesirable or unhelpful effect of this avoidance?	
What are you doing to try to block out painful thoughts or feelings?	
What are the undesirable or unhelpful effects of these strategies?	

TIP

Use what you've learn from analyzing your avoidance and blocking out to help guide your activity scheduling in the "Actively Attacking Your Depression" section later in this chapter.

When you're depressed, focusing your attention on almost anything other than your internal thoughts is likely to lead you to feel at least a little better. Accepting the presence of distressing thoughts and images as part of depression but then choosing to turn your attention to other things will probably help your depression to stabilize rather than worsen.

Reckoning with Rumination

The word *rumination* has its origins with the way cows repeatedly chew over grass ("chewing the cud") as part of their digestive process. Humans also spend time ruminating, by going over things in their minds, but with more harmful results. Generally, when they feel depressed, people ruminate over past events that can't be changed or questions that can't be answered, such as:

- What if . . .?
- If only . . . (I'd done things differently).
- Why do I feel this way?
- Why didn't I do things differently/make different choices?

Identifying where and when you ruminate is half the battle, because this knowledge will help you avoid getting caught up in it. Recognizing what you tend to ruminate about will also help you sidestep this toxic trap.

EXAMPLE

Rachael has been depressed since she separated from her husband. A feature of her depression is that she often ruminates about the way her relationship broke down. Table 10-3 shows how she identified her rumination patterns.

TABLE 10-3 Rachael's Recognizing Rumination Record

Which time(s) of day are you most likely to ruminate?	In the morning and at night if I wake up.
Where are you when you tend to ruminate?	Lying in bed, in my bedroom, or in the bathroom.
What kinds of activities are you doing when you ruminate?	Trying to get back to sleep or getting dressed and ready to go to work.
What do you commonly ruminate about?	I try to work out why things broke down with my husband. I try to figure out why I can't snap out of this depression.

Now carry out your own analysis of your rumination in Worksheet 10-3.

WORKSHEET 10-3 My Recognizing Rumination Record

Which time(s) of day are you most likely to ruminate?	
Where are you when you tend to ruminate?	
What kinds of activities are you doing when you ruminate?	
What do you commonly ruminate about?	

Actively Attacking Your Depression

An *activity schedule* is a diary sheet for each day with times of the day clearly marked in two-hour blocks. It's one of the most (if not *the* most) effective psychological tools you can use to combat depression. This tool is often overlooked or underused by both therapists and sufferers because it seems too simple, but research shows it works.

Getting active again is a vital step to beating depression. Because depression saps motivation and promotes lethargy, your activity schedule can really help you to get on with daily tasks you may be avoiding. Research shows that the simple action of planning your daily activities and allocating specific times to specific tasks greatly increases the likelihood of carrying them out. When you get started using an activity schedule, your motivation to do the things you once enjoyed and found rewarding will begin to return.

TIP

You can use your activity schedule for a number of jobs:

- Recording a week's activity to provide a baseline to return to in future weeks to compare your progress against.
- Beginning to steadily face up to things you've been avoiding and becoming more activated.

- Reducing blocking-out behaviors and replacing them with more rewarding or productive activities.
- Structuring your daily routines to give your appetite and sleeping patterns the best possible chance of returning to normal. By "normal," we mean eating regular meals three times a day and getting roughly eight hours of sleep each night.
- Planning your day or week to help get chores done, keep social engagements, and set aside time for hobbies and interests.
- Monitoring to make sure that you *gradually* increase your activities in a steady and realistic way instead of overloading yourself with all the things you think you should do.

Worksheet 10-4 is an example of an activity schedule.

WORKSHEET 10-4 Activity Schedule

	Monday	Tuesday	Wednesday	Thursday	Friday	Saturday	Sunday
6–8 a.m.							
8–10							
10–12							
12–2							
2–4							
4–6							
6–8							
8–10 p.m.							

Now complete your own activity schedule to record your typical week for your baseline. Use subsequent forms to gradually increase your levels of activity. Use the assessment in Worksheet 10-2 to guide you in deliberately targeting for change those avoidance and blocking-out behaviors you identified as being part of the maintenance of your depression.

	Monday	Tuesday	Wednesday	Thursday	Friday	Saturday	Sunday
6–8 a.m.							
8–10							
10–12							
12–2							
2–4							
4–6							
6–8							
8–10 p.m.							

	Monday	Tuesday	Wednesday	Thursday	Friday	Saturday	Sunday
6–8 a.m.							
8–10							
10–12							
12–2							
2–4							
4–6							
6–8							
8–10 p.m.							

	Monday	Tuesday	Wednesday	Thursday	Friday	Saturday	Sunday
6–8 a.m.							
8–10							
10–12							
12–2							
2–4							
4–6							
6–8							
8–10 p.m.							

IN THIS CHAPTER

» Identifying obsessional problems

» Re-appraising responsibility

» Facing fears and stopping rituals

Chapter 11

Overcoming Obsessions and Cutting Out Compulsions

Obsessive-compulsive disorder (OCD), health anxiety, and body dysmorphic disorder (BDD) are examples of obsessional problems, which can be extremely distressing and interfere greatly in people's lives. This chapter shows you how these problems are maintained and offers some key techniques for overcoming them. Fortunately, specifically tailored CBT has proven to be successful in helping people overcome each of the obsessional problems we discuss in this chapter.

Observing Obsessive Behavior

Of course, a self-help book can't give you a formal diagnosis on whether you're suffering from an obsessional problem, but this section has checklists of common features of three of the most prevalent obsessional problems. You can use these checklists to get a sense of whether this applies to you. As we show, understanding your problem is a critical step in ridding yourself of excessive and disabling anxiety, obsessions, and preoccupations.

TIP

If you can identify obsessions and/or compulsions in the following sections, and they cause you distress and/or interfere with your life, you may want to show the lists to your doctor and discuss possible diagnosis and treatment for OCD.

REMEMBER

The way you cope with your obsessions may be part of maintaining them — in other words, your solution may be the problem. Understanding this concept is a really important part of recovering. Use Chapter 7 to help you build a profile of the strategies you're currently using that are fueling the problem.

Checking out OCD

OCD is in the top ten most disabling illnesses, according to the World Health Organization. This illness is characterized by *obsessions* (distressing thoughts, images, impulses, or doubts), and *compulsions* (rituals and regimented behaviors that a person feels compelled to perform).

Work through Worksheet 11-1 to figure out whether you have any of the features of OCD.

WORKSHEET 11-1 Obsessions Checklist

❑	Distressing unwanted religious, blasphemous, sacrilegious thoughts or images intrude into my mind.
❑	I'm greatly troubled by intrusive thoughts or images of violent acts such as stabbing, pushing, hitting, and burning.
❑	Unacceptable or inappropriate sexual thoughts or images repeatedly enter my mind against my will and cause me distress.
❑	I frequently worry greatly about contamination from dirt, germs, bodily fluids, excrement, chemicals, sticky substances, or other material.
❑	I frequently worry greatly that I may lose something important or regret throwing something away.
❑	I often worry that I may be responsible for a bad event, such as a fire, flood, car accident, or burglary, through not being careful enough.
❑	My obsessions cause me significant amounts of distress.
❑	My obsessions are on my mind for at least an hour each day.
❑	My obsessions interfere with my ability to function in important areas of my life, such as my social life, work, family life, and relationships.

The first six items on Worksheet 11-1 can help you identify the type of obsessions that trouble you. These are very common types of OCD. Checking off even one is sufficient to indicate that you're suffering from OCD. Many people have more than one form of this disorder, however, so don't be alarmed if you check more than one of the first six items.

The last three items on the worksheet help you determine how severe your problem is and how much it's disrupting your life. OCD is what is called a *spectrum disorder*, which means that it can range in severity. People with mild OCD may find their obsessions irksome but not be bothered by them for more than an hour each day and their OCD doesn't stop them from living a normal life. If you have more severe OCD, you probably find your obsessions very distressing and distracting; your obsessions are on your mind for at least an hour and possibly several hours every day. The more severe your OCD, the more it impedes your ability to function. Everyday tasks like locking doors, going to work, interacting with friends and family, getting dressed, and taking care of household chores can become extremely time-consuming when you have moderate to severe OCD. Happily, no matter how severe your OCD, CBT can help you to overcome it.

OCD is a broad topic. There are many different forms of OCD, and discussing each one in depth is unfortunately beyond the scope of this chapter. CBT treatment has been proven effective with all sorts of OCD problems and the principles outlined in this chapter (as well as the exercises in Chapters 5 and 9) can really help you. You may also want to consult other books that deal exclusively with OCD. We recommend a book by Rob Willson and David Veale called *Overcoming Obsessive Compulsive Disorder* (Robinson and Constable).

Discovering body dysmorphic disorder

The American Psychiatric Association says that BDD is characterized by a preoccupation with an imagined defect in appearance or markedly excessive attention to a minor physical defect. BDD is a profoundly distressing and disabling problem that goes far beyond imagined ugliness. Sufferers tend to be very preoccupied with their appearance and highly afraid of being humiliated because of what they perceive as their "revolting" or "freakish" looks.

Use Worksheet 11-2 to check for any symptoms of BDD.

WORKSHEET 11-2 BDD Symptoms Checklist

❑	I spend more than an hour each day worrying about my appearance.
❑	I believe that I look ugly or unacceptable, despite being reassured by others that this is not the case.
❑	I worry that I will be embarrassed or humiliated because of my appearance, especially if I don't conceal or camouflage my defect(s).
❑	I tend to compare my appearance to that of other people, including people I encounter in my real life and those in magazines and on TV.
❑	I spend a lot of time thinking about how I could improve or camouflage my appearance through cosmetic or dermatological procedures, clothing, dietary supplements, exercise, makeup, and so on.

If you check off three or more items, you're probably suffering from BDD. The same sort of CBT techniques that work for OCD can help you overcome BDD. You can use the worksheets in this chapter to help you understand and beat BDD.

Highlighting health anxiety

Hypochondriasis is the old term for health anxiety. This term has largely been dropped by professionals because it suggests someone who is constantly suffering from different ailments and is a bit neurotic. In fact, real health anxiety can be severely distressing. It involves being preoccupied with constant worries about having or developing serious illnesses. It is also sometimes referred to as "illness anxiety disorder," but whatever you call a persistent and distressing worry about your health, it's far from being silly or attention-seeking.

Use Worksheet 11-3 to help you recognize features of health anxiety.

WORKSHEET 11-3 Health Anxiety Checklist

❑	I spend at least an hour a day worried about being ill or thinking that I am ill with cancer, heart disease, multiple sclerosis, AIDS, or something similar despite having been given medical reassurance that I'm healthy.
❑	I have a strong sense that I am vulnerable to illness.
❑	I worry that if I'm not vigilant for signs of illness, I might miss something important.
❑	I worry a lot that anxiety itself may cause harm.

If you checked off the first item, that alone probably indicates that you have health anxiety. If you checked the first item and one or more other items, the probability that you suffer from health anxiety increases.

OCD, BDD, and health anxiety all respond very well to CBT treatment. The same CBT exercises are effective in overcoming all three of these disorders, which is why we include them all in the same chapter. We urge you to read Chapters 5 and 9 for more techniques to help you defeat these disorders.

Checking out compulsive behaviors

Compulsions are actions that you feel compelled to carry out over and over again or in a precise and exact manner. Health anxiety, OCD, and BDD all involve compulsive actions and rituals. Rituals and compulsions are largely similar in that you feel duty-bound to complete them and feel very uncomfortable and anxious if you're somehow prevented from doing so. Rituals, however, are often more elaborate than straightforward compulsions. For example, you may feel compelled to get dressed in a precise order and go through a highly specific ritual for putting on items of clothing. Or you may have a ritual about how you brush your teeth. You may be very particular about how much toothpaste you use, how many times you brush each layer of teeth and so on. An example of a compulsion may be feeling like you need to check that you've locked the door ten or more times.

The problem with compulsions and rituals is that the more you carry them out, the more you reinforce the idea that you *need* to keep on carrying them out.

Use Worksheet 11-4 to go through the list of common compulsions. If you carry out any of the actions listed in the worksheet more than three times, you're doing them excessively and more than is considered necessary by most people without obsessional problems. Similarly, if the time you devote to tasks listed in the worksheet means that you neglect other duties or are late for appointments, you're doing them to excess.

The kinds of excessive behavior highlighted in this worksheet underpin and maintain your obsessional problem. When you're aware of your individual rituals and compulsions, you know what you need to be doing less of.

TIP

It can be useful to monitor and record just how many times you check things, repeat words or phrases, ask for reassurance, or engage in other rituals. You can also record exactly how much time you spend on certain tasks. Doing this can help you fully realize the degree to which compulsions are interfering with your life.

WORKSHEET 11-4 Compulsions Checklist

❑	I frequently check things such as locks, water taps, gas taps, and electrical items more often than is necessary.
❑	I spend an excessive amount of time washing.
❑	I frequently seek reassurance from my partner, friends, or family (for example, asking repeatedly for reassurance that nothing bad is about to happen, that you don't have a disease or that you look "normal" or "acceptable").
❑	I frequently repeat words and phrases in my mind, or replay images.
❑	I spend an excessive amount of time putting things in order, tidying, or making things "just so."
❑	I have an excessive amount of clutter and hoarded items in my home.
❑	I try hard to push upsetting thoughts out of my mind.
❑	I become significantly distressed if I'm prevented from or am interrupted in carrying out my rituals.
❑	My compulsions interfere with my ability to function in important areas of my social life, work, family life, and relationships.

REMEMBER

Carrying out compulsive and ritualistic actions is a symptom of the disorders mentioned previously. Bear in mind that reducing and stopping these actions is a major element in overcoming your obsessional problems.

Assessing and Acting against Obsessional Attitudes

Research has narrowed down the common underpinnings of obsessional problems. Intolerance of doubt and uncertainty; excessive responsibility; and a need for control over your mind, health, or attractiveness are common characteristics of obsessive thinking. See if any of the following examples strike a chord:

- If a thought or image of harm happening to myself or others occurs to me, it means I am responsible for preventing that harm.
- I need to be certain that my fear will not come true.
- I should be able to control the thoughts, doubts, images, or sensations I have.
- Because an upsetting thought or image comes from my mind, it must say something about me — that I'm bad, evil, dangerous, or otherwise disturbed.
- If something bad happens and I have not taken all possible steps to prevent it, I am to blame for it happening.

The exercises in the following sections are aimed at helping you fight back against the attitudes that drive your obsessive behavior.

Pitting Theory A against Theory B

If you've read any of the other chapters in this book before this one, you're familiar with the idea that the more extreme the meaning you give to an event, the more extreme your emotional response to it is likely to be.

Theory A is the negative, catastrophic definition you give to your problem. For example: "An intrusive thought about abusing a child means I must want to do it, and that proves I'm a pedophile," or "An imperfection in my appearance means I'm hideous and will be totally humiliated if I approach someone I find attractive," or "This lump on my skin means I have a cancer that hasn't been detected, I'll die in a few months, and my children will be devastated."

Theory B is a more realistic and likely definition you choose to give to your problem. So, "Intrusive thoughts about abusing a child means I've got OCD and I'm worrying obsessively about being a pedophile," or "An imperfection in my appearance is something I focus on too much because I have BDD," or "I'm worried about this lump because I have health anxiety, not cancer."

Worksheet 11-5 gives you a structure for developing a less threatening and more accurate theory for your obsessional problem. Then it's up to you to adopt the theory that best fits the facts — Theory B! Next strive to behave as if you really believe that Theory B is correct. When you act according to Theory A, you engage in all sorts of rituals and compulsions like those described in Worksheet 11-4 which only makes your obsessions worse. Acting according to Theory B leads you to resist compulsions and rituals and re-engage in other activities that help you overcome your obsessions.

EXAMPLE

For many years Sharon had experienced obsessive thoughts about harming her daughter. She used Table 11-1 to work out a theory to help her deal with her problem.

TABLE 11-1 Sharon's Constructing a Workable Theory Worksheet

Intrusive thought, doubt, image, impulse, urge, bodily sensation, or area of concern:	
Whenever I'm near an object that could potentially do someone harm, such as a knife or scissors, I have an image of hurting my child with that object.	
Theory A (upsetting/negative theory)	**Theory B (alternative theory)**
This means I am an evil and dangerous person who should be locked up and never see her child again.	This means I am extremely worried about being dangerous to my child and am afraid of her coming to harm.
What can I try to do to treat my problem as if Theory B is correct?	
I need to try to worry less about being dangerous and interpret intrusive images as reflecting what I actually don't want to happen. This means training myself to become more comfortable with sharp/potentially dangerous objects, like I used to be a few years ago and most people are. I also need to let my intrusive images and doubts pass through my mind without making them so significant and without fighting them or seeking reassurance.	

Now consider a Theory A and a less disturbing Theory B for your own obsession, using Worksheet 11-5.

WORKSHEET 11-5 My Constructing a Workable Theory Worksheet

Intrusive thought, doubt, image, impulse, urge, bodily sensation, or area of concern:

Theory A (upsetting/negative theory)	Theory B (alternative theory)

What can I try to do to treat my problem as if Theory B is correct?

Realistically appraising responsibility

Excessive responsibility leads to excessive worry and guilt, and to trying excessively hard to prevent bad things that lie outside of your control from happening. It lies at the very heart of many obsessional problems. Reducing your tendency to assume excessive responsibility for causing or preventing harm, monitoring your health, or being humiliated on the basis of your appearance, is a big help in reducing your obsessions themselves. So, aim to deflate your inflated responsibility and practice nonextreme thinking to aid breaking free from OCD and related problems.

EXAMPLE

Clive worries excessively about passing on toxic substances and bodily fluids to other people and their becoming ill or dying as a result. Table 11-2 shows how he assigned responsibility for his problem.

TABLE 11-2 Clive's Realistic Responsibility Pie Chart

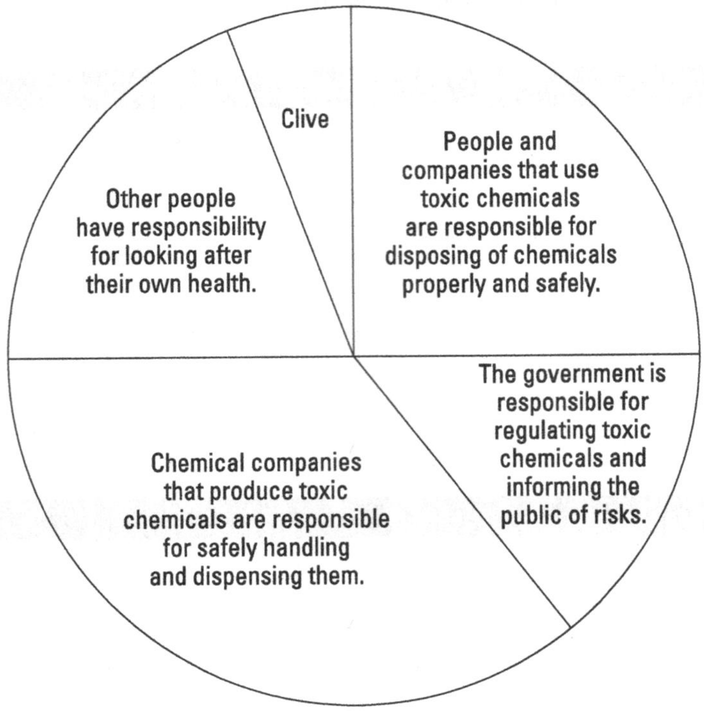

To work out your responsibility pie chart, first fill in Worksheet 11-6. The first rating is important because it represents the amount of responsibility you take before you actually analyze other contributing factors. Generally, you'll give yourself an unreasonable and inflated amount of personal responsibility for your feared event in the first instance. Also, be sure to list all contributing factors before yourself and place yourself within the pie last. Otherwise, you risk overlooking factors besides yourself and giving yourself an overly generous slice of the pie.

WORKSHEET 11-6 My Assigning Responsibility Worksheet

Define your feared event:	
Rate how much responsibility (0% to 100%) you would give yourself if this feared event occurred:	

List all the factors you consider would contribute to your feared event, placing yourself last on the list.	
Now allocate a portion of responsibility to each of the factors you listed, putting yourself in last.	

Use the percentages from Worksheet 11-6 to fill in your own pie chart in Worksheet 11-7.

WORKSHEET 11-7 Your Realistic Responsibility Pie Chart

Steering in the right direction

"How can you know for sure?" is the question we get asked a *lot* by our clients with obsessional problems. "How can you be sure I won't cause someone harm?" "How can you be sure I'm not ill?" "How can you be sure I won't get ill?" "How can you know I won't be rejected and humiliated?" "How can you be sure I'm not dangerous to children?" The answer, of course, is that we can't be sure of any of these things. But we can be pretty sure that if you keep searching for answers to these doubts and uncertainties, you're likely to maintain your obsessional problem.

If you identified an obsessional problem in yourself and are worried about something, you can't be certain that your fear won't come true. However, you can be fairly sure that you're likely to overestimate the chances of disaster. This knowledge has a very important implication: Instead of worrying, you can choose to safely assume that things are okay and then act accordingly.

Think of your mind as a boat traveling along a wide river. As you sail, the left side of the river represents "assuming the worst" and the right side, "assuming things will be okay." Now, as you sail down the river that is navigating the world, you notice that wind (anxiety) and current (obsessions) move the boat toward the shore of assuming the worst. So, to avoid colliding with the shore, you need to steer your boat toward the shore of assuming things will be okay, at least until the current and wind subside.

EXAMPLE

Mike worries that he'll inadvertently cause harm to people. For example, if he's walking down the street, he fears he might accidentally push someone into oncoming traffic. Table 11-3 shows how he started to combat his bias.

TABLE 11-3 Mike's Taking Control Worksheet

Trigger:	Passing a woman in the street.
What I tend to assume:	That I will hurt her.
How I act as a consequence:	I give people a wide berth as much as I can and repeatedly look backward or retrace my steps to check for signs of an accident.
The results of thinking and acting in this way:	It slows me down, and I realize I'm acting quite strangely. It also only reassures me for this one moment, and I often worry that I might have hurt another person while I was distracted checking the original person.
Alternative (assuming things are okay) assumption:	That a doubt or image of knocking someone into oncoming traffic reflects my brain being overly alert to this kind of danger. I can afford to assume I haven't caused anyone harm.
How I can act as if I'm assuming things are okay:	Keep moving without excessive caution and without looking or listening for signs of an accident.

Now, in Worksheet 11-8, identify the kinds of unhelpful catastrophic assumptions you would benefit from steering away from.

WORKSHEET 11-8 My Taking Control Worksheet

Trigger:	
What I tend to assume:	
How I act as a consequence:	

The results of thinking and acting in this way:
Alternative (assuming things are okay) assumption:
How I can act as if I'm assuming things are okay:

TIP

Use this exercise sparingly to help set the course against your obsessional problem. Avoid using it if you sense that you're doing so to gain reassurance that you're definitely not going to act on your obsessions and are absolutely safe from doing so. Otherwise, you can end up making this worksheet another ritual! Instead, use it to recognize the benefits of acting according to your alternative assumption that things are okay.

People with obsessional problems like OCD, BDD, and health anxiety typically demand cast-iron guarantees that certain bad things won't happen. Demands for certainty can very rarely be met, which is why they produce anxiety. So, when you're working to overcome obsessional problems, it's important to learn to tolerate doubt and uncertainty.

Reining in Rituals

In addition to deliberately confronting triggers for your fears, doubts, and intrusive thoughts, you need to reduce and stop the rituals and compulsions you use in response to those obsessions. This section offers some suggestions for controlling rituals. (For more advice on deliberately confronting your fears, see Chapter 9.)

Checking out and changing your termination criteria

One of the keys for cutting out rituals is to become aware of why you finish a session of washing, checking, seeking reassurance, or performing some other ritualistic behavior. This reason is known as your *termination criteria*. People who wash their hands excessively, for example, tend to finish washing when they *feel right*, whereas the average person finishes washing their hands when their hands look clean enough (if they were visibly dirty to begin with) or just goes on autopilot to do a convenient quick wash after using the toilet because they don't regard it as all that important. Table 11-4 lists helpful and problematic reasons for stopping a behavior.

TABLE 11-4 **Good and Not-So-Good Reasons to Stop Compulsive Behavior**

Problematic Reasons	Ordinary, Acceptable Reasons
It feels right.	That's long enough; any more is too much hassle.
I'm comfortable.	It's convenient to do it this way.
It's "just so."	I can see that it's done and can live with the doubt that it's not.
I feel sure.	I've taken enough care, I don't have to be certain. That's as much care as most people take. Let's get on with the next task/appointment.

EXAMPLE

Harold washes his hands at least 30 times a day for several minutes at a time, using very hot water and antibacterial soap. Table 11-5 shows how changing his termination criteria helped him to cut down.

TABLE 11-5 **Harold's Changing Criteria Worksheet**

The ritual or compulsion I want to reduce or stop:	My excessive handwashing.
The unhelpful criteria I tend to use to end this ritual or compulsion:	When I feel completely sure I've removed any trace of germs and get a sense of relief.
The alternative criteria I'm going to train myself to use to end my action:	To make handwashing quick and functional. To stop once I have briefly lathered my hands with soap and rinsed it off. I only need to wash for more than a few seconds if I can see dirt on my hands without carefully examining them.

Use Worksheet 11-9 to discover a point at which to stop your rituals.

WORKSHEET 11-9 **My Changing Criteria Worksheet**

The ritual or compulsion I want to reduce or stop:	
The unhelpful criteria I tend to use to end this ritual or compulsion:	
The alternative criteria I'm going to train myself to use to end my action:	

Recording and resisting rituals

Keeping a record of the rituals or compulsions you carry out is a simple yet surprisingly helpful step in cutting them down. A chart that records the frequency of your rituals helps you to:

- See just how often you use them and improve your awareness.
- Record your progress.
- Boost your motivation to resist!

EXAMPLE

Mark is troubled by a fear of causing harm to people in the street through his negligence. This leads him to constantly check when he passes people to ensure that he hasn't hit them or tripped them. Mark is constantly looking over his shoulder to make sure people he's been near are unhurt. When he walks down the street, he keeps his arms close to his sides and won't carry sharp objects or large bags in case he injures someone. When he gets home, Mark carefully checks all his clothing for any traces of blood, which may mean that he's unknowingly caused another person injury. Table 11-6 shows his ritual record sheet.

TABLE 11-6 Mark's Ritual Record

Ritual/Compulsion	SUN	SUN	MON	TUES	WED	THURS	FRI	SAT
Checking over my shoulder when I pass people in the street to be sure I haven't hit or tripped them.	5×	5×	3×	1×	0	11×	13×	2×
Checking my clothes for traces of blood when I return home.	2×	2×	2×	1×	0	6×	6×	2×
Pulling my arms tightly to my body and checking that they stay in that position.	10×	10×	12×	4×	0	6×	6×	2×

REMEMBER

You might be carrying out rituals in your head as well as in your behavior, so record mental rituals too.

Use Worksheet 11-10 to identify rituals you want to reduce. Stop your compulsions and start recording!

WORKSHEET 11-10 My Ritual Record

Ritual/Compulsion	SUN	SUN	MON	TUES	WED	THURS	FRI	SAT

IN THIS CHAPTER

» Understanding low self-esteem

» Acknowledging self-acceptance as an alternative to low self-esteem

» Acting according to acceptance attitudes

» Making personal improvement

Chapter 12
Lifting Low Self-Esteem

Rating yourself as "good" or "bad," a "success" or a "failure," "worthy" or "worthless" on the basis of your achievements or circumstances is extremely common. But just because it's common practice doesn't make it good practice. In fact, attaching your self-opinion to external conditions is at the very root of self-esteem problems. Your opinion of yourself is vulnerable to plummeting if your existing state of affairs isn't maintained. Life is unpredictable and prone to change, so your mood and view of yourself can shift wildly if you consistently anchor your value to your job, relationships, financial situation, and so on.

Even the term *self-esteem* is problematic because it implies that a person can be given an accurate overall rating even if the person doing the rating is you! Assessing a piece of jewelry or a diamond and estimating its overall market value is easy. People, however, are living, changing creatures and far more complex than inanimate objects. An alternative to self-esteem is the concept of *self-acceptance*.

Cognitive behavioral therapy (CBT) encourages you to stop giving yourself overall or global ratings altogether. Instead, accept yourself as a fundamentally worthwhile person and rate only individual aspects of yourself, your lifestyle, your behavior, and so on.

In this chapter, we expand on the concept of self-acceptance and offer you some practical exercises for applying an accepting attitude toward yourself and others.

TIP

You can use most of the exercises in the chapter to increase your tolerance of other people, too. The same rules for self-acceptance apply to accepting others. Practicing an attitude of "other acceptance" can help you put a stop to unhealthy anger, jealousy, and hurt.

Acquiring Self-Acceptance

All human beings are equal in worth. Stop for a moment and consider how much you agree with that statement. Isn't all human life sacred? Isn't that why murder is a crime regardless of who's killed? Essentially, most of us are taught that human beings have *intrinsic* value and worth (meaning we're valuable and worthy just because we exist). But we frequently behave as if some people are worthier than others.

We commonly attach too much importance to (or overvalue) certain things such as wealth and social status. You may mistakenly assume that people who possess these prized conditions or traits are superior to yourself or others who lack them. At the same time, you may attach too little importance (or undervalue) aspects of your personhood such as generosity, social responsibility, and kindness.

REMEMBER

Comparing yourself to others on the basis of external conditions leads you to feel either superior or inferior. Both positions are unhealthy because you're putting down yourself or others.

Acquiring self-acceptance (and acceptance of others as well) means that you're able to recognize that we're all equal in worth but unequal in specific aspects. So, you may be an excellent cook and a poor driver, while your neighbor may be the exact opposite. You're still both worthy individuals — you just have different strengths and limitations. One of the first steps toward self-acceptance is noting particular conditions to which you typically attach your self-worth.

Worksheet 12-1 is a checklist of general areas or domains against which people frequently judge their overall worth. Check off the ones that resonate with you; then add a couple of your own not included in the list.

WORKSHEET 12-1 External Conditions Checklist

❑	Academic/educational qualifications
❑	Career or job success
❑	Creativity/artistic talents
❑	Ethnicity
❑	Fame/celebrity status
❑	Family background
❑	Intelligence
❑	Mental health
❑	Parenting skills
❑	Physical attractiveness/fitness
❑	Physical disabilities
❑	Physical health
❑	Quality of relationships

❑	Religious observance
❑	Social popularity/social ease
❑	Socioeconomic status
❑	Wealth/material possessions
❑	____________________
❑	____________________

Now that you've pinpointed the areas that you tend to give yourself a global rating on, you can use this knowledge to help yourself overcome low self-esteem and to adopt self-acceptance instead. The techniques offered in the following sections can help you to do so.

Realizing reasons not to rate yourself

Human beings are too complex to be given an overall rating. We're all a mixed bag of good, bad, and neutral traits. Sure, there are things about yourself or your life circumstances that you may want to improve, but doing so doesn't up your worth. Making positive changes where possible may help you to enjoy life more, but your human worth remains constant.

You probably have areas that you're dissatisfied with but that you're unable to improve or alter. For example, you may not be artistic or you may not be a social butterfly, and that's just the way you are. Sometimes you're better off just accepting reality and focusing on other skills and talents that you *do* possess. Rating yourself negatively because of your limitations can lead to emotional problems such as anxiety, depression, and shame.

REMEMBER

Your emotional problems aren't solved by rating yourself as "bad" or "worthless" for having them in the first place. Kicking yourself when you're down isn't the most effective way of getting yourself back on your feet. If you rate your entire worth based on just one aspect of yourself, you're making the part-whole error: judging (and probably condemning) your whole self based on one or two parts of yourself. Don't do it. Judging yourself in this way is bad news.

As a human being, you're always changing and growing from the day you're born until the day you die. You're also unique and individual — no one else on the planet is exactly the same as you. Your human complexity involves all your past, present, and future experiences, deeds, and adventures.

Use Worksheet 12-2 to list reasons *not* to give yourself a global rating.

WORKSHEET 12-2 Reasons Not to Rate Myself

Giving myself a global rating is inaccurate because I'm ever-changing. These are some ways in which I'm a changing and developing human being:	
I'm too complex to be able to accurately rate or judge myself on the basis of one or more individual traits or actions. My complexities as a human being include:	
As a human being I'm unique. Some of my unique traits, skills, limitations, likes, and dislikes include:	

Leaving behind loathsome labeling

In addition to unhelpfully giving yourself negative global ratings, you probably call yourself names — and nasty ones at that. You may call yourself nasty names silently in your own head, or you may even say them out loud at times.

WARNING

Even if you don't think that you really *mean* the hateful things you call yourself, they can have a negative impact on your self-opinion. So, if you don't mean it, don't say it! And even if you do mean it, stop it!

The names you call yourself can further erode your sense of worth plus reinforce negative core beliefs (see Chapter 15 for more on core beliefs and how to change negative ones). Another term for name calling is *labeling* (see Chapter 2 for more about labeling). Some typical examples of loathsome labeling include expressions such as:

I'm inadequate.

I'm worthless.

I'm weak.

I'm no good.

I'm a failure.

I don't matter.

I'm defective.

I'm stupid.

I'm unlovable.

I'm pathetic.

I'm useless.

I'm a loser.

I'm bad.

I'm disgusting.

I'm inferior.

I'm crazy.

The main method of losing loathsome labels from your life is to resist using them. It's like breaking a habit. Catch yourself in the act and refuse to call yourself horrible labels — either inside your head or out loud.

TIP

One of the tactics we sometimes use with patients is to record each time they call themselves negative names. Doing this can help you to see just how often you resort to name calling and can help remind you to stop.

Instead of calling yourself globally negative labels, try to label only your *actions* and be very specific about what aspect of your actions you're displeased with. So, instead of saying "I'm a total loser," specify what you've lost by saying something like "I lost my job," "I lost the golf match," or "I lost the promotion." Being specific helps you to accept that you're capable of losing sometimes but acknowledge that you're also capable of winning sometimes. Hence, no one is ever a "total loser."

Also, substitute more accurate names and labels for the globally negative ones you typically use. You don't need to veer into wildly positive self-statements like "I'm fantastic" or "I love myself" — in fact, we strongly discourage you from doing so for two reasons:

- You're unlikely to truly believe such globally positive things about yourself, especially if you've been battling low self-esteem for some time.

» These statements, although positive, are still unhealthy because they're global and unrealistic. No one is ever totally bad and, therefore, no one is ever totally good. Instead, try using alternative self-statements that are balanced and realistic.

Table 12-1 shows some appropriate alternatives.

TABLE 12-1 **Healthy Alternatives to Labels**

Loathsome Label	Alternative Healthy Self-Statement
I'm inadequate.	I have skills and talents.
I'm worthless.	I'm a worthwhile person.
I'm weak.	I have both strengths and weaknesses.
I'm no good.	I have many good qualities.
I'm a failure.	I'm a fallible human being capable of both success and failure.
I don't matter.	I have significance.
I'm defective.	I may have certain defects (like any person), but I'm not defective.
I'm stupid.	I can do stupid things sometimes, but that doesn't mean I'm stupid.
I'm unlovable.	People can love me, and I am worthy of being loved.
I'm pathetic.	I have capabilities.
I'm useless.	I do many useful things.
I'm a loser.	I'm a normal person who can both win and lose.
I'm bad.	I'm a person with both good and bad traits.
I'm disgusting.	I'm acceptable.
I'm inferior.	I have equal worth to others.
I'm crazy.	Even if I sometimes do crazy things, I'm not totally crazy.

EXAMPLE

Rajesh anchors his self-worth to his career success and his social popularity. He often tells himself that he's inadequate and a total failure if he makes a blunder at work or embarrasses himself even slightly in a social setting. Often, Rajesh feels anxious before social events and work meetings. Because of his beliefs that he *must* succeed in his career and be popular, Rajesh often experiences unhealthy negative emotions such as shame and depression when his personal rules are not wholly met. He doesn't give himself much room for human error. Rajesh used Table 12-2 to readjust his self-labeling and assess the effects of doing so.

After you generate some healthy alternative statements to replace your loathsome labels, you need to reinforce your belief in them. Practice saying your healthy alternatives to yourself several times every day — particularly in situations in which you would typically resort to loathsome self-labeling. Also, act as if you truly believe your healthy alternative. For example, if you truly believe "I'm worthwhile," then you look after your health, join in social activities, voice your views and opinion, and make eye contact with others. The more you act according to the new way you want to think of yourself, the more you will come to believe in its truth.

TABLE 12-2 Rajesh's Loathsome Labels and Alternatives List

Areas I commonly rate my whole self on the basis of:	My career and job success. My popularity and social ease.
What negative labels do I most often use about myself?	I'm a failure. I'm useless. I'm unlikable.
What are three good reasons for losing these labels?	1. I feel really bad about myself and depressed when I call myself these things. 2. I tend to avoid social outings and work stuff when I'm thinking of myself in line with these labels. 3. I decide that I can't improve and give up trying to reach goals when I'm stuck in name-calling behavior.
What are helpful self-accepting alternatives for these labels?	Everyone makes work errors and social gaffes from time to time, not just me. I'm a human being capable of success and failure just like any other person on the planet. Just because I make mistakes doesn't make me totally useless. I do plenty of things that are useful. Lots of people seem to enjoy my company, and I have several friends. Just because I may put my foot in my mouth sometimes or feel a bit awkward socially doesn't mean that I'm not likeable. No one can be everybody's cup of tea.

In order to successfully change a habit, you need to stick with it for a minimum of three weeks. You'll notice changes after one week or even after a few days, but you need to keep on practicing alternative healthy ways of thinking about yourself for several weeks. In time, and with deliberate effort and practice, thinking in positive and balanced ways about yourself will become more automatic. In other words, you'll have developed a new constructive thinking habit.

Table 12-3 shows how Rajesh monitored his progress.

TABLE 12-3 Rajesh's Three-Week Progress Report

After one week:	It takes a lot of reminding and effort to resist calling myself nasty names. I obviously do it a lot more than I realized.
After two weeks:	I feel generally better about myself and am better able to stick with uncomfortable situations when I'm resisting calling myself names and labeling myself negatively.
After three weeks:	It's getting much easier to resist name calling. I find that I'm thinking in a more balanced and helpful way about work and social situations almost automatically. I feel less depressed and ashamed. Plus, I like myself more than I did three weeks ago.

In Worksheets 12-3 and 12-4, list your own nasty name-calling habits and record the results of refusing to call yourself names anymore.

Take notice of the positive changes, benefits, and overall effects as you shed your loathsome labels in Worksheet 12-4.

WORKSHEET 12-3 Your Loathsome Labels and Alternatives List

Areas I commonly rate my whole self on the basis of:	
What negative labels do I most often use about myself?	
What are three good reasons for losing these labels?	
What are helpful self-accepting alternatives for these labels?	

WORKSHEET 12-4 Your Three-Week Progress Report

After one week:	
After two weeks:	
After three weeks:	

Acting on Acceptance

Self-acceptance beliefs and attitudes have the following characteristics:

- **They make logical sense.** For example, just because you *prefer* not to make mistakes doesn't mean that you *must* not make them.
- **They're consistent with reality.** For example, you're capable of making mistakes. Thus, giving yourself permission to screw up reflects the reality of your capacity to screw up now and then.
- **They're helpful.** For example, if you give yourself room for error, you won't be unduly depressed when you make a mistake. You'll be better able to make amends or solve problems if you're not absorbed in condemning yourself for your errors.

REMEMBER

Rating your whole self on one component of your behavior isn't helpful. Figure 12-1 gives you a more visual example of your human complexity. It also highlights the silliness of giving yourself a global label.

The big *I* drawn in Figure 12-1 represents your *whole* self — past, present, and future; good, bad, and neutral. Absolutely every last little thing about you. The smaller *i*'s represent your various behaviors, traits, skills, attributes, talents, experiences, dreams, limitations, mistakes, upsets, and so on.

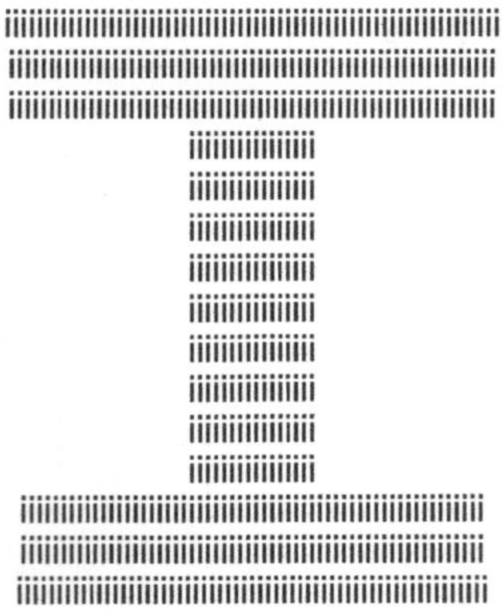

FIGURE 12-1: Which do you see first, the big *I* or all the little ones?

Adding Up the Evidence

Self-acceptance may seem like a pretty straightforward concept, but like many CBT principles, it's considerably harder to put into practice. Because it isn't easy, self-acceptance needs to be rehearsed, rehashed, and revisited time and again before you begin to feel the positive effects. The more proof or evidence that you can gather to support your attitude of self-acceptance, the more you'll reinforce it as true.

Follow these steps to complete Worksheet 12-5:

1. **Describe a negative event or situation in which you called yourself nasty names.**
2. **Record the unhealthy label you gave yourself in your own words.**
3. **Record your alternative healthy self-statement.**
4. **Look for and record evidence in the situation that supports your healthy self-accepting attitude and contradicts your unhealthy negative label.**

EXAMPLE

Table 12-4 provides an example of how Rajesh worked to reinforce his self-acceptance attitudes.

TABLE 12-4 Rajesh's Evidence Epistle

Situation:	Spilling my drink and stumbling over my words when I arrived at an after-work social evening.
Negative label:	I am a total loser and not likeable.
Self-accepting alternative attitude:	Okay, so I got a bit flustered. I'm not a loser, but I am a fallible person, and I'm still likeable despite this minor social blip!
Evidence supporting my self-accepting attitude:	Everyone laughed and joked about my spilling the drink. A colleague instantly went to the bar and bought me another. Everyone chatted with me and asked me questions as though nothing serious had happened. My desk-mate pulled me onto the dance floor. No one gave me funny looks or the cold shoulder because of my awkwardness.

Now reinforce your self-acceptance attitudes using Worksheet 12-5.

WORKSHEET 12-5 My Evidence Epistle

Situation:	
Negative label:	
Self-accepting alternative attitude:	
Evidence supporting my self-accepting attitude:	

Now check Table 12-4 again and include any extra evidence that you may have overlooked or discounted the first time round.

Feeling fine about human fallibility

You're human and, hence, fallible. You make mistakes. Deal with it. Your fallibility is inevitable. Perfect people don't exist. So, instead of putting yourself down, making yourself ashamed and depressed about mistakes, insisting that you *must* do better, or writing yourself off completely, face up to your fundamental fallibility.

Worksheet 12-6 helps you to embrace your ability to make gaffes, slip-ups, minor errors, or major screwups and still think of yourself as a basically okay person. Give it a whirl.

WORKSHEET 12-6 My Feeling Fine about Fallibility Form

Recent event(s) that I'm putting myself down for:	
How is putting myself down affecting my mood?	
How is putting myself down affecting my behavior?	
Review the event(s) again. Did I do something bad or behave poorly?	
Did I make a mistake or fail at something?	
Considering my human fallibility, can I take a more compassionate or forgiving view of myself in light of these recent events?	

(continued)

WORKSHEET 12-6 ***(continued)***

How can I make amends for poor or bad behavior, if appropriate?	
How can I rectify a mistake or failure, if appropriate?	
In light of these events, are there conditions I can strive to improve or change?	
In light of these events, are there elements of them that I can strive to accept as they are?	
How will accepting myself as fallible motivate me to get on with solving my problems?	
How will accepting myself as fallible benefit my mood and self-opinion?	

Being very specific

An antidote to global rating is to be *very specific* when judging your actions, deeds, or intentions. So, instead of telling yourself what an utter failure you are, ask yourself in what *specific* way you have failed on this occasion. Instead of labeling yourself as utterly incompetent, ask yourself in which *specific* area you've behaved incompetently. Own up to the nitty-gritty, fine details instead of just throwing your whole self out of the window with the dirty bath water.

EXAMPLE

Table 12-5 shows how Rajesh got specific.

TABLE 12-5 Rajesh's Specific Synopsis Sheet

What exactly happened?	I was a bit nervous and foolish when I first arrived at an after-work social event.
What specific aspect of my/others' performance, behavior, or emotional response am I displeased with?	I spilled my drink and spoke incoherently.
How can I put my displeasure into perspective given my understanding of myself/others as mistake-making human beings?	Okay, so I spilled my drink and stammered. Not the end of the world. The rest of the evening went well, and even if it hadn't, it wouldn't mean that I'm useless or unlikeable. It would simply mean that I get anxious in social situations. Not a major crime but a personal inconvenience that I'm trying to surmount. My social anxiety has more negative impact on me than it does on those around me. So, I don't really need to worry about what other people are thinking of me quite so much.

When you judge yourself harshly and are unforgiving, you're probably doing the same to others. Judging is a double-edged sword that can ultimately negatively affect your personal relationships. So, use Worksheet 12-7 on both yourself and others! When using the worksheet on another person, remember to resist globally rating them on the basis of their actions. Be specific about what they've done or failed to do that you're displeased with. Finally, remind yourself that others are fallible, too — just like you. Applying these basic principles of acceptance to others, as well as to yourself, can greatly reduce disharmony in relationships.

WORKSHEET 12-7 My Specific Synopsis Sheet

What exactly happened?	
What specific aspect of my/others' performance, behavior, or emotional response am I displeased with?	
How can I put my displeasure into perspective given my understanding of myself/others as mistake-making human beings?	

Using the best friend technique

It's often easier to be understanding and compassionate with the people you love than yourself. You may find that you can forgive and overlook shortcomings in the people you care about but find it difficult to cut yourself the same slack. Learning to be more understanding and compassionate with yourself is an important part of self-acceptance and promotes good emotional health. Ever heard of double standards? One rule for you and another rule for someone else? Think of a recent event that you may be beating yourself up over. Now imagine that your best friend or someone you care about came to you berating themselves about the same event. What would you say to your loved one? Use Worksheet 12-8 to highlight what you would say to your best friend if they were in your situation. Next make a real effort to apply the same advice to yourself.

WORKSHEET 12-8 Your Best Friend Form

What exactly happened?	
What am I telling myself about what happened? What does it mean about me?	
Would I advise my best friend or loved one to hold this view of themselves about the event?	
If not, why not?	
What would I say to my best friend or loved one in the same circumstances?	
How can I apply the same advice I would give to a friend or loved one to myself?	

Accepting and Improving Yourself at the Same Time

Perhaps you think that accepting yourself means that you can surrender self-improvement and let yourself off the hook for any bad actions you may take or good actions you neglect to execute. We hope not, because that really isn't our message. On balance, if you accept yourself as fundamentally worthwhile in view of your shortcomings or bad behaviors, you're in a better place to work on them than if you condemn yourself. We suggest that you simultaneously give yourself room to be less than perfect and still strive to make personally important changes. Doing so really is a recipe for self-improvement success.

Selecting specific areas for self-improvement

If you want to make improvements to your personal behavior and your life in general, being extremely specific is best. Saying "I want to be a better person" may be true, but it doesn't give enough information to work with. The detail is what matters. (See Chapter 8 for more on goal setting.)

Try out Worksheet 12-9. Do it now, and then do it again, after reading or rereading Chapter 8.

WORKSHEET 12-9 My Specific Areas for Self-Improvement

What emotional problems do I want to overcome?	
How would I like to feel differently? (See Chapter 6 on finding your feelings.)	
What aspects of my behavior do I want to change?	
How would I like to behave differently?	
In which specific situations would I like to behave and feel differently?	
How will changing the way I feel and behave in these situations be of benefit to me? (Think short, medium, and long term.)	
Which aspects of my life circumstances do I want to improve?	

What action do I need to take to initiate these improvements?	
What steps can I take — and when — to help me make basic changes to my circumstances?	

Embracing personal responsibility

Other people or world/life events don't wholly mess us up. The meanings we *assign* to these events do a far more thorough and comprehensive job of that.

Poor Rajesh is tired! He's working hard on his own issues. Try Worksheet 12-10 on your own to discover your personal meanings. We think you'll survive.

WORKSHEET 12-10 My Personal Responsibility Reckoning Record

What happened? (Be clear and precise.)	
What personal meanings am I ascribing to the situation or event?	
Am I making any thinking errors that lead me to feel unhealthy emotions?	
What, if anything, did I do that was poor or bad in context of the situation?	
How can I attempt to make amends if appropriate or necessary?	
How can I take a compassionate view of myself in light of the circumstances? (Think of what you would say to a close friend or loved one.)	
Am I wholly responsible for the event?	
Who else may have some degree of responsibility for the event?	

REMEMBER

When you take *appropriate* responsibility for your behavior and your emotions you're better able to make effective changes. When you blame other people or life conditions/events for your disturbed emotions or self-destructive behavior, you're giving up your power to make things better.

Regularly Reviewing Reasons for Self-Acceptance

Self-acceptance takes practice. Sometimes you may find believing in and acting according to your new attitudes easy. Other times, doing so is more difficult. Worksheet 12-11 may help you to see the sense of self-acceptance attitudes when your conviction is waning.

Review the work you've done in this chapter and record whatever answers you find the most persuasive in this final worksheet.

WORKSHEET 12-11 Your Reasons for Self/Other-Acceptance

My self/other-acceptance attitude:	
Why does it make sound logical sense to hold this attitude?	
Why is this attitude true? How does this attitude fit with reality?	
In what specific ways is it helpful or useful for me to hold this attitude?	
How does holding this attitude positively benefit my mood?	

TIP

You can use Worksheet 12-11 as a cheat sheet. To keep the concepts fresh in your mind, carry it with you and consult it every so often (or when you feel a self-battering session coming on).

IN THIS CHAPTER

- » Knowing the difference between healthy and unhealthy anger
- » Acquiring accepting attitudes
- » Practicing healthy assertion
- » Appreciating yourself as you are

Chapter 13
Maintaining Relationships

Your ability to get along with others depends on your ability to be accepting of them and to experience healthy negative emotions instead of unhealthy ones, such as rage, hate, and fury. (Take a look at Chapter 6 for an explanation of healthy and unhealthy negative emotions.) Unhealthy anger is a common reason for relationship problems. Another common cause of interpersonal difficulties is low self-esteem (see Chapter 12).

In this chapter, we help you to work out what type of anger you most often experience and to get better at being healthily angry. We also give you a few exercises to strengthen your acceptance of yourself and others — thereby increasing your chances of developing satisfying and functional relationships.

Overcoming Outrage

Everyone does it from time to time — loses their cool, blows their top, goes berserk. Some behave in this way more often than others, though. Losing your temper can cause problems in your romantic life, family relationships, friendships, and work life.

Recognizing whether unhealthy outrage is the type of emotion you're experiencing is the first step in overcoming it. This section helps you discern the difference between irrational rage and appropriate annoyance.

Identifying healthy anger

Let's have a look at the aspects of healthy anger. When you're healthily angry, you tend to be thinking in a balanced and accepting way about others. You believe that someone has broken one of your personal rules without deciding that they really must *not* do so. You still feel in control of yourself and you behave in an assertive but nonthreatening manner.

Choose a recent or typical example when you got angry, and use the checklist in Worksheet 13-1 to identify aspects of healthy anger that apply to your thoughts, behaviors, and physical reactions.

WORKSHEET 13-1 Aspects of Healthy Anger Checklist

Thinking Aspects
❑ Holding strong preferences about how others behave
❑ Allowing others to live according to their own personal rules
❑ Strongly preferring that others treat you well and neither disrespect nor ridicule you
❑ Desiring that other people and life conditions don't get in the way of your pursuing your goals
❑ Thinking realistically about whether other people have deliberately acted badly toward you
❑ Considering that both you and the other person may be right and wrong to some degree
❑ Making an effort to understand the other person's point of view
Action Aspects
❑ Asserting yourself respectfully
❑ Staying in the situation and trying to resolve any disagreement
❑ Asking the other person to modify their behavior while respecting their right to disagree with you
❑ Looking for evidence that the other person may not have behaved with malicious intent
Physical Aspects
❑ Some degree of muscular tension
❑ Minor shaking or trembling
❑ Feeling a bit hot or flushed
❑ Slightly elevated heart rate

Seeing aspects of unhealthy anger

Anger of the unhealthy variety is typified by certain ways of thinking and acting in addition to certain physical sensations. Generally, unhealthy anger means that you're thinking in very harsh ways about someone else and behaving in an intimidating manner (that you may later regret). The sensation usually feels pretty uncomfortable and can be all-consuming.

REMEMBER

As a rule, *unhealthy anger* lasts longer and is more intensely uncomfortable than its healthier version.

Think of a recent or typical example of a time when you became angry. Use the checklist in Worksheet 13-2 to check off the aspects of unhealthy anger that apply to you.

WORKSHEET 13-2 Aspects of Unhealthy Anger Checklist

Thinking Aspects
❑ Rigid demands or rules about how other people must or must not behave
❑ Insisting that others must not disrespect or ridicule you
❑ Demanding that others and life conditions do not get in the way of your getting what you want, when you want it
❑ Assuming that other people have deliberately acted in an undesirable or unpleasant way toward you
❑ Taking the stance that you're totally right and others are totally wrong
❑ Refusing to consider the other person's point of view or opinion
Action Aspects
❑ Either actually attacking or wanting to attack another person verbally and/or physically
❑ Getting back at the other person in subtle ways such as sabotaging their job or relationship (which is known as passive aggression in psychological terms)
❑ Venting your anger on innocent parties such as other people in your life, animals, or objects
❑ Fantasizing about and plotting revenge
❑ Sulking or freezing the other person out
❑ Looking for evidence that the offense was both malicious and is likely to be repeated
Physical Aspects
❑ Muscular tension
❑ Trembling or shaking
❑ Clenched jaw
❑ Feeling hot and flushed
❑ Elevated heart rate

Having had a look at the difference between healthy and unhealthy anger through using the checklists, you may now be in a better position to decide which type of anger you most frequently experience.

Counting the Cost of Losing Your Cool

Getting unhealthily angry can have negative consequences on your relationships and your life in general. Sometimes you may think that your rage has positive benefits that healthy annoyance wouldn't bring about. You're probably wrong. Usually you're more articulate and effective at making your points if you're not fuming with hostility.

EXAMPLE

Paul hates other people telling him what to do. He tells himself that he can't stand it when other people try to assert control over him. Even when his girlfriend makes a minor request, he sees it as an imposition and becomes very defensive. Paul also has trouble at work because he thinks his boss is belittling him if he's anything other than complimentary about his work. He's lost many jobs as a result of his angry outbursts. Recently, Paul had a serious argument with his girlfriend because she disagreed with him about vacation plans. He shouted at her and accused her of "treating me like an idiot" for questioning his choice of destination. During the argument, he pushed her forcefully against a piece of furniture, badly bruising her back. As a result, Paul's girlfriend has refused to go on vacation with him and is rethinking the future of their relationship. Paul now feels guilty for hurting his girlfriend and is kicking himself for his behavior. Table 13-1 shows how Paul counted the cost of his unhealthy anger.

TABLE 13-1 Paul's Counting the Cost of Losing His Cool Worksheet

Recall a recent or typical situation in which you became unhealthily angry:	My girlfriend disagreed with me about where to go for our summer vacation.
Who or what were you angry with?	My girlfriend, for challenging my opinion and plans.
What did your unhealthy anger lead you to do?	I shouted at her and called her rude names. I threatened her and pushed her into the bookshelf.
What effect did your unhealthy anger have on the other person involved and/or your relationship with them? (Think both short and long term.)	She cried, looked hurt and frightened, and ran out of my apartment. Now she won't come on vacation with me and is thinking seriously about breaking up with me.
What effect did your unhealthy anger have on the situation/problem? (Think both short and long term.)	It made the problem much more serious than it needed to be and has created a really upsetting and painful situation between myself and my girlfriend. The vacation is totally off.
What effect did your unhealthy anger have on you? (Think both short and long term.)	I felt really out of control at the time of the argument. I now feel guilty for hurting my girlfriend and am very worried that she'll dump me for being so violent.

Use Worksheet 13-3 to help you count the cost of losing your cool.

WORKSHEET 13-3 My Counting the Cost of Losing My Cool Worksheet

Recall a recent or typical situation in which you became unhealthily angry:	
Who or what were you angry with?	
What did your unhealthy anger lead you to do?	
What effect did your unhealthy anger have on the other person involved and/or your relationship with them? (Think both short and long term.)	

What effect did your unhealthy anger have on the situation/problem? (Think both short and long term.)	
What effect did your unhealthy anger have on you? (Think both short and long term.)	

TIP

Chapter 8 contains a cost-benefit analysis (CBA) form that you may find helpful for further weighing the costs and benefits of both healthy and unhealthy anger.

Lengthening Your Fuse

Okay, so perhaps you're identifying that you often feel unhealthily angry and that it has some pretty negative results. What's next? Dealing with your anger may be challenging, but if you want to enough and are prepared to put in some serious hard work, you can do it.

If you have strict rules that you demand others and the world adhere to at all times, then you're prone to unhealthy anger if they break your rules. Giving others the right to hold and voice their own opinions is a good first step toward experiencing healthy anger. Also, having preferences for how others behave but not insisting that everyone *must* do as you wish helps you to avoid unhealthy outrage.

Paul used the questions in Table 13-2 to work toward a healthier version of anger.

TABLE 13-2 Paul's Fuse-Lengthening Formula

Recent or typical situation in which I became unhealthily angry:	My girlfriend disagreed with me about where to go for our summer vacation.
What was I demanding of the other person/situation?	She must agree with me and she must not challenge me about where to go.
Was I insisting that I was right and the other person was wrong? What about?	I was insisting that I was right about where to go on vacation and that she was wrong to question my choice.
Was I refusing to allow the other person to disagree with me or to hold a different opinion or set of values to my own?	Yes, I completely discounted her opinion and ideas. I shouted her down and got very aggressive.
What is a more flexible and tolerant attitude I can hold about the other person/situation?	I'd rather that my girlfriend agreed with me about vacation plans, but there's no reason that she has to. I can stand her disagreement and it doesn't mean that I'm weak or ineffectual if she disagrees with me.
How might holding this new attitude help me to resolve the problem?	I'd probably listen to her and not become loud and unpleasant. She may have a valid point, and I might be wise to listen to her point of view. Also, if I hadn't gone totally ballistic, we may still be going on vacation together and she may not be thinking about breaking up with me.
How might holding this new attitude benefit the other person involved?	My girlfriend wouldn't be afraid, insulted, and physically injured. She may feel appreciated and understood rather than bullied and abused.

REMEMBER

When completing the worksheets in the remainder of this chapter, certain questions may not apply to you. Their relevance depends on whether you're unhealthily angry with another person or with the world/life conditions.

Following Paul's example, use the questions in Worksheet 13-4 to help you turn your unhealthy-anger-producing demands into flexible preferences that lead to healthy anger.

WORKSHEET 13-4 Your Fuse-Lengthening Formula

Recent or typical situation in which I became unhealthily angry:	
What was I demanding of the other person/situation?	
Was I insisting that I was right and the other person was wrong? What about?	
Was I refusing to allow the other person to disagree with me or to hold a different opinion or set of values to my own?	
What is a more flexible and tolerant attitude I can hold about the other person/situation?	
How might holding this new attitude help me to resolve the problem?	
How might holding this new attitude benefit the other person involved?	

Embracing Effective Assertion

Learning to be assertive takes a lot of practice, so give yourself permission to get it wrong a few times before you get it right. The best recipe for assertion is to accept both yourself and the other person as flawed human beings who can make mistakes. Then listen to the other person and really think about what you want to say in response. This process is especially relevant if you're in the throes of disagreement or on the receiving end of critical comments.

Healthy assertion is about getting your point across and standing up for your rights when others are treating you unfairly or poorly. Unlike aggression, assertion doesn't mean proving to another person that you're right and they're wrong. Assertion is intended to be a civil exchange with the aim of resolving a difference and/or reaching a compromise. When you're being assertive, you tend to do the following:

- Speak respectfully to the other person without name calling or using offensive or abusive language.
- Avoid intimidating, unduly upsetting, or diminishing the other person.
- Give the other person a chance to tell you their views.
- Refrain from any violence or threat of violence.
- Engage in discussion with the other person instead of trying to score points or win an argument.
- Strive to resolve differences if possible or agree to disagree on a point.

REMEMBER When resolving a disagreement, you need to find an environment private enough to talk when both of you have time. Keep in mind that conditions don't have to be perfect for you to discuss issues with another person, but it helps to minimize possible distractions. If it's a work issue, you may want to book an appointment to speak to your colleague or boss.

You can use Worksheet 13-5 to work through a disagreement with another person and review the benefits of using the assertion principles discussed in this section.

WORKSHEET 13-5 My Assertion Action Plan

Before the Meeting:	
What time and place have I set for the discussion?	
What specific points do I want to voice? How can I both stick to my point and be respectful when doing so?	
Can I remind myself to take responsibility for my feelings instead of blaming or condemning the other person/situation?	
After the Meeting:	
In what ways can I learn from or use any constructive criticism or feedback from the other person?	
Is there a grain of truth in what the other person is saying about me, my behavior, or the situation?	
How can following these steps potentially benefit both me and the other person involved?	

Putting Yourself on Par with Your Peers

Low self-opinion can lead to all sorts of social difficulties. Viewing yourself in this way can lead to unhealthy anger, as described in the previous sections. It can also lead you to compare yourself negatively and harshly with others. You may feel socially anxious because you fundamentally believe that others won't like you or accept you just as you are.

One of the very best ways (if not the *only* way) to truly enjoy social interaction, make friends, and maintain relationships is to consider yourself equal in human worth to all others. Holding this opinion may sound pretty easy, but like many CBT principles, putting it into practice is considerably harder. Your sense of equality involves giving up your need to *be superior* in order to not *feel inferior.* It also involves being your *true self* and allowing others to like or dislike you on that basis, and vice versa. Considering yourself equal also involves being able to accept, embrace, and even rejoice in your own ordinariness. Most of us are mostly average in most respects. And that's normal and just fine, if you let it be so.

EXAMPLE

Simone believes that she must be liked and approved of by others at all times. If she senses that someone doesn't completely like her, she becomes depressed or hurt. Simone tells herself that being disliked or rejected proves that she's a totally unlikable person. Because of her demands to be liked and approved of, Simone goes out of her way to please other people. Sometimes she pretends to be interested in things she knows little about in an attempt to impress others. Simone craves social contact, but because she's so afraid of being disliked, she often feels very anxious in social situations. Recently, Simone was invited to a friend's wedding. Prior to the wedding, she became very anxious about her appearance and whether she would know the other guests. During the wedding supper, Simone was placed at a table with five other guests, none of whom knew each other very well. The other guests chatted and got to know one another over the meal. Simone was so focused on what they might be thinking about her that she lost a lot of the conversation and tripped over her words a bit. Finally, she withdrew from the conversation altogether and berated herself for being a "social freak." One man at Simone's table was very outgoing and made a lot of jokes. He made a few good-natured remarks about how quiet Simone was during the meal. Simone felt hurt by his remarks and resented him for drawing attention to her. "What an insensitive creep," she thought. "How *dare* he call attention to me." Simone felt low for a few days after the wedding and continued to put herself down for being awkward. She also blamed her friend for placing her on that table with that "horrible man" who had "ruined" her evening. Table 13-3 shows how Simone came to grips with the crux of her self-opinion problem and her tendency to blame others for her bad feelings.

TIP

See Chapter 12 for much more about self-acceptance and how to develop it!

Now do the same exercise as Simone in Worksheet 13-6 and see if it helps you to readjust your self-opinion for the better! Also, see if you can recognize where you may be missing an opportunity to laugh at yourself or the situation.

WARNING

You can give "yes" or "no" answers to the questions in this worksheet. Giving yourself specific examples for each question will be more helpful to you, though.

Hopefully, you'll now be more equipped to nurture your relationships with others and to deprive your unhealthy anger attitudes of further fuel.

TABLE 13-3 Simone's Putting Herself on a Par Page

When do I typically put myself down? (Cite a recent example.)	At my friend's wedding, when I got anxious and awkward during the supper.
What are some good reasons for believing in my inherent human worth?	I'm a fallible, complex, and ever-changing human being. I can make mistakes like anyone else. My social unease is only one part of my whole self. Being rejected or disliked isn't nice, but it's also not a sign that I'm totally unlikable. I can't be a hit with everyone, and trying too hard to please others ends up costing me a lot of energy. I can like myself even if I don't always get obvious approval from others within a social group.
Am I allowing myself to be an individual without trying too hard to impress or please other people?	No. In this wedding situation I was utterly focused on making a good impression and avoiding any negative judgments from the other guests. My personality took a back seat.
Am I accepting others as individuals and allowing them to have their own personalities, tastes, and idiosyncrasies, whether I agree with them or not?	No. I totally blamed the outgoing man at the table for making me feel anxious. I also called him a creep and a horrible man (in my head) because I didn't like his way of socializing.
Am I devaluing or putting down others in order to feel better about myself?	Not really, but I suppose that by putting down the loud man I made myself feel less responsible for my own social anxiety.
Am I taking myself too seriously?	Definitely! How important is a wedding supper in the grand scheme of things anyway? So I was anxious and it showed. Why am I making such a big deal about it days after the event?
Am I taking the opinions/actions of others too seriously?	Definitely! I'm still worried and obsessing about what the other five guests are thinking about me days after the event. They've probably forgotten about me by now or are certainly more focused on their own lives than on my social awkwardness.
Am I taking the situation too seriously?	Yes. It wasn't a life-or-death situation, for heaven's sake. I was one guest out of hundreds.
How can I get myself to lighten up and let the laughter leak out?	I could laugh at my ridiculous way of thinking at the time and for the few days following. I could appreciate that the loud man was only being friendly and trying to get me to relax. It's kind of funny now to think about how nutty my thinking was at the time. It's laughable to assume that those five people spent most of the supper (or the days after) concentrating on my social problems. They have their own lives!

WORKSHEET 13-6 My Putting Myself on a Par Page

When do I typically put myself down? (Cite a recent example.)	
What are some good reasons for believing in my inherent human worth?	
Am I allowing myself to be an individual without trying too hard to impress or please other people?	

(continued)

WORKSHEET 13-6 ***(continued)***

Am I accepting others as individuals and allowing them to have their own personalities, tastes, and idiosyncrasies, whether I agree with them or not?	
Am I devaluing or putting down others in order to feel better about myself?	
Am I taking myself too seriously?	
Am I taking the opinions/actions of others too seriously?	
Am I taking the situation too seriously?	
How can I get myself to lighten up and let the laughter leak out?	

4

Forging into the Future

IN THIS PART . . .

This part helps you look at long-standing beliefs and ways of thinking that may affect you in the present. We help you challenge old and unhelpful beliefs about yourself, others, and the world at large. We give you the tools to make new beliefs more permanent, and to focus on further personal development.

We can't ignore the possibility of relapse, so in this part, we give you a chance to plan for and troubleshoot possible problem recurrence. We finish up by helping you live in a positive way, even after you've largely defeated your initial problems.

IN THIS CHAPTER

» Linking early experiences with present beliefs

» Getting to know your core beliefs

» Creating healthy new beliefs

Chapter 14 Examining and Changing Long-Standing Beliefs

Past experiences and early childhood situations can influence the way you think about yourself and others, and how you make sense of the world in your present life. You learn certain messages from your parents, other relatives, teachers, and peers. Sometimes these messages are helpful and other times they aren't. As you get older, you often reassess the validity and usefulness of some of your early beliefs and ideas. Other times you don't re-evaluate ideas you took as gospel truth in your early life and continue to live according to these philosophies and beliefs.

In this chapter, we introduce you to some techniques to help you unearth your core beliefs and replace unhelpful inaccurate beliefs with new and helpful ways of thinking.

Uncovering Your Core Beliefs

In cognitive behavioral therapy (CBT), long-standing, enduring beliefs about yourself, people, or the world are called *core beliefs*. Core beliefs are generally global and absolute in nature. So, usually your core beliefs are 100 percent true at all times, and you may ignore or misinterpret evidence that contradicts them. If you think of core beliefs as being at the very *heart* (or *core*) of your belief system — and the way you understand yourself and all the things around you — you can begin to see how important they are to your mental and emotional health.

Beliefs adopted in early life tend to be very tenacious and difficult to shift. Even if you know that you hold an unhelpful belief such as "I'm unlovable" or "I'm weak" or "The world is dangerous," refraining from thinking and acting according to that damaging (yet often strongly held) belief can be very difficult. Identifying and understanding the ways in which your past experiences have influenced the beliefs you *still* hold is a useful first step to overcoming negative core beliefs.

Sorting out the three types of core beliefs

Core beliefs are ways of thinking about and making sense of the world around you and the people in it — yourself included. Healthy, positive core beliefs help you adjust to negative circumstances, promote positive self-opinion, and contribute to your forming rewarding relationships. Many people develop reasonably rational and healthy core beliefs in childhood or update and change their ways of thinking as they grow older.

Core beliefs are generally formed in childhood and early life; they're often influenced by repeated messages you received from others and/or your environment. Similar and repeated experiences are called *themes*. Negative early experiences like poor parenting, death of loved ones, abuse, illness, injuries, accidents, bullying at school or at home, rejection from peers or family, or growing up in an area with a lot of poverty and crime contribute greatly to the development of unhealthy core beliefs. Unhealthy negative core beliefs impede your ability to problem-solve and adjust to negative circumstances, undermine self-esteem, and may cause relationship problems.

Your core beliefs determine how you conduct yourself in relationships and in your overall life. They inform what you expect the world to be like and how you expect others to treat you. Your core beliefs influence your *personal rules* (demands that you put on yourself for your behavior) and your *automatic thoughts* (thoughts that just seem to pop into your head in certain situations).

Core beliefs fall into three main categories:

- **Your beliefs about yourself** inform the way you understand your own worth. For example, if you experienced harsh criticism, neglect or abuse as a child, you may have learned to think of yourself as weak or inadequate.
- **Your beliefs about *other people*** also frequently have their roots in early life. Again, if you suffered traumas or very negative treatment from others, you may adopt the belief that people are dangerous or untrustworthy.
- **Your beliefs about *life in general and the world*** help determine your general attitudes. If you grow up in a deprived or unpredictable environment, you may develop negative beliefs about the world and life. Beliefs that the world or life is dangerous, cruel, or unfair are examples of the kinds of beliefs negative life conditions may give rise to.

Healthy core beliefs about the world, yourself and other people may include "The world is mostly a good place" or "Most people are decent" or "I'm a worthwhile person." Positive early experiences of life conditions, parents, and other family are likely to give rise to healthy core beliefs.

EXAMPLE

Mary's mother was an alcoholic and very unpredictable in her moods. Sometimes she was violent toward Mary. Mary's mother would often leave her alone in the house at night. As a result, Mary formed the core belief about herself that "I'm unlovable" because it seemed to make sense of her mother's neglect and abuse. Mary also developed a core belief that "Other people are unreliable" and "The world is a scary and lonely place." Because her core beliefs are so deeply entrenched, they impact greatly on how Mary makes sense of her current experiences.

Recently Mary's boyfriend of six months broke up with her. He explained to Mary that he didn't think they were well-suited and that he wasn't ready for a long-term relationship with her. Mary used Table 14-1 to examine how her core beliefs determined her understanding of the breakup.

TABLE 14-1 **Mary's Core Belief Breakdown**

My core beliefs about myself:	I'm unlovable.
My core beliefs about others:	Other people are unreliable.
My core beliefs about the world/life:	The world is frightening and lonely.
Recent situation/event:	My boyfriend ended our six-month relationship.
My negative automatic thoughts about the event (how my core beliefs determine what the event means to me):	He was right to break up with me. I'm not good enough to keep a boyfriend interested in me for long. I deserve to be alone. Other people will abandon me and leave me alone, too.
My personal rules and demands (how my core beliefs will lead me to act in the future based on this event/experience):	I should not rely on other people to stay with me. I must not allow myself to be abandoned again. I must try harder to be lovable, or I'll always be alone. I shouldn't give others any reason to be displeased with me.

You can see that Mary's unhealthy negative core beliefs lead her to make some extreme conclusions about herself, other people, and the future based on the recent breakup.

Use Worksheet 14-1 in the same way Mary did to see if you can identify your core beliefs and how they may be influencing your understanding of a recent event in your life. Getting familiar with your beliefs and their effects is the first step in changing them to healthier, more positive alternatives.

WORKSHEET 14-1 **My Core Belief Breakdown**

My core beliefs about myself:	
My core beliefs about others:	
My core beliefs about the world/life:	
Recent situation/event:	

(continued)

WORKSHEET 14-1 *(continued)*

My negative automatic thoughts about the event (how my core beliefs determine what the event means to me):	
My personal rules and demands (how my core beliefs will lead me to act in the future based on this event/ experience):	

Bringing past relationships into the light of the present

Your relationships with your family members and, in particular, your parents have a lot of influence over the ideas you develop about yourself. Other important people in your early life — such as neighbors, extended family, siblings, friends, first loves, teachers, or religious leaders — also can have a significant impact on the beliefs you form.

EXAMPLE

Lester is the middle child. His parents were loving but often overlooked Lester because his older brother was very intelligent and charming and his younger sister had learning difficulties. Lester was an average child, but very responsible and capable, so his parents could rely on him to do things on his own. Lester often felt like an outsider in his own family. At school, Lester did well, but his teachers often compared him to his intelligent older brother or told him how lucky he was not to struggle like his little sister. He had friends, but Lester had trouble making lasting relationships. As a teenager, Lester's first real girlfriend eventually broke up with him to date a more popular boy. Another girl went out with Lester for a while, but it turned out that she was more interested in his older brother and they ultimately broke up. In his adult life, Lester has assertion problems at work and occasional episodes of depression. He's often jealous and suspicious in his romantic relationships.

Lester used Table 14-2 to help him better understand the role events and individuals played in the early development of his core beliefs.

TABLE 14-2 Lester's Early Experiences Worksheet

Who were the most significant people in my life during childhood, my teenage years, and my early adult years?	My parents, brother, and sister My math teacher, who I really liked My first and second girlfriends My classmates
Were there recurring themes to some of my early experiences?	My parents often gave me less attention than they gave my brother and sister. Teachers compared me to my brother and sister, even my math teacher, who told me that I should study more to be as good at math as my brother. My first girlfriend left me for a boy that I thought was more popular and likable than me. My second girlfriend liked my brother more than she liked me.
What beliefs did I learn from these experiences?	That I'm easily overlooked and less important than other people like my brother and sister. I learned that I'm lucky to get any positive attention from others. I suppose I also believe that women will only stay with me until they find someone better.

Through the worksheet, Lester is beginning to get an idea of how his past influenced his present way of thinking and how it contributes to some of his current emotional problems.

WARNING

Although you may be able to accurately attribute certain core beliefs you hold to events and/or the actions of people from your past, this is *not* an exercise in assigning blame. If you blame your past or your parents for your current problems as an adult, you're likely to stop yourself from moving on and getting better. Past aspects of your life may have *contributed* to the unhelpful ways you think and act in the present. However, you're the one who now has the choice to revamp your ideas and live in a new and more fruitful way. Don't let yourself get sucked into the quicksand of your past. Instead review your past with the purpose of better understanding and improving your present life.

Worksheet 14-2 can help you understand which significant people in your life have contributed to your core beliefs. Also, recording recurring experiences in your life (or themes) can help you recognize how specific events may have further contributed to the core beliefs you hold.

Use Worksheet 14-2 to record some of your early formative experiences.

WORKSHEET 14-2 My Early Experiences Worksheet

Who were the most significant people in my life during childhood, my teenage years, and my early adult years?	
Were there recurring themes to some of my early experiences?	
What beliefs did I learn from these experiences?	

EXAMPLE

Lester's analysis of his past relationships helped him fill in Table 14-3 to better understand what fundamental beliefs he holds in these three areas.

TABLE 14-3 Lester's Three Camps of Beliefs Record

What are my core beliefs about myself?	I'm unimportant. I'm inadequate.
What are my core beliefs about other people?	Other people are superior to me. People will leave me eventually.
What are my core beliefs about the world/life?	Life is difficult. The world is against me.

Giving some thought to the way you make sense of yourself, others, and the world is useful. Consider the types of core beliefs you may hold in these three areas. By getting a sense of your core beliefs, you're in a good position to challenge some of them.

Use Worksheet 14-3 to record your considerations. Show this worksheet to your CBT therapist if you're working with one.

WORKSHEET 14-3 My Three Camps of Belief Record

What are my core beliefs about myself?	
What are my core beliefs about other people?	
What are my core beliefs about the world/life?	

Catching your core beliefs interacting

Your core beliefs don't exist in isolation. Instead, they tend to interact and reinforce one another. If you hold a core belief about yourself like "I'm weak," "Others are strong and dangerous," or "Life is harsh and difficult," you can see how you may easily become depressed and feel powerless to solve problems. Looking more closely at how your core beliefs interact can help you see why you may keep having the same kinds of problems.

EXAMPLE

Lester asks a girl from work on a date but she said no because she already has a boyfriend. Lester makes sense of this rejection according to his three camps of core beliefs. Table 14-4 shows how Lester's core beliefs play off one another.

TABLE 14-4 Lester's Belief Interaction Chart

Core Belief	Effect on Meaning Assigned to the Situation
Self: I'm unimportant. I'm inadequate.	Molly is too good for me. Her boyfriend is more important than I am as a person. If I were a better person, she might have agreed to date me.
Others: Other people are superior to me. People will leave me eventually.	Molly is better than me, and so is her boyfriend. I could never keep the interest of a girl like Molly anyway. Someone else would take her from me.
World/life: Life is difficult. The world is against me.	It took a lot of courage to ask Molly out, and it was all in vain. Romance never works out for me.

Hopefully, you can see with Lester's example that his beliefs in all three areas influence the meanings he assigns to being turned down by Molly. Also, you can probably see that the beliefs he holds about himself, others, and the world are reinforced by one another. Looking at Table 14-4, it's easier to understand how Lester became quite depressed over this rather minor rejection.

Now try working out how your beliefs interact with each other in Worksheet 14-4. Think of a recent situation in which you became emotionally disturbed. Fill in your beliefs on the chart (you can refer to Worksheet 14-3) and then think about how they may have contributed to the meaning you assigned to the event.

WORKSHEET 14-4 My Belief Interaction Chart

Core Belief	Effect on Meaning Assigned to the Situation
Self:	
Others:	
World/life:	

Digging Up Your Core Beliefs

Sometimes, unearthing your precise core beliefs can be tricky. Often you may not hear your core beliefs in their absolute form. Usually you're more aware of your negative automatic thoughts (NATs), which we talk about in Chapter 3. For example, if you held a core belief of being a failure, you may not actually say this to yourself very often. More likely you say things to yourself like "Here I go screwing up again" or "I never do anything right."

The following sections offer more exercises that can help you pin down the nature of your core beliefs if you're having trouble.

Doing a downward arrow

The downward arrow technique is simple: Start by identifying a situation or event in which you felt an unhealthy negative emotion, such as guilt, shame, or depression (see Chapter 6 for more on unhealthy negative emotions).

What happened and who else was involved? The emotions you feel in response to adverse events are more likely to be unhealthy ones (like deep depression) rather than healthy ones (like intense sadness) when your core beliefs are unhealthy and negative.

Next, ask yourself what the situation *means* about you, others, or the world. Your answer will probably be an NAT. Keep asking yourself what your answers *mean* to you until you finish with a global label or statement. The statement you finish with is your core belief. You can also do a downward arrow for all three types of core beliefs separately.

EXAMPLE

Table 14-5 shows how Lester did a downward arrow on his situation of being turned down by Molly when he asked her out on a date. He used the technique to arrive at his core belief about himself.

TABLE 14-5 Lester's Downward Arrow

Situation

Molly turned me down when I asked her for a date.

↓

What does this mean about me:
Molly doesn't think I'm good enough for her.

Others:

The world:

↓

What does this mean about me:
She'd rather go out with someone interesting like her current boyfriend.

Others:

The world:

↓

What does this mean about me:
I'll never have a decent relationship with a girl I really like.

Others:

The world:

↓

What does this mean about me:
No girl will ever find me attractive.

Others:

The world:

↓

What does this mean about me:
I'm inadequate.

Others:

The world:

REMEMBER

You can use the downward arrow technique to boil down your thinking about any type of situation, past or present, until you arrive at a core belief. You may need to complete the downward arrow a few times until you arrive at a core belief.

Use Worksheet 14-5 to get started.

WORKSHEET 14-5 My Downward Arrow

Situation

↓

What does this mean about me:

Others:

The world:

↓

What does this mean about me:

Others:

The world:

↓

What does this mean about me:

Others:

The world:

↓

What does this mean about me:

Others:

The world:

↓

What does this mean about me:

Others:

The world:

Taking note of themes

Another way of journeying to the core of your beliefs involves tracking familiar themes in your thinking. You can review your A-B-C forms in Chapter 3 to find recurrent themes that point to a core belief. *Themes* include ways of thinking about yourself, others, and the world that you tend to revisit over and over. So, if you often have thoughts about yourself that seem to boil down to the same theme such as inadequacy, failure, or insignificance, this gives you a strong clue as to what your core belief is about yourself.

EXAMPLE

Lester notes that he often thinks thematically consistent things about himself, others, and the world in lots of different negative situations. Take a glance at Lester's list of thinking themes in Table 14-6.

TABLE 14-6 Lester's Thinking Themes

About myself:	My opinions don't really count.
	Other people are more capable at work than I am.
	I don't succeed socially.
	I'm lucky to get any positive attention from others.
About other people:	People are better at things than I am.
	I shouldn't upset other people by voicing my opinions or disagreeing with them.
	People always leave me for someone better.
About the world/life:	I never seem to get the good things in life that other people get.
	Other people seem to negotiate life more easily than I do.

By looking at his list of thinking themes, Lester can begin to take an accurate guess at what core beliefs he holds.

Use Worksheet 14-6 to see whether you recognize themes in your own thinking.

WORKSHEET 14-6 My Thinking Themes

About myself:	
About other people:	

About the world/life:

Forming a Formulation

In this section, you put all your hard work together on one handy form. Pulling all this information together reminds you where your core beliefs may have come from, how they lead you to think in everyday situations, and what behaviors they promote. Your formulation can also remind you of the beliefs that you want to change and the reasons why.

Follow these steps to complete your formulation form in Worksheet 14-7.

1. **In the first box, record early events or past experiences that you think contribute to the development of your core beliefs.**
2. **In the second box, write down your unhelpful core beliefs about yourself, others, and the world/life.**
3. **In the third box, record the rules, demands, or codes that you expect yourself to live by or other people and the world to live by.**

   These assumptions are formed *due* to your core beliefs. For example, Lester's rules include: "I must not assert myself" and "I must seek people's approval to make sure they don't reject me."
4. **In the fourth box, list things you do to avoid triggering your core beliefs or unhelpful things you do to cope with your core beliefs.**
5. **In the fifth box, list your strengths as an individual and things in life you have going for you.**

WORKSHEET 14-7 My Formulation Form

FORMULATION OF MY BELIEFS AND RULES

RELEVANT EARLY/ PAST EXPERIENCES	→	CORE UNHELPFUL BELIEFS I am . . ., The world is . . ., Other people . . .	RULES/ ASSUMPTIONS If . . . then . . ., Demands about self, the world, others.

AVOIDANCE AND COMPENSATORY BEHAVIORS Situations you tend to avoid or things you do excessively as a consequence of your beliefs/rules	WHAT I'VE GOT GOING FOR ME List your personal strengths and assets

Creating Constructive Core Beliefs

Identifying your core beliefs can be a bleak exercise. After you do it, though, you're ready to change those beliefs and adopt new ones. Consider good (and more balanced) ideas you have that contradict your negative beliefs, and think about how you can use this information to construct new ways of viewing yourself, others, and the world. Especially remind yourself of positive experiences you've had with other people, traits and characteristics you like about yourself, and anything you've experienced that suggests the world has many good things to offer. Then scribble down a few of those better, more accurate beliefs.

TIP

You may find it helpful to make a list of life experiences and personal attributes that contradict your unhelpful core beliefs. Remember to include positive experiences with others. Then use your list to develop more balanced and accurate core beliefs.

EXAMPLE

Lester listed his more constructive beliefs in Table 14-7.

TABLE 14-7 Lester's Constructive Core Beliefs

Information That Contradicts My Negative Core Beliefs	More Helpful/Constructive Beliefs I Can Adopt
My work colleagues often ask my opinion on procedures and seek my input during meetings.	**Self:** I'm basically okay and on a par with other people.
I have two friends that have stuck by me even when I've been depressed.	**Others:** People are as worthy as me, no more and no less. Some people have been my friends for a long time.
A girl who works in the coffee shop near work often flirts with me.	**World/life:** Life can be difficult, but it also can be good. Good things do happen to me.
I have a decent job and a comfortable home that I obtained through my own efforts.	
I'm generally polite and kind to others.	
Other people are often friendly toward me.	
My boss gave me a pay raise last year.	

Now rework your core ideas using Worksheet 14-8, keeping in mind that your constructive core beliefs should be statements about yourself, others, and the world that you can *genuinely* imagine eventually *truly* believing in.

WARNING

Changing your negative core beliefs isn't tantamount to sugar-coated positive thinking. So, be wary of replacing a negative belief such as "I'm inadequate" with something over the top like "I'm fantastic!" First, no one is totally fantastic, nor is anyone totally inadequate. Both are global statements. Second, if you've spent years thinking of yourself in a negative way, you're highly unlikely to believe in an overly positive view of yourself. Instead, try to come up with reasons why your negative core beliefs are not 100 percent true. Work on generating balanced, optimistic, and realistic alternative views.

WORKSHEET 14-8 Your Constructive Core Beliefs

Information That Contradicts My Negative Core Beliefs	More Helpful/Constructive Beliefs I Can Adopt
	Self:
	Others:
	World/life:

Assigning New Meanings to Old Events

As a child, young adult, or even later in life, you may have given idiosyncratic meanings to certain life events and experiences. These meanings are often the foundation of negative core beliefs. Fortunately, you can now reassess the meanings you attached to these events and assign new and more accurate meanings to them. In doing so, you can further your work toward generating healthier beliefs.

EXAMPLE

Lester attached the meaning "I'm unimportant and inadequate" to the experience of his parents overlooking him and attending to his brother and sister. He attached the same meaning to the event of his teachers comparing him to his siblings. Lester used Table 14-8 to challenge and change these meanings and, thus, create healthier core beliefs.

When Lester was rejected by two girlfriends, he attached the meaning "Other people are superior to me" and "People will leave me" to the events. He used Table 14-9 to confront and revamp his beliefs about other people.

TABLE 14-8 **Lester's Meaning Sheet about Himself**

Event: Parents ignoring me and giving more attention to my siblings

Old Meaning	New Meaning
I must not be as important to my parents as my brother and sister are.	My parents may not have been aware of ignoring me. My brother was very gregarious and commanded a lot of attention. My sister had problems, and it's understandable that my parents devoted much of their attention to her. It may have been more a case of circumstances that I ended up being overlooked rather than a true reflection of my importance to my parents.
Old Core Belief	**New Core Belief**
I am unimportant and inadequate.	I have importance just like everyone else. I'm adequate just like everyone else.

TABLE 14-9 **Lester's Meaning Sheet about Others**

Event: My first girlfriend breaking up with me to date a popular boy. My second girlfriend having a crush on my older brother.

Old Meaning	New Meaning
My brother and other boys are better than me. There must be something about them that makes my girlfriends prefer them to me. People I get close to will leave me for someone else eventually.	Okay, so I had bad luck with my first couple of girlfriends. They may have left me for other people or liked my brother, but that doesn't mean that other people are better than me. It just means that those two girls preferred other people. That can happen to anyone, not just me. Just because I lost my relationships with two girlfriends doesn't mean that everyone I get close to will leave me. Some may and some may not. I've already survived rejection, and I can survive it again if it happens.
Old Core Belief	**New Core Belief**
Others are superior to me. People will leave me eventually.	I am equal in worth to other people. Not everyone I get close to will leave me.

You can also use this worksheet to form new beliefs about the world/life. We haven't provided an example here, but you complete it in exactly the same way.

Wrestle those grisly beliefs to the ground using Worksheets 14-9, 14-10, and 14-11.

WORKSHEET 14-9 **My Meaning Sheet for Myself**

Event:

Old Meaning	New Meaning

Old Core Belief	New Core Belief

WORKSHEET 14-10 My Meaning Sheet about Others

Event:

Old Meaning	New Meaning

Old Core Belief	New Core Belief

WORKSHEET 14-11 My Meaning Sheet about the World/Life

Event:

Old Meaning	New Meaning

Old Core Belief	New Core Belief

Well done! You're now on your way to changing the way you feel and act (for the better) by changing your core beliefs.

REMEMBER

The more negative your life experiences, the more extreme the beliefs you developed are likely to be. You can use the techniques described throughout this chapter to confront and deal with any life event, even very traumatic or long-lasting ones. We don't expect your experiences to mirror Lester's; we only use him as an example to show you how to use the worksheets. Everyone is unique and has a unique background, including you.

IN THIS CHAPTER

» Moving new beliefs from your head to your heart

» Practicing your new beliefs

» Putting your new beliefs to the test

» Living according to your new beliefs

Chapter 15

Consolidating Conviction in Your New Core Beliefs

So, you've done a lot of work and now you've got a set of healthy beliefs that you want to strengthen (Chapters 1, 2, 3, and 12 cover healthy beliefs in detail). Learning to live with a new set of beliefs takes yet more work. You need to reprogram your brain to make sense of situations in a new way. Unhelpful core beliefs tend to be very rigid and long held, so a fair bit of retraining is necessary for your new healthy beliefs to become second nature. Persistence and patience are also needed. Most people we see for cognitive behavioral therapy (CBT) can fairly readily recognize the self-defeating nature of their unhealthy beliefs, come up with better ways of thinking, and understand that their new beliefs make sense. But very often we hear patients say, "I know these new beliefs will help me, but I just don't *really believe* them yet." In CBT parlance, we call this division between what you *know* to be true and helpful and what you actually *believe*, the *head–heart* or *head–gut* issue. This chapter is devoted to helping you resolve the *head–heart* conflict.

REMEMBER

You've probably been living according to your unhealthy core beliefs for many years — maybe most of your life. So it's understandable that your thinking automatically veers that way when you encounter a negative life event. But habits *can* be broken — even if doing so is difficult and feels awkward at first. Imagine that you break your dominant arm badly — the one you write with and use for most tasks. As the doctor puts you in a cast from your wrist to your shoulder, you realize that you'll have to rely on your other arm for several weeks. At first, it feels very weird and uncomfortable, everything is difficult, and you doubt that you'll be able to brush your teeth and hair until your arm is mended. But over time, your brain adjusts to your altered circumstances and, before you know it, you're doing things relatively easily. Changing your belief system is a bit like this example.

Spotlighting Beliefs You Want to Strengthen

Healthy beliefs have the following characteristics:

- **They're flexible and preference based.** Instead of insisting that you must meet certain criteria, you prefer a specific outcome or desire to achieve a specific goal, but you also accept the possibility of failing to do so. You leave room for normal human error and random life events. So, instead of "I *must* not fail!" you may have the healthy belief "I'd *prefer* not to fail, but there is no reason that I absolutely *must* not."
- **They include a sensible if-then statement.** Instead of concluding extreme negative things about yourself, others, or the world based on a singular event, you can put the event into a healthy perspective. So, instead of "*If* I fail at something, *then* it proves that I am a total failure" you may believe "*If* I fail, *then* it's bad but not terrible and it just means that I am a normal fallible person."
- **They include a positive and realistic general truth.** Instead of assigning global negative ratings to yourself, others, or the world, you allow for the coexistence of good, less good, neutral, and bad elements. So, in place of a belief such as "I'm worthless" or "The world is terrible," you may have "I am basically okay" or "The world is complex and has both good and bad parts."

The first step is to make note of the beliefs that you want to subscribe to for each of three main categories:

- **Yourself:** Your self-opinion and ideas about your worthiness
- **Other people:** Your view of others and how you expect them to behave generally or toward you specifically
- **The world/life:** Your expectations of how the world will treat you and how life is likely to unfold for you and/or others

Chapters 14 and 15 discuss these three types of core beliefs in depth.

Preparing a Portfolio of Persuasive Arguments

A good way of generating lots of sound arguments to support your new beliefs is to create a portfolio of good sound reasons that they make sense. All you need to do is record your ideas about why your new healthy beliefs make sense, reflect reality, and help you to function.

TIP

Make sure your beliefs hold to these basic guidelines:

- **They're true and consistent with reality.** Ensure that your new beliefs or philosophies don't distort the facts of any given situation or event or deny the actual situation or event.
- **They're flexible and preference based.** They leave a margin for error. They recognize that you and other humans are fallible and capable of both success and failure at any given task or endeavor. They acknowledge that life is full of random events and that complete certainty is rarely possible.
- **They're balanced and not extreme.** You resist using judgmental, absolute, harsh labels to describe yourself, others, or the world. Instead, you strive to use descriptive terms that include the complexity and changeability of you, other people, and life itself.
- **They're sensible and logical.** Construct new beliefs that make good sense and are logically sound.
- **They're helpful to you.** Your new beliefs should be ways of thinking that can assist you in reaching your goals and lead to mental/emotional health.

EXAMPLE

Agatha has a core belief that she's a failure. She is very hard on herself and gets depressed at the slightest sniff of failure. Agatha works very hard to avoid failing at anything she does because, to her, any failure or mistake means that she is a total failure as a person. Often, Agatha avoids experiences such as taking her driving test and going for new jobs because she is too terrified of the possibility of failure. Agatha has worked hard to change her belief that she is a failure. Table 15-1 shows how she used a worksheet to help increase her conviction in a healthy alternative belief about herself.

TABLE 15-1 Agatha's Portfolio of Persuasive Arguments

Healthy core belief about myself:	I prefer not to fail, but there is no reason that I must not do so. Failing at things means that I am a normal person, capable of both succeeding and failing.
What reasons show that my belief is true?	Anybody can fail sometimes, even at important things, and so can I. If failing at one or more things meant that I was a total failure, then I would never be able to succeed at anything. The truth is that I have succeeded at lots of things in my life. It's true that I prefer not to fail, but it's also true that no reason exists why I should not fail from time to time. Even people I respect have failed at things. For example, my best friend failed her driving test three times, and I don't think that she's a total failure.
How does my belief reflect reality?	Reality shows that I can (and do) make mistakes and fail sometimes. So, if I insist that I must not fail, I am denying reality. My new belief reflects reality because it accepts the possibility that I can potentially both fail and succeed at tasks. It is normal for people to fail, and my new belief acknowledges this point.
In what ways is my belief flexible?	My new belief allows me to prefer to succeed and to strive to reach my goals, but it also allows me to accept the possibility of failure. After all, to err is human and I'm human. My new belief makes it possible for me to fail at important (or less important) things without deciding that I'm a total failure and becoming depressed.
In what ways is my belief balanced and not extreme?	My new belief is balanced because it is realistic and desirable to not fail, but it's not the end of the world if I do. I also do not have to put myself down in extreme and nasty ways if I do fail at something.

(continued)

TABLE 15-1 *(continued)*

What reasons show that my belief is sensible and logical?	It makes sense to prefer not to fail, but it is illogical to insist that therefore I must not fail. Just because I ***want*** to succeed it doesn't follow logically that I ***must*** succeed. When I do fail at something, it makes sense to feel disappointed because it's a negative event. But it also makes sense to review possible reasons for my failure and to try again if it's appropriate. It makes logical sense that one failure does not make me a total failure as a person.
How will holding this new belief be helpful to me?	I will feel disappointed or sad when I fail but not depressed and full of self-loathing. I'll probably enjoy life more because I won't see everything I do as a test of my overall worth. I'll be more likely to take some risks and try new things because I won't be so worried about getting it wrong.

Agatha now has a comprehensive portfolio of arguments that support her new core belief. She can use this portfolio to help her when she struggles with resurgence of her old, unhealthy belief system. Agatha can also review her portfolio regularly to help resolve the head–heart issue.

You can use Worksheet 15-1 to generate arguments in defense of your new core beliefs about others and the world at large, as well as about yourself as Agatha does!

WORKSHEET 15-1 Your Portfolio of Persuasive Arguments

Healthy core belief:	
What reasons show that my belief is true?	
How does my belief reflect reality?	
In what ways is my belief flexible?	
In what ways is my belief balanced and not extreme?	
What reasons show that my belief is sensible and logical?	
How will holding this new belief be helpful to me?	

You can repeat this exercise if you find yourself feeling emotionally disturbed in response to a particular life event. Emotional disturbance (see Chapter 6) is a reliable indicator that you're thinking in a rigid and unhealthy manner. You may want to do an A-B-C form (see Chapter 3) on the event and then repeat this worksheet to renew your conviction in your healthy beliefs.

If At First You Don't Succeed, Try, Try Again

Finding yourself thinking and acting according to your old negative core beliefs, even after a lot of effort on your part to embrace new ones, can be pretty discouraging. Remind yourself that doing so is a normal part of change and resume your efforts. In this section, we give you some additional arsenal for aiming the big guns at your unhelpful beliefs.

If you find yourself faltering in your attempts to change your beliefs, take a moment to reflect on what you've discovered about yourself thus far. Also, think about positive changes (no matter how small) you've made. Record them for future reference on Worksheet 15-2.

WORKSHEET 15-2 My List of Positive Changes

Acting accordingly

One of the best ways of truly embracing new beliefs and ways of thinking is to behave as if you already *really* believe them. The way you act or behave has a big impact on your thinking. So, if you deliberately act *against* your negative core beliefs, you're simultaneously eroding them and building up your new beliefs. We call this process the *acting "as if"* exercise. This exercise is extremely helpful, so practice it often. Here are some steps to help you get acting "as if":

1. **Record you healthy new belief on a piece of paper.**
2. **Consider what the people in your life would notice if they could see positive changes in you. Think how your behavior would be different if you truly believed in your new way of thinking about yourself, others, and/or the world.**

Think of people you know who seem to hold the healthy core belief that you want to strengthen. How do they behave in ways that reflect that way of thinking?

3. **Identify times that you can devote to test-driving behaviors that match your new core belief.**

EXAMPLE

Let's take a look at Agatha again. Her old core belief was that she is a failure.

Now have a look at how Agatha got into acting "as if" in Table 15-2.

TABLE 15-2 Agatha's "As If" Actions

New core belief:	I prefer not to fail, but there is no reason that I must not do so. Failing at things means that I am a normal person, capable of both succeeding and failing.
If I truly believed this, how would I act/behave?	I'd start driving lessons. I'd take on new tasks at work. I'd approach my boss about a promotion. I'd join the local bar trivia team. I'd shake off minor failures and refuse to condemn myself.
When can I practice these healthy actions?	I'll book driving lessons on Monday. I'll speak to my boss after the staff meeting on Wednesday. I'll go to the bar and join a trivia team tonight.

Take a leaf from Agatha's book and do Worksheet 15-3 for yourself. Try to be specific about times when you can act in line with beliefs that you want to strengthen. Doing so will help you to move from intention to action.

WORKSHEET 15-3 My "As If" Actions

New core belief:	
If I truly believed this, how would I act/behave?	
When can I practice these healthy actions?	

Now get out there and act in the ways you've identified!

You can also use Worksheet 15-3 to identify ways of acting according to healthy beliefs about others and the world. For example, you may think of behaviors that go with a belief such as "Other people are mostly decent and trustworthy" or "Life includes both bad and good events."

Digging out and defeating doubts

Having some doubts or reservations about the truth of your new core beliefs and associated behaviors is natural. When you first start acting according to new ways of thinking, you may feel as though you're going against the grain.

You need to really look at any doubts you may have about making changes. That way, you can deal with them before you're in a tricky situation and your old beliefs are triggered. Facing your misgivings, qualms, or niggling worries about your new beliefs helps you to strengthen them. The zig-zag technique is a useful way of digging out and defeating doubts. Here are the steps for using this technique and filling in Worksheet 15-4:

1. **Record the belief that you want to strengthen in the upper-left box. Rate how strongly you believe it is true from 0 percent to 100 percent.**
2. **In the second box, record one of your doubts or arguments *against* your healthy belief.**
3. **In the third box, record an argument that challenges your doubt and *defends* your healthy belief.**
4. **In the fourth box, record another one of your doubts and *attack* your healthy belief again.**
5. **In the fifth box, again record an argument that challenges your doubt and *defends* your healthy belief.**
6. **Repeat this process of attacking and defending your healthy belief until you've dealt with all your doubts.**

   WARNING

   Make sure you stop on a defense of the healthy belief not on an attack!
7. **Re-rate how strongly you believe in the new core belief from 0 percent to 100 percent.**

   The strength of your conviction in your new belief is likely to go up after using this technique. If it hasn't, you may need to repeat the process or defend your belief more vigorously. If you're seeing a CBT therapist, you can show them your zig-zag and they can help you see where you may have missed good defenses.

EXAMPLE

Agatha knows that she really *wants* to start living according to her new core belief. But in her heart, she has some residual thoughts about whether her new way of thinking about herself is actually true.

Agatha used the zig-zag form in Table 15-3 to confront her troublesome thoughts.

Agatha increased her conviction in her healthy belief to 80 percent, which is a solid percentage. The type of doubts she recorded are very common and often obstruct positive change.

TABLE 15-3 Agatha's Zig-Zag Form

THE ZIG-ZAG FORM

HEALTHY BELIEF

I prefer not to fail but there is no reason that I must not do so. Failing at things means that I am a normal person, capable of both succeeding and failing.

Rate conviction in Healthy Belief 30%

ATTACK

But if I fail at a lot of things or at all really important things, such as work or relationships, then that must mean that I am a total failure.

DEFENCE

No, it doesn't! It may be more inconvenient and disappointing to fail at important things but it still doesn't make me a total failure. Even if I fail many times it is still possible that I will succeed at some of the things I try. If I were a total failure, the I would only be able to fail and that is not what has happened in reality. Lots of people fail at things that are important to them – not just me. So failing really just means that I am a normal human being.

ATTACK

But if I hold this new belief, I will stop working so hard to succeed and I'll become lazy and complacent.

DEFENCE

Allowing myself to fail without putting myself down will help me to take risks and do new things. I will still be motivated to work hard because I prefer to do well. Instead of being driven by a fear of failure, I'll push myself to do things that are important to me because they are worth doing.

ATTACK

But if I try to do something and fail at it, other people will think that I'm a loser. I'll make a fool of myself. If other people think that I'm a total failure, it must be true.

DEFENCE

First of all, I don't know for sure what other people think of me. Even if others do think that I'm foolish to try something or that I'm a failure – that doesn't make it true. I can't control what other people think of me but I can decide how to think about myself. If I constantly worry about other people's opinions of me, I'll never try anything. If other people treated me like I were a failure it would be hard to cope with but I can choose to disagree with them. At the end of the day, I can survive the discomfort of being ridiculed or criticized by other people.

Re-rate conviction in Healthy Belief 80%

Do your own zig-zag on one of your healthy new core beliefs about yourself, other people, or the world. You can use the form in Worksheet 15-4 again and again, so make some copies before you get started.

WORKSHEET 15-4 My Zig-Zag Form

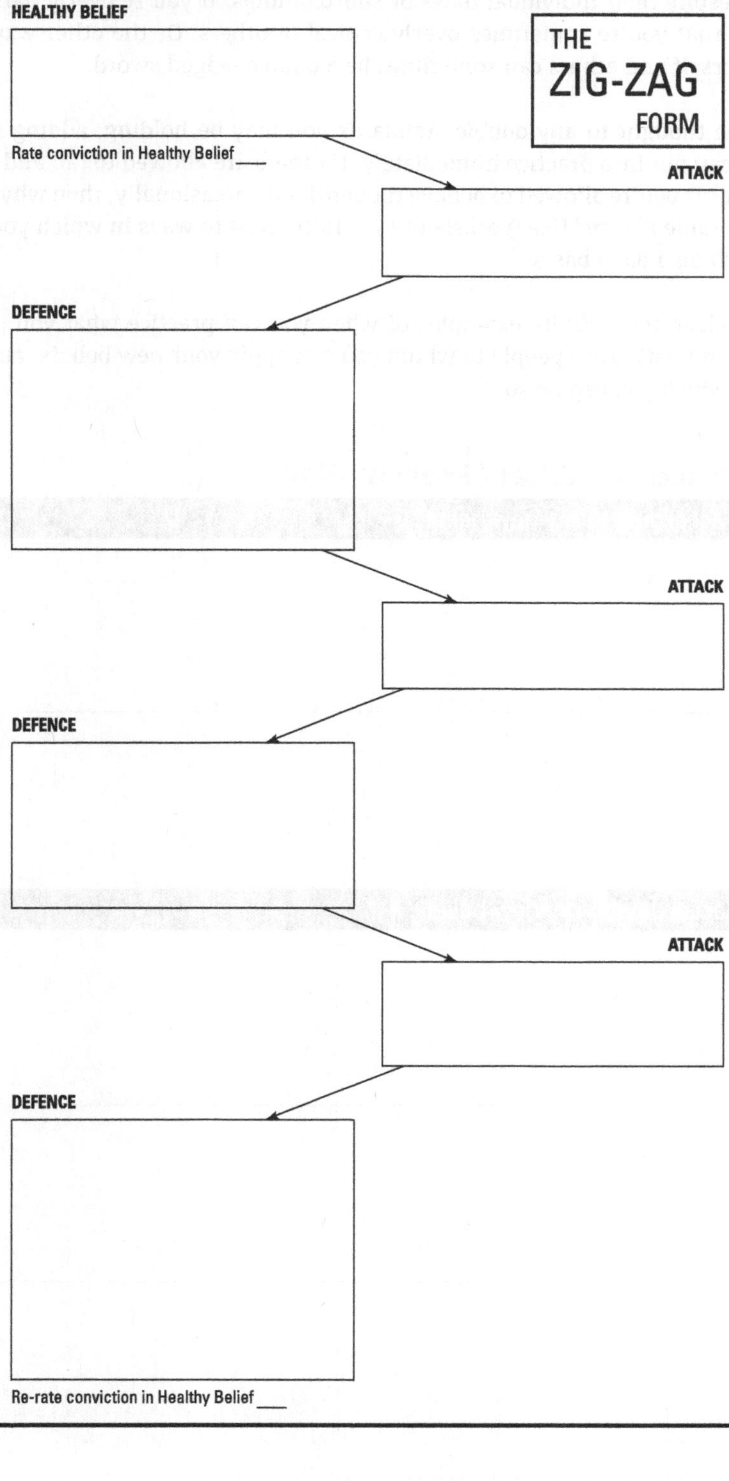

Practicing what you preach

If you're trying to endorse a new belief about yourself, applying the same rule to other people and vice versa makes sense. So, if, like Agatha, you're trying to give yourself permission to fail sometimes, give others the same permission, too. Or if you're trying to believe that you're basically likable (warts and all!), then consider that other people are basically acceptable and worthy despite their individual flaws or shortcomings. If you're overly harsh on yourself, you may find that you're sometimes overly critical of others. Or the other way around — beliefs about yourself and others can sometimes be a double-edged sword.

Give some thought to any double standards you may be holding, adding *specific* suggestions that you can put into practice immediately. If others are allowed to fail and mess up, then why aren't you? If you're allowed to behave thoughtlessly occasionally, then why aren't your friends given the same liberty? Use Worksheet 15-5 to commit to ways in which you can practice what you preach on a daily basis.

Think of clear and definite examples of when you can practice what you preach. Also clearly identify (and list) other people to whom you can apply your new beliefs, and list specific situations in which you can do so.

WORKSHEET 15-5 My "Practicing What I Preach" Plan

How can I treat myself according to my new belief?
When?
Where?

How can I treat others according to my new belief?
Who?
When?

How can I treat others according to my new belief?
Where?

How can I live in the world according to my new belief?
When?
Where?
Who else may be involved?

Considering what you'd want a loved one to believe

Another method for increasing your belief in a new healthy way of thinking is to ask yourself what you want someone who you truly love to believe. Would you want your child, niece, cousin, best friend, or partner to hold your new healthy or old unhealthy belief? Hopefully, you'd recommend your healthy belief to anyone you care deeply about. Think about why. These reasons are likely to be good arguments that will help to further your conviction in the truth and usefulness of your new way of thinking.

EXAMPLE

Agatha thought about her three-year-old son and what attitude she would like him to have toward failure. She used Table 15-4 to highlight the reasons she wants her son to hold a healthy core belief about failing at things in his life.

REMEMBER

Perhaps the best way of imparting healthy self-belief and well-balanced worldviews to your loved ones is to model them!

You can use Worksheet 15-6 to make your own arguments for passing a healthy belief on to others in your life. If the belief makes sense for them, it makes sense for you.

TABLE 15-4 Agatha's Belief for Her Loved One

Who is someone I really love and care for?	Max, my three-year-old son.
What is my healthy core belief?	I prefer not to fail, but there is no reason that I must not do so. Failing at things means that I am a normal person, capable of both succeeding and failing.
What are the reasons that I recommend this way of thinking?	I love Max no matter whether he succeeds or fails. I'd never want Max to think he was a total failure — even if he failed every exam he ever took! I want him to consider failure a normal part of life and not a huge catastrophic event. I also want Max to be happy with who he is and not always be judging himself according to how well he does. I'll never think of Max as a failure, and I certainly don't want him to torture himself about his mistakes and shortcomings in the way that I've tortured myself. I think Max will lead a fulfilling and satisfying life if he holds this healthy belief.
How will this belief help my loved one?	It will prevent Max from becoming depressed about failures. He will also be able to try new things and push himself to give his best effort instead of being paralyzed by fear of failure. It will save him from anxiety and worry prior to exams, job interviews, asking people out on dates, and more. This belief will help Max to have a robust sense of his own intrinsic self-worth. Max will also be less affected by the negative judgments of others if he holds this healthy belief about himself. This belief will ultimately help Max to pursue his goals in life.

WORKSHEET 15-6 My Belief for My Loved One

Who is someone I really love and care for?	
What is my healthy core belief?	
What are the reasons that I recommend this way of thinking?	
How will this belief help my loved one?	

Nurturing Nice New Beliefs

After you develop new healthier beliefs and start acting according to them, it can be very useful to keep a record of the benefits you and the people in your life hold as a result. Doing so not only further consolidates your conviction in your new ways of thinking but also gives you a turbo boost if your enthusiasm wanes or old beliefs raise their ugly heads. Take a bit of time to thoroughly record the positive effects of acting on new beliefs and to acknowledge positive responses from other people.

Worksheet 15-7 provides a format for getting going.

WORKSHEET 15-7 My Positive Data Log

My healthy core belief:	
What recent experiences have I had that support this belief?	
What positive reactions have I had from other people when acting according to this new belief?	
What positive changes to my life (however small) have occurred as a result of acting according to this new belief?	
What other evidence do I have that this new belief is helpful to me? (Include positive effects on your emotions and behaviors.)	
Are there any ways in which holding this new belief has been helpful to other people in my life?	

IN THIS CHAPTER

» Anticipating setbacks and relapse

» Recovering from a relapse

» Developing yourself

» Looking ahead

Chapter 16

Delving into Personal Development

A common reason for problems reappearing is complacency. So, you need to nurture the positive changes you're making to your thinking, behavior, and emotions.

Constantly practicing your new ways of thinking and related behaviors and not taking your improved mental health for granted can help to prevent relapse. For example, if you make changes to your thinking but then return to old unhealthy ways of behaving, you put your gains at risk. Consistently acting in line with your new beliefs (see Chapter 15 for tips on how to do that) and moving toward your goals (turn to Chapter 8 for advice on getting goal-directed) helps you to stay on track.

Unfortunately, despite your best efforts, setbacks can and often do occur. One of the best ways of dealing with relapse is to be prepared for it! In this chapter, we offer guidelines for making a relapse prevention plan and pursuing personal development, thereby making serious setbacks less likely.

Being Realistic about Relapse

It would be nice if the road to recovery were a straight and sure path with no detours. In reality you can expect to have difficult periods and to experience setbacks when trying to overcome your psychological problems. To some extent, relapse is a normal part of recovery.

WARNING

Panicking or catastrophizing (taking a relatively minor event and imagining nightmare scenarios resulting from it) about setbacks often can lead to a more serious return of symptoms. Try to view setbacks as disappointing but not disastrous. You can use them as an opportunity to further consolidate your understanding of core CBT techniques. Be compassionate with yourself when in the grips of a relapse instead of giving yourself a hard time about it. Have a look at Chapter 21 for inspiration.

Use Worksheet 16-1 to get started on your relapse prevention plan.

TIP

When completing the worksheets in this chapter you may wish to review work you've done from other chapters to jog your memory.

WORKSHEET 16-1 Your Problem/Goal Review

What were my original target problems?
Emotional problems:
Behavioral problems:
Practical problems:
What are my goals in relation to these problems?
Emotional goals:
Behavioral goals:
Practical goals:
What positive changes/progress have I made thus far?
Emotional progress:
Behavioral progress:

What positive changes/progress have I made thus far?

Practical progress:

What are the benefits of positive changes I've made thus far?

Emotional benefits:

Behavioral benefits:

Practical benefits:

Ideally, this exercise reminds you how far you've come and renews your motivation to continue the good work.

An ounce of prevention

This step in your relapse prevention plan is about — you guessed it — prevention or troubleshooting. First, recall the ways of thinking, feeling, and acting that maintained or worsened your target problems. Now try to imagine scenarios that may come up in the future and trigger these old unhealthy ways of thinking, behaving, and feeling. Next imagine yourself coping successfully with your trigger situation by thinking and acting in constructive healthy ways. The "A pound of cure" section, later in this chapter, has further advice on troubleshooting potential difficulties.

You can use Worksheet 16-2 to structure your troubleshooting. The idea is to help you spot potential setbacks before they truly take hold. You may want to revisit Chapters 14 and 15 to help you better use this worksheet. These chapters discuss core beliefs and how to replace old destructive beliefs with new constructive ones in depth.

WORKSHEET 16-2 My Troubleshooting Tableau

What negative core beliefs have I been working on eroding?

Self:

Others:

World:

(continued)

WORKSHEET 16-2 ***(continued)***

What healthy alternative core beliefs have I been working on strengthening?
Self:
Others:
World:
What thinking errors do I typically make?
What types of situations or conditions typically trigger my unhealthy core beliefs/thinking errors?
Past environmental triggers (include illness, financial worry, work hassles, seasonal changes, household bills, moving house, and so on):
Past interpersonal triggers (include relationship conflicts with family, friends, colleagues, and so on):
What possible triggers can I look out for in the future?
Environmental triggers:
Interpersonal triggers:
What destructive behaviors have I used in the past to try to cope with my problems?
What early warning signs can I look out for that may signal my problems returning?
Unhealthy negative emotions:
Negative changes to my thinking:
Negative changes to my behavior:

TIP

If you've been working with a CBT therapist, involve them in drawing up your relapse prevention plan. Your therapist is likely to provide valuable input on obstacles they may anticipate based on the literature, their experience, or what they know about your past triggers and beliefs.

A pound of cure

Often we hear our patients say things like "I really hope I don't get depressed again" or "I'm keeping my fingers crossed that I stay well." These sentiments are completely normal and understandable. But our advice is "Don't leave staying well to chance!" Don't ignore early warning signs — nip your recurring problem in the bud! Be confident that whatever strategies you used to get better in the first place are more than likely to work again.

For example, if some of the strategies described in Chapter 3 really helped you to manage your negative thoughts, record your preferred strategies and remind yourself to use them again if your symptoms return. If sticking to an activity schedule helped you to overcome depression (see Chapter 10), note that down and use it again when you notice a dip in your mood. Or perhaps the behavioral experiments found in Chapter 4 helped you to confront your anxieties — if so, make a note of these, too.

Worksheet 16-3 provides a convenient reminder of helpful strategies you've used before and can reuse anytime you need them.

WORKSHEET 16-3 My Pound of Cure Compendium

What areas do I most need to keep working on in order to maintain my gains?	
Which specific CBT strategies aid me most in overcoming my emotional/behavioral problems?	
What helpful beliefs and attitudes do I want to keep practicing and strengthening?	
What are the most helpful behavioral techniques I've used to overcome my problems?	
Who can I go to for additional support if I start to struggle?	
Professionals:	
Friends:	

(continued)

WORKSHEET 16-3 *(continued)*

Family:	
Support groups:	

If you've been prescribed medication before and found it beneficial, talk to your doctor if you relapse. Sometimes the right medication at the right time can prevent a more serious resurgence of symptoms.

WARNING

Never self-medicate. Don't restart leftover medication from previous prescriptions. Always consult your doctor about any medication you take.

Getting Back to Your Personal Values and Hobbies

Another way of keeping yourself on the straight and narrow is to think about what's important to you. Sometimes emotional problems take up so much of your attention that you can lose sight of your own personal values. Now that you're on the road to recovery, you can turn your attention to the kind of world you want to live in. Perhaps you value fairness or environmental initiatives. Your personal values may be specific to your home life or apply more broadly to your community, your city, and the planet.

People tend to be most content when they're involved in meaningful, absorbing activities. Because CBT focuses on goals regarding your problems, it also recognizes the benefit of working toward broader goals based on what's important to you. Acting in line with your personal values and engaging in activities that you enjoy or consider worthwhile helps you to stay psychologically healthy.

Take a minute now to make a note of your personal values in Worksheet 16-4.

WORKSHEET 16-4 My Personal Values

What values do I hold for myself, my family, and my friends?	
What broader values do I hold for my community, the human race, and the planet?	

REMEMBER

Filling your life with meaningful activities consistent with your values can help keep your mood on an even keel.

Acting consistently

After you assess your personal values, you can identify ways of putting them into practice more often. We're not suggesting that you make it your mission to singlehandedly rid the world of crime or stop global warming — not necessarily. But we do suggest living in a manner that reflects what's important to you. Doing so can promote a sense of well-being and of involvement with the world around you — good news for your continued mental health.

Pinpoint particular ways (however small) in which you can strive to act consistently with your values. Use Worksheet 16-5 for each of your identified values. Include simple value-based tasks such as reading to your children, recycling, donating to a charity, and eating locally grown foods.

WORKSHEET 16-5 My Value-Based Activities

One of my personal values:	
What specific action can I take to promote this value?	
Where?	
When?	
With whom?	
How often?	

Reinstating personally significant practices

Your hobbies and interests may have been neglected due to your psychological problems. Now is the time to reintroduce practices that you used to enjoy and that gave you a sense of achievement. Activities such as gardening, playing sports, reading, visiting museums, going to movies, and traveling are all valid ways of filling up your life. Now that you have more time for enjoying yourself, you may want to start new projects or take up new hobbies.

Jot down some ideas in Worksheet 16-6.

WORKSHEET 16-6 My Personally Significant Practices

What activities did I use to enjoy and would now like to reintroduce?	
What activities would I like to start?	

Looking at Your Lifestyle

Striking a balance between your personal life and your work life is part of keeping emotionally and physically well. Keeping the different aspects of your life fairly balanced helps to ensure that you don't overdo some things and neglect others.

Use Worksheet 16-7 to take stock of your current lifestyle. Base your answers on a weekly average over the past three to four weeks.

WORKSHEET 16-7 My Current Lifestyle Checkup

Question	Answer
How many (if any) days have I worked later than usual or taken work home with me?	
How many times have I been out socially?	
How many evenings and/or weekends have I allocated to spending time with friends and/or family?	
How often have I gotten some form of exercise?	

Question	Answer
How many hours/days have I spent on hobbies or activities that interest me?	
How much time have I allocated to taking care of household duties?	
How do I usually relax in the evenings?	
How much time have I spent on self-help or continued CBT practice?	
What other activities have I spent time on?	
Which activities could I benefit from devoting more time to per week?	
Which activities could I benefit from spending less time on per week?	
Which times/days can I allocate to neglected activities in the coming week?	

Look at your answers to Worksheet 16-7. Is your time roughly divided between various activities (both work and play), or is it concentrated in one or two particular areas such as work or household duties? Are you devoting enough of your time to activities that help keep you emotionally and mentally healthy, such as socializing, relaxation, and exercise?

Everyone's life circumstances are different, so there are no hard and fast rules about how much time you should dedicate to any singular activity. However, relaxation is very important because it gives your body and mind a chance to recharge. Relaxation activities can include pretty much anything that helps you to chill out and unwind. Walking, reading, meditating, sitting down with a cup of tea and looking out the window, listening to music, or chatting with a friend are all fine examples of relaxation activities. You benefit from spending at least one hour a day doing something relaxing.

Exercise is also good for both physical and mental health, but most of us don't get enough of it. Aim to increase your exercise wherever you can. Walk to the shops instead of getting the bus or driving. Take the stairs instead of the elevator. Raising your heart rate through exercise for at least 20 minutes three times per week is acceptable. The more exercise you get, the better.

Try to spend at least a couple of hours on the weekend or in the evenings on hobbies like gardening, painting, cycling, or whatever you're interested in doing. Spend a minimum of one evening or day each week with your family and/or friends.

Aim to spend a minimum of two hours per week reviewing the CBT strategies that helped you overcome your problems. Practice is key to staying well. You can plan to practice self-help techniques at various times during your week instead of doing all your practice in a two-hour chunk.

In general, strive to keep work duties confined to office hours. Not everyone works 9 to 5 but the principle is to stick to working during the hours you're paid to do so.

REMEMBER

Obviously, you'll have times when work or family responsibilities, for example, temporarily require most of your energy and attention. During times of crisis, you naturally and appropriately have to concentrate on the issue and not on yourself. Just remind yourself to restore the balance afterward.

If you're wondering where you'll find the time to do more exercising, studying, or socializing — or any of the activities that you're currently not doing enough of — try slotting these pursuits into times when you're usually just watching TV or working late.

Going Boldly Where You Haven't Gone Before

Let's assume that you've largely overcome your problems and you have an eye out for possible relapse risks. You've taken up some hobbies and values-based activities and are managing to maintain a pretty balanced lifestyle. Great, well done! Perhaps you may now want to think about your goals for the future. Think about longer-term personal development goals such as furthering your career, changing careers, moving, traveling, and so on.

Fill out Worksheet 16-8 to help you clarify any goals you may have for the future and what steps you need to take in order to achieve them. (Chapter 8 shows you how to set effective goals.)

WORKSHEET 16-8 My Future Goals

My Personal Development Goals	Steps I Need to Take to Achieve My Goals
In the next 6 to 12 months:	
In the next one to two years:	
In the next five years:	

IN THIS CHAPTER

» Getting past emotions that obstruct recovery

» Asking for a little help

» Keeping up with positive practices

Chapter 17

Rupturing Roadblocks to Recovery

On your way to overcoming your psychological problems, you're likely to stumble once, twice, or even three times — doing so isn't unusual. You may feel like you've struck a brick wall, which can be discouraging, but we promise this is normal and all part of the process of moving forward.

Obstacles to positive change come in several forms: Sometimes you may unwittingly block your own progress through faulty thinking leading to unhelpful emotions such as shame or guilt. Other times you may be aware of deliberately (or almost deliberately) practicing self-sabotage. Why? Well, any change (even positive change) can be daunting, risky, hard work, and even frightening. You may find yourself putting obstacles in your way because staying "as you are" seems temporarily more attractive than putting yourself through a lot of effort and discomfort to overcome your problems.

Whatever the reasons for getting stuck, this chapter focuses on how to rupture roadblocks on your route to a robust recovery.

Exorcising Emotions that Bind You

A common roadblock to recovery is *secondary emotional problems*, a term used to describe feeling bad about your original, or *primary*, problem. Examples could be feeling guilty about being depressed or feeling ashamed about having panic attacks. Guilt or shame often mean that you're putting yourself down for having psychological difficulties. Guilt, shame, and pride are three of the most common types of secondary emotional problems:

- **Guilt** often emerges as a secondary emotional problem in depression. Depression can lead you to withdraw from other people and avoid social contact. You may believe that you're neglecting your loved ones because of your depression and make yourself feel guilty. When you're depressed, everyday tasks can feel overwhelming and you may not be able to function effectively. You may make yourself feel guilty about letting tasks build up or failing to fulfill obligations. It's common for depressed people to berate themselves for being unproductive. Secondary guilt about the effects of your depression can worsen your mood.
- **Shame** is often a secondary emotional problem for people with anxiety disorders such as panic attacks or obsessive-compulsive disorder (OCD). If you think that your anxiety problem means that you're weak or foolish, you're probably making yourself feel ashamed about experiencing anxiety. Because OCD typically involves unwelcome intrusive thoughts and images that you find unacceptable, it's very possible that you feel shame about having these OCD symptoms in the first place.

  Shame can stop you from talking to others about your problems or seeking professional treatment. It can also mean that you become defensive about your problems or even unwilling to change for fear of "losing face."
- **Pride** attends many emotional problems. Often people think that they should be able to overcome their emotional problems without any outside support. Especially if you consider yourself "someone who copes," value your independence, and/or see psychological problems as unacceptable weaknesses, you may be too proud to admit to yourself or others that you need help. Pride can even prevent you from embarking on a course of self-help because you believe that you should know all the answers yourself without needing to consult books. Pride can also increase the likelihood that you get bogged down with blaming other people for your problems instead of focusing on the steps you can take to recover.

Secondary problems can really stop you in your tracks. These types of unhealthy emotions may prevent you from talking to other people about your situation or from seeking valuable professional help. They can also frequently lead to unhelpful behaviors such as avoidance and denial and actually worsen the symptoms of your primary problem. As you work through this chapter, we hope you'll consider how humility, self-compassion, forgiveness, tolerance, and understanding can help you break free.

EXAMPLE

Silas has OCD (see Chapter 11). He experiences unwanted thoughts about harming children and animals. Silas thinks that nobody would understand his problem and that his thoughts mean that he's a bad person. He feels very guilty about having intrusive, upsetting thoughts.

Silas used Table 17-1 to shed light on his secondary emotional problem.

See Chapter 6 for clarification about healthy and unhealthy negative emotions.

You can use Worksheet 17-1 to put your finger on any secondary emotional problems you may be experiencing.

TABLE 17-1 Silas's Secondary Emotions Worksheet

My primary problem:	I've been diagnosed with OCD. I have lots of really unpleasant thoughts about hurting children and small animals.
Unhealthy negative emotions I have about this problem (my secondary emotional problem):	I feel guilty about the thoughts I have, but I can't control them. I feel like a bad and nasty person for having such dark and unacceptable thoughts.

WORKSHEET 17-1 My Secondary Emotions Worksheet

My primary problem:	
Unhealthy negative emotions I have about this problem (my secondary emotional problem):	

If, like Silas, you've identified guilt or another unhealthy negative emotion about your primary problem, your next step is to work on overcoming these obstructive feelings.

Giving up on guilt

Sometimes your disorder may lead you to think in ways that aren't in keeping with your morals, as in the case of Silas, earlier in this chapter. His OCD means that he thinks about hurting the very creatures he believes deserve protection. Or your depression may impede your ability to do things that you consider to be important, such as caring for your family or performing well at work. Making yourself feel guilty about your illness is all too easy. But guilt only makes you feel worse and delays your improvement.

Instead of focusing solely on the negative effects of your illness and on what you're unable to do as a result of your problems, try being more understanding and compassionate with yourself. The person who suffers most from your OCD, depression, anxiety, or other problem is *you*. Remind yourself that you're only human and that although your psychological problems may be negatively impacting others in your life, making yourself guilty about this reality won't fix anything. You're not neglecting your duties or family deliberately out of malice; this is just a regrettable side effect of many different psychological problems. In Chapter 6, we discuss the differences between healthy and unhealthy negative emotions like guilt.

Silas's primary problem is having OCD-intrusive thoughts about harming children and small animals, which lead to feelings of guilt. He used Table 17-2 to help him let go of guilt and move in a goal-directed direction.

In Table 17-3, Silas records ways giving up on guilt can help him in his recovery from OCD. Use Worksheet 17-2 to highlight the benefits of giving up your own guilt about your emotional problem. Consider how guilty thinking may be eating up your time and worsening your mood. How would you be acting differently if you were guilt-free?

TABLE 17-2 Silas's Giving Up on Guilt Guide

Guilt-Producing Thoughts	Guilt-Removing Arguments
I shouldn't be having these thoughts.	Unwanted thoughts are a feature of OCD.
These thoughts mean that I'm bad.	Thoughts aren't actions. These thoughts mean that I have OCD, but they don't mean anything else about me.
Decent people don't think like this.	Everyone has unwanted thoughts from time to time.
My thoughts are dangerous.	I certainly don't like having these thoughts, and I wish I didn't. But the only person who is suffering from my OCD is me. I'm not inconveniencing, harming, or damaging anyone else by having unpleasant and intrusive thoughts.

TABLE 17-3 Silas's Guilt-Free Benefits

How giving up on guilt will be helpful to my recovery:
I'll be better able to focus on getting treatment for my OCD. I'll be willing to talk to other OCD sufferers about their experiences and share my own. I still won't like the thoughts, but I won't feel so devastated about having them in the first place. I won't be judging myself as a bad person for having thoughts that I don't want. I'll believe that I deserve to get help and to get better.

You may find that you need to work hard to generate convincing and credible arguments in opposition to your guilty feelings. Having to make a big effort is *not* a sign that your guilt is appropriate; instead, it's a side effect of thinking in a self-punishing way for a long time.

Now use Worksheets 17-2 and 17-3 to exorcise your guilty thoughts and feelings about your primary problem.

WORKSHEET 17-2 My Giving Up on Guilt Guide

My Primary Problem:	
Guilt-Producing Thoughts	Guilt-Removing Arguments

WORKSHEET 17-3 My Guilt-Free Benefits

How giving up on guilt will be helpful to my recovery:

Refusing to play the shame game

Shame is a slimy little emotion that can get you stuck. Heave out humiliation and shame by giving yourself permission to be both human and fallible. Instead of ridiculing, belittling, or denigrating yourself for having psychological problems, try being a bit more compassionate and understanding with yourself. Remember that as a human being, you don't expect to never become physically ill or to be injured in some way. So, why should you expect yourself to always be in tip-top mental and emotional shape?

It makes sense to dislike having psychological difficulties, but if you make yourself ashamed of your problems, you're telling yourself that you must not have them. That just doesn't make sense.

Think of as many reasons as you can to counteract your shame. Try reminding yourself that however uncomfortable and undesirable your problem is, this is a normal part of being human and there is no reason that you shouldn't be experiencing psychological difficulties.

You may be surprised by the support and concern you receive from other people in your life, too. You may expect to be rejected on the basis of your problems when, in reality, people want to help. Be prepared to be pleasantly surprised by some of the reactions you get from those who care about you.

EXAMPLE

Neha has panic attacks. She finds it very difficult to go into supermarkets or other busy shops. Neha is ashamed of her problem, so she tries to hide her anxiety from people. She hasn't told anyone about her problem because she thinks it makes her weak and that other people will also think she's weak and pathetic if they know. (Turn to Chapter 9 for more on anxiety and panic and how to treat them.)

Neha put her shame-provoking thoughts about her panic attacks down on paper in Table 17-4 and disputed them using evidence against them.

TABLE 17-4 Neha's Heaving Out Humiliation Worksheet

My primary problem: Panic attacks	
Shame-Producing Thoughts	**Shame-Disputing Arguments**
Only weak people and wimps panic for no reason.	All the literature I've read and websites I've visited say that all sorts of people from all walks of life have anxiety disorders. Panic attacks are actually very common.
People will think less of me if they find out that I suffer from panic attacks.	Some of my friends or colleagues may have a similar problem. People like me for lots of reasons, and my panic is just one small part of who I am.
I should be able to stop my panic.	In time, I can learn to overcome my panic attacks. If I tell myself that I must not panic and beat myself up when I do, I just make the problem worse. Obviously, I'd prefer not to panic, but there's no reason that I absolutely shouldn't have panic attacks. I'm human, not a robot.

Neha then used Table 17-5 to list how saying goodbye to her shame could help in overcoming her panic attacks.

TABLE 17-5 Neha's Heaving Out Humiliation Benefits Worksheet

How heaving out humiliation and shame will help in my recovery:
Shame leads me to try to hide or stop my anxiety symptoms, which makes me even more anxious and likely to panic.
Humiliation stops me from going outdoors and socializing, which means that I feel isolated and lonely.
If I stop making myself ashamed about having panic attacks, I'll undertake exposure exercises and get some support.

Now you can give the shame and humiliation your primary problem produces the heave-ho by working through Worksheet 17-4.

WORKSHEET 17-4 My Heaving Out Humiliation Worksheet

My primary problem: Shame-Producing Thoughts	Shame-Disputing Arguments

Use Worksheet 17-5 to list how sending shame scurrying can help with your recovery.

WORKSHEET 17-5 My Heaving Out Humiliation Benefits Worksheet

How heaving out humiliation and shame will help in my recovery:

Paralyzing problematic pride

You may be surprised to realize that your pride can, indeed, hinder progress. If you tell yourself that you should be able to get better on your own or know all the answers to your problems, you may be too proud to seek professional help. Your pride may also stop you from confiding in others about your problems for fear of appearing weak or flawed. You may even be reluctant to admit your problems to yourself and instead exhaust yourself trying to mask them or insist that you "pull yourself together."

EXAMPLE

Pablo has a pride problem. Actually, he is depressed and has been for several months, but he keeps telling himself to pull himself together and get over it. Unfortunately, Pablo just feels worse about himself when he can't get over his depression on his own. Simultaneously, he also thinks that self-help techniques won't work for him and that he should know how to get over his depression instinctively. Pablo used Table 17-6 to tackle his paralyzing pride problems connected to his depression.

TABLE 17-6 **Pablo's Prevailing over Pride Page**

My primary problem: Depression	
Pride-Based Thoughts	Balanced Thoughts
I'm intelligent, so I should be able to work out this problem on my own!	Even the brightest people need help and guidance with things outside their knowledge base occasionally. Depression can happen to anyone no matter how smart they are.
I'm a strong person, and I can fight this on my own.	Depression is not a sign of weakness. Ultimately, I'll be the one who fights my own depression, but that doesn't mean that I can't seek help or guidance to do so.
If I thought self-help techniques would work, I'd have done them a long time ago!	Actually, I can't really help myself without knowing how to. Maybe professional advice would put me on the right track.

Pablo then considered how overcoming his pride could help him conquer his depression in Table 17-7.

TABLE 17-7 **Pablo's Putting Pride Aside Benefits**

How putting aside my pride will aid my recovery:
I may actually research depression more fully and see what's out there in terms of treatment.
I may be more inclined to talk to my doctor about my situation and maybe even take medication for a while.
I'll tell the people closest to me how I'm feeling instead of shutting them out and avoiding them. They might understand me and give me some extra support.

Is pride getting in the way of owning up to your primary problem or seeking help to overcome it? If you think so, put pen to paper and fill in Worksheet 17-6.

WORKSHEET 17-6 **My Prevailing over Pride Page**

My primary problem:	
Pride-Based Thoughts	Balanced Thoughts

Now use Worksheet 17-7 to record how letting go of your pride can bring big benefits.

WORKSHEET 17-7 My Putting Pride Aside Benefits

How putting aside my pride will aid my recovery:

Letting Others Help Bear the Burden

You get by with a little help from your friends . . . or do you? After you've dealt with some of your problematic secondary emotions, can you elicit a little support from others? We hope so because sorting out your problems on your own is a lonely business.

A big (and not so very rare) obstacle to recovery is hiding your problems away and refusing to let others in on how you're feeling. You may conceal your problem as a result of shame, guilt, pride, or fear of burdening others. We urge you to take the risk of approaching others. Even if your friends or family don't totally understand your particular problem, they may well be willing to try.

REMEMBER

Other people may be far more understanding, compassionate, and empathetic than you give them credit for when you're feeling low.

WARNING

Thinking that everyone in your life will be ready and willing to give you a bit of support or care in your time of need is nice, but that isn't always the case. If you're already feeling low, talking to someone who's unlikely to give you the kind of attention you need right now makes little sense. So, if your best friend is great to go out dancing with but has very little patience or understanding about anxiety problems, she may not be the ideal candidate to talk to about your panic attacks. Looking for support from unsuitable sources can give you a negative experience with opening up and may put you off the idea altogether. So, give some thought to who you think is suitable to lend you support.

Make a list of the people in your life who you may be able to talk to openly and honestly about your emotional and/or behavioral problem. Worksheet 17-8 walks you through identifying sympathetic family and friends and recording the type of support you can expect from each. Don't forget about professional people and well-established support groups.

A doctor can prescribe appropriate medication and refer you for therapy. A friend may be able to empathize with your problems because they've been through a similar experience. Another friend may be better able to give you financial advice and help you develop strategies for resolving practical problems. Your mom may give you milk, cookies, and sympathy but really not understand your problem. Your siblings may be able to give you some much-needed childcare or help around the house. The possibilities entirely depend upon your own circumstances and the people in your life. The point is to think about the different types of support you need and who in your life is most likely to be able to provide it.

TIP

If you're afraid of their reaction, ask yourself how you'd react if they came to you with the same problem. Chances are, you'd be very willing to help them however you could. So, take the plunge and lean on others a little.

WORKSHEET 17-8 My Suitable Sources of Support Sheet

Who in my life is most likely to understand my current problem?	
What specific forms of support do I need most right now?	
Which specific friends or family members can I seek support from?	
What kind of support am I most likely to get from each of the people listed?	
Who can I approach for professional help?	
What support groups can I join or look into?	

REMEMBER

Look to the people in your life to give you the kind of support you think they're most likely to be able to provide.

Persisting with Practice

Practice may be tedious, but it's absolutely essential. If you really want to bust through blockages, you have to persevere. Most people find sticking to difficult and uncomfortable tasks hard — even when they know that those tasks are in their long-term best interest. But you *can* overcome your effort and discomfort intolerance in the short term if you seriously consider why doing so is worthwhile. Very often, *doing* something about your problem is actually easier than *thinking* about it.

Worksheet 17-9 helps you to stick with goal-directed action (see Chapter 8). The worksheet also gives you a chance to review techniques that have helped you to get better. Chapter 3 describes the A-B-C form that Mortimer found helpful. Chapter 10 gives you advice on beating depression, and Chapter 9 addresses anxiety. You may also have used strategies offered in Chapter 11 to overcome your obsessional problems. Use the worksheet to further plan and persist with your recovery.

EXAMPLE

Mortimer has social anxiety. He rehearses what he says before he says it, leaving little room for spontaneity. He replays social events in his head after they're over and looks for gaffes he may have made. Mortimer also pays very close attention to how others are responding to him during a social interaction. If he thinks he has made a poor impression, Mortimer berates himself harshly and calls himself a selection of horrible names for being socially awkward. He often drinks too much to quell his nerves and then finds that he regrets it the next day because he worries that he has made a fool of himself when drunk. Mortimer has been working hard to overcome his social anxiety but hit a wall recently when he thought he'd done enough and didn't want to push himself any further.

Mortimer used Table 17-8 to help him get back on the road to recovery and to persuade himself to persist with goal-directed practices.

TABLE 17-8 Mortimer's Persistence Policy

What is my primary problem?	Social anxiety.
What are my goals for my primary problem?	To feel concerned but not anxious about my performance socially.
What techniques have helped me thus far?	Fixing my attention on other people and my environment. Listening to what others are saying and responding without preparing a speech. Sitting or standing in a central position during a social outing. Using an ABC form.
What is my helpful attitude/belief about my primary problem?	I'd prefer not to make social errors, but there is no earthly reason why I must not. If I do make a gaffe, it simply means that I made a social error like anyone else can do. I can still think of myself as a worthwhile and likeable person in the face of social unease.
In what ways, do I need to push myself in order to advance my progress?	I should really go to the holiday party at work and try to stand in the middle of the room. I need to make conversation without pre-planning it when I go out with friends. I should try to talk to people who I think are above me or wouldn't like me when I'm out and see what happens. Even if they reject me, I'll live.
Why is it worth pushing toward overcoming my problem? (Be specific.)	I'll get rid of this social anxiety and feel appropriately nervous or concerned about social outings in the long run. I'll be better able to make friends and socialize rather than sit at home alone. Ironically, I'll probably appear more interesting and attractive to others when I'm socially relaxed than when I'm freaking out about what they might be thinking about me. I might get up the nerve to ask a girl I really fancy at work out for a drink. And if I do ask the girl out for a drink, I'll be able to talk to her normally without having to go to the bathroom every five minutes because I'm so anxious!

How can I be compassionate with myself about setbacks and my reluctance to continue?	As anyone with social anxiety knows, deliberately going into social situations that you could otherwise avoid is terrifying. I'm doing great by continuing to try. Even if I screw up on one occasion, I can learn from it. I'm only human and born to make mistakes. Everyone has setbacks, and I'm no different. I'm a whole, complex, changing individual and my social unease is only one small part of who I am in total. Besides, I'm not the only person in the world with social anxiety! Lots of people have it. So, I don't need to beat myself up about it.
What behaviors do I most need to resist in order to overcome my problem?	Monitoring myself for signs of anxiety such as shaking, blushing, and sweating. Planning what to say before I open my mouth. Sticking to safe areas such as the sides of the room, the bar, or my seat. Talking only to people I know and feel reasonably comfortable with. Drinking too much too quickly in an attempt to quell my nerves. Replaying the social event and battering myself for any minor social gaffes.
What behaviors do I most need to foster in order to overcome my problem?	Going out more often. Inviting myself along to after-work drinks. Keeping my attention trained outward on other people and my environment. Speaking without preparing in advance. Making small talk with people I don't know well. Drawing a line under any social outing after it has ended and resisting the urge to review it and judge my performance. Monitoring my alcohol intake closely during a social event and not allowing myself to have a drink solely for the purpose of relieving my anxiety.
When can I allocate time to practice CBT, both behavioral and thinking based?	I can think in a healthy way about social unease and social blips every day — especially before I enter the office and during any social banter throughout the workday. I can go out every Friday night with people from work. I can join a weekly club that interests me and force myself to meet new people. I can practice saying hello to people in the street, the bus driver, and baristas on a daily basis and remind myself that though I'd really like them to respond in kind, they don't have to! I'm likeable even if I get a poor response from others sometimes.

Now that you've seen how Mortimer has renewed his commitment to his goals and revived his general get-up-and-go, see if you can use Worksheet 17-9 to the same effect for your own problems.

TIP

You may want to review some of the previous chapters to help you get to the guts of your given problem. Have a flick through the table of contents and look at the chapters that you think might be most relevant to you right now.

WORKSHEET 17-9 My Persistence Policy

What is my primary problem?	
What are my goals for my primary problem?	
What techniques have helped me thus far?	
What is my helpful attitude/belief about my primary problem?	
In what ways do I need to push myself in order to advance my progress?	
Why is it worth pushing toward overcoming my problem? (Be specific.)	
How can I be compassionate with myself about setbacks and my reluctance to carry on?	
What behaviors do I most need to resist in order to overcome my problem?	
What behaviors do I most need to foster in order to overcome my problem?	
When can I allocate time to practice CBT, both behavioral and thinking based?	

IN THIS CHAPTER

» Taking appropriate responsibility and worthwhile risks

» Getting involved with life by holding healthy attitudes

Chapter 18
Putting into Practice Principles of Positive Living

Life is about more than overcoming psychological problems. When you've sustained recovery from your difficulties for a while, it may be time to look at how you live your life and see whether you can do so more positively.

In this chapter, we briefly outline the types of personal principles and attitudes that can help you get the most out of life, including seeking out positive experiences and dealing effectively with negative ones.

Receiving Your Ration of Responsibility

Obviously, bad things do happen, and often you can't do much to change them. But you can try to identify where you may have some responsibility for what happened or for how you respond to the event. Taking responsibility isn't about blaming yourself or others for a negative event or situation. You're not fault finding as such. Instead, taking responsibility is about empowering yourself to either change a negative situation by problem solving (if possible) or, alternatively, adapting and adjusting to conditions.

EXAMPLE

Patrick is very sensitive to rejection from women. He isn't very confident about his attractiveness to the opposite sex. Patrick finds it hard to imagine that any woman would be interested in him. Susan, a bartender at Patrick's favorite bar, caught his eye a few months ago. Although he hangs around the bar in order to be near Susan, Patrick freezes up whenever she tries to make conversation with him. As a result, Patrick seems aloof and disinterested. Jack, a friend of Patrick's, also likes Susan. Patrick compares himself negatively to Jack and considers Jack much better looking and more charming than himself. Last weekend, Jack asked Susan out for dinner and she said yes. Patrick is furious with Jack for callously moving in on his love interest. He's also very hurt that Susan agreed to date Jack and sees it as a huge personal rejection and as further proof of his unattractiveness. Patrick used Table 18-1 to see if he could take some responsibility for what happened with Jack and Susan. Using the worksheet also helped him to see how his reactions to the negative event were making things worse for himself.

TABLE 18-1 Patrick's Responsibility Ration Record

Identified negative event or situation:	Jack asked out Susan and she said yes. They had dinner together last weekend.
Which people or conditions contributed to the negative event or situation occurring?	Jack, Susan, the local bar environment, and my failure to make a move before Jack did.
Can I take a degree of personal responsibility for what occurred?	I suppose my fear that Susan would reject me if I expressed my interest in her led me to appear aloof. I didn't ask her out even though I had plenty of chances, and I didn't even speak to her much when she tried to talk to me. I didn't tell Jack how much I like Susan, so he didn't know that I'd be upset if he asked her out.
How can I take personal responsibility for my emotional and behavioral responses to the negative event or situation?	I'm getting angry with Jack for something he doesn't know he did to offend me. Not talking to him or going to the bar with him as punishment is a bit off. I'm basically sulking but not telling Jack why I'm angry. I'm making myself all hurt and wounded about Susan going out with Jack, but she hasn't betrayed me. She doesn't even know that I like her. Comparing myself negatively to Jack and deciding that I'm a geek and he's totally cool is just making me feel really depressed and hopeless. Jack's a good looking, nice guy, but he's not Superman.
How might taking appropriate personal responsibility help me to resolve the event or situation or adjust healthily to it?	It will help me to stop taking the whole thing so personally and stop making myself angry, hurt, and depressed. I'll be better able to talk to Jack and let him know my feelings for Susan. I'll be better able to recognize that I've possibly missed my chance with Susan and accept that she and Jack are dating. It may help me to stop comparing myself to Jack and instead accept that we're different people, with different traits and personalities. I'll be better able to move on and look for someone else I like and try to overcome my social unease in order to ask her out.

Now that Patrick has shown you the ropes, take a swing yourself in Worksheet 18-1.

REMEMBER

If someone has violated your human rights or you've been traumatized by an accident or a tragic life event, you're *not* responsible for what has happened. However, you can still take personal responsibility for the rest of your life and how you'd like to live it. To a degree, you can choose how you emotionally respond to very negative life events.

WORKSHEET 18-1 My Responsibility Ration Record

Identified negative event or situation:	
Which people or conditions contributed to the negative event or situation occurring?	
Can I take a degree of legitimate responsibility for what occurred?	
How can I take personal responsibility for my emotional and behavioral responses to the negative event or situation?	
How might taking appropriate personal responsibility help me to resolve the event or situation or adjust healthily to it?	

Finding that Flexibility Feeds Fun

Often being stuck in your ways indicates rigid and unyielding ways of thinking about life. The more rigid your personal rules about yourself, others, and the world, the more vulnerable you are to experiencing emotional disturbance and life problems. Rigid thinking limits your ability to creatively adapt to changing life circumstances. This attitude also leads you to avoid taking risks of any kind.

If you want to change from rigid to flexible thinking, you need to acknowledge that *want* does not equal "have to get." So, if you *want* to succeed at a task but don't insist that you *have to* succeed, then you're thinking flexibly and leaving room for error.

REMEMBER

If you want to have fun, you have to be flexible! Otherwise, you'll never try anything new or a bit risky, even when doing so is worth it. Consider Patrick and his unexpressed adoration of Susan from the preceding section. Look at how Patrick handled his rigid thinking in Table 18-2.

TIP

Refer to Chapter 2 for more on thinking errors and demands. Also check out Chapters 14 and 15 for more on core beliefs about yourself, others, and the world. Head to Chapter 6 for an explanation of healthy and unhealthy negative emotions.

Flexible thinking generally leads to healthy negative emotions in the face of negative events and to effective problem-solving.

TABLE 18-2 Patrick's Finding Flexibility Form

What situation or event (past, present, or future) am I thinking about rigidly?	Jack and Susan going out together for dinner. My not asking Susan out first or telling Jack that I liked her.
What specific rigid demands am I making?	***Self:*** I must be attractive to the opposite sex. I must not be rejected by Susan. ***Others:*** Jack must not ask out Susan. Susan must not reject me for Jack. ***World:*** The Jack-and-Susan situation is totally unfair and it shouldn't be happening!
How is my rigid thinking negatively impacting my emotions? (List any unhealthy negative emotions.)	Anger, depression, and hurt.
How is my rigid thinking negatively impacting my behavior? (List any destructive or self-defeating behaviors.)	Sulking with Jack and refusing to spend time with him. Comparing myself negatively to Jack and putting myself down as unattractive. Being sullen with Susan and giving her the cold shoulder.
What are more flexible attitudes I can adopt about the situation or event that may help me to feel less disturbed and act more constructively?	***Self:*** I'd rather be attractive to the opposite sex, but I don't have to be! I don't want to be rejected by Susan, but there's no reason she must not reject me. If I'm rejected by Susan, or any other woman, it means that those women didn't like me. It doesn't mean that I'm wholly unattractive or unlikable. ***Others:*** I'd prefer it if Jack hadn't asked out Susan, but there's no reason he shouldn't. I'd prefer it if Susan chose me over Jack but she doesn't have to! Neither Jack nor Susan has to do what I want them to do. ***World:*** The Jack-and-Susan situation is unfortunate and disappointing but not unfair. It's the way it goes, and I can deal with it if I choose to do so!

Worksheet 18-2 is your chance to go from rigid to flexible.

WORKSHEET 18-2 My Finding Flexibility Form

What situation or event (past, present, or future) am I thinking about rigidly?	
What specific rigid demands am I making?	***Self:*** ***Others:*** ***World:***
How is my rigid thinking negatively impacting my emotions? (List any unhealthy negative emotions.)	

How is my rigid thinking negatively impacting my behavior? (List any destructive or self-defeating behaviors.)	
What are more flexible attitudes I can adopt about the situation or event that may help me to feel less disturbed and act more constructively?	*Self:* *Others:* *World:*

Understanding Uncertainty and Lack of Control as Unavoidable

Trying to control events that aren't within your control and to gain certainty about things that you can't be certain about is pretty disempowering. The truth is, you, along with the rest of the human race, live with uncertainty and limited control over life events every single day, whether you choose to acknowledge it or not. No one, not even you, is all-knowing and all-powerful. So, try as you might to get absolute certainty about future events or to control random events and other people, you just can't do it. Accepting uncertainty and limited personal control can help you overcome anxiety and enjoy life fully.

EXAMPLE

Patrick confronts his demands for certainty and control by using Table 18-3.

TABLE 18-3 Patrick's Uncertain, Uncontrollable, and Unavoidable Record

Negative situation or event (past, present, or future):	Jack and Susan dating.
What aspects of the situation am I trying to control?	Susan being attracted to Jack and vice versa. Jack asking Susan out in the first place.
What aspects of the situation am I trying to gain certainty about?	I was insisting on being certain about how Susan felt about me before asking her out. I tried to be certain that Susan wouldn't reject me. I insist on certainty that people (like Susan) think as much of me as they do of others (like Jack).
Are these aspects of the situation within my control?	No. I can't control what other people feel, think, and do. Jack and Susan can act however they choose to act, no matter how hard I insist that they do what I want them to do.

(continued)

TABLE 18-3 ***(continued)***

Is it possible to be certain about these aspects of the situation?	No. Even if Susan reassured me that she liked me as much as Jack, she can always change her mind in the future. I can't be certain that Susan won't reject me, and if I never ask her out, I'll never know. Also, Susan may not reject me today, but I can't be totally certain that she won't reject me at some point in the future. Rejection is a risk, no matter who I date. I spend a lot of time searching for clues about how other people feel about me and guessing what they're thinking about me. But even a well-researched guess is not a guarantee.
How are my attempts to gain control and certainty affecting my ability to adjust to the situation or event?	In general, I feel very anxious in social situations. I get self-conscious in situations that I can't control or in which I can't be certain that I'm making a good impression. My demands for certainty and control have stopped me from asking Susan out. My demands for certainty and control have also led me to feel angry and hurt about Jack and Susan dating.

Use the same questions in Worksheet 18-3 regarding your own situation to see where you may be demanding (in vain) that you get certainty or control.

WORKSHEET 18-3 My Uncertain, Uncontrollable, and Unavoidable Record

Negative situation or event (past, present, or future):	
What aspects of the situation am I trying to control?	
What aspects of the situation am I trying to gain certainty about?	
Are these aspects of the situation within my control?	
Is it possible to be certain about these aspects of the situation?	
How are my attempts to gain control and certainty affecting my ability to adjust to the situation or event?	

Letting Life Be Unfair

Life is a jumble of positive, negative, and neutral events. Moreover, life isn't always fair. Sometimes things happen that are undeserved. Life just doesn't seem to stop and consider who deserves a good or bad thing to happen to them at any given time. Instead, life events seem to occur in a pretty random way.

Imagine you experience a negative event and conclude that life is unfair and that you've been victimized. Thinking in this way may be understandable, but dwelling on unfairness can ensnare you in unhealthy emotions and prevent you from making things better for yourself. Sometimes taking a second to consider whether what you're experiencing is truly unfair or, more accurately, bad, unfortunate, or even tragic is worthwhile. We're not saying that unfair things don't happen, because they most certainly do. But life is unfair to everyone from time to time, not just to you.

Patrick challenged his victim mentality by asking himself the questions in Table 18-4 about the Jack and Susan situation.

TABLE 18-4 Patrick's Letting Life Be Unfair List

Negative situation or event:	Jack and Susan dating.
Aspects of the situation or event that I think are unfair:	Jack asking out the woman I like. Susan agreeing to date Jack before I got a chance to ask her out myself. Jack always gets the girl. Everyone always likes Jack more than me because he's so charming. It's unfair that I'm not a social butterfly like Jack. It's not fair that I'm a social moth!
Am I mislabeling any aspects of the situation as unfair when to view them as bad, unfortunate, or tragic is more accurate?	It's unfortunate that I was too anxious to ask Susan out before Jack did. It's bad that she agreed to date him when I wanted to go out with her. It's not unfair that Jack is socially skilled and I'm anxious in social situations. We're different, that's all. If Jack had known that I liked Susan and asked her out anyway, he may have been acting unfairly. I still think it's unfair that Jack always gets the girl!
What arguments can I use to convince myself that accepting life's potential to be unfair is in my best interest?	If I keep thinking that life is unfair only to me, then I'll just give up. I can do something to improve my social skills and to overcome my social anxiety. But if I think of my problems as unfair, then I'm less likely to bite the bullet and make some changes. It may be unfair that Jack gets the girls and I don't. But that's life, and if I start taking some risks by talking to women, then I might level the playing field a bit more. Lots of guys have trouble approaching women, not just me. So, if social anxiety is an example of life's unfairness, then I'm not the only one affected! By accepting that life can and will be unfair from time to time, I'll be better able to problem-solve because I'll spend less time being hurt, being resentful, and whining.

Think of a recent negative and/or unfair life event that you've experienced. See if you can use Worksheet 18-4 to help you take a more proactive stance on resolving it, if possible, or at least adjusting to it.

WORKSHEET 18-4 My Letting Life Be Unfair List

Negative situation or event:	
Aspects of the situation or event that I think are unfair:	
Am I mislabeling any aspects of the situation as unfair when to view them as bad, unfortunate, or tragic is more accurate?	
What arguments can I use to convince myself that accepting life's potential to be unfair is in my best interest?	

Taking Risks and Making Mistakes

Sometimes mistakes are well worth making and risks are well worth taking. The trick is to be able to go for it when you think doing so is in your best interests *and* to believe you're able to cope with the consequences of any mistakes, poor outcomes, or bad decisions. If you believe that making mistakes is unacceptable, you'll be unlikely to take any form of risk for fear of failure. Accepting yourself as a fallible human being capable of both success and failure can help you to take worthwhile risks.

EXAMPLE

Patrick recognized some personal risks he's been avoiding because he fears rejection. To Patrick, rejection means that he's an unattractive and unlikable person overall. He used Table 18-5 to help him weigh up personal risks and to be more compassionate with himself.

TABLE 18-5 Patrick's Risk Assessment

Risks I'd like to take but am avoiding:	Asking a woman out on a date.
Why am I avoiding taking action?	I'm afraid of being rejected. It would prove to me that I'm unattractive.
Realistically, what's the worst thing that could happen if I take this risk?	I could be rejected in an unpleasant way. I'd make myself feel depressed.
Can I imagine surviving the worst-case scenario?	I suppose being rejected would be bad but not as terrible as I've been telling myself. I could decide to accept it and resist putting myself down as an unattractive loser. You win some, you lose some. I can choose to feel sad about being rejected but not depressed. Rejection means that someone doesn't want to date me; it doesn't make me an ugly loser.

Is it worth it to me to take this risk even if I don't get my desired outcome? If so, why?	Yes. Even if a woman I like turns down my invitation to go out, I'll at least have tried. It's good practice for me to talk to women and take the risk of asking them out. I also get the chance to become more robust about rejection. It would help me to believe that I can survive rejection.

Write up your own risk assessment using Worksheet 18-5.

WORKSHEET 18-5 My Risk Assessment

Risk I'd like to take but am avoiding:	
Why am I avoiding taking action?	
Realistically, what's the worst thing that could happen if I take this risk?	
Can I imagine surviving the worst-case scenario?	
Is it worth it to me to take this risk even if I don't get my desired outcome? If so, why?	

Striving for Self-Acceptance over Other-Approval

Having other people think well of you is nice. Being approved of by others is a good thing, most of the time. Wanting to be liked is okay, too. However, *nobody* can be a hit with *everybody.*

If you believe that you *have* to be approved of by everyone you meet, you'll run into emotional trouble. You'll probably spend a lot of time worrying about what others think of you, try so hard to please others that you surrender your own needs and opinions, be a bag of nerves in social settings, lose your spontaneity, or act in ways that you think will impress others.

You stand a far better chance of enjoying social interactions, making meaningful relationships, and expressing your own unique personality if you see approval from others as a bonus rather than a necessity. Accepting yourself doesn't mean becoming vain or arrogant and disregarding the opinions of others completely. Self-acceptance means seeing yourself as an equal to others and being comfortable in your own skin. We cover the concept of self-acceptance in detail in Chapter 12.

EXAMPLE

Take a look at how Patrick uncovered some of his approval-seeking attitudes in Table 18-6.

TABLE 18-6 Patrick's Other-Approval Account

Broad description of situation or event (think of a specific recent or typical event in which you sought other people's approval):	Recently, I wanted to ask Susan out on a date and let her know that I liked her.
Whose approval am I seeking in this situation?	Susan's.
What specific type of approval am I seeking from this person?	I wanted her to find me attractive and think of me as cool and intriguing.
Am I putting myself down about any specific aspects of myself when I sense that I'm not getting approval?	Yes. I decide that I'm ugly, dull, and a total loser with women.
What arguments can I use to convince myself that accepting myself is a good idea, even in the absence of approval from this person?	If I accept myself, I'll be able to ask women like Susan out. Even if I get turned down, I won't put myself down so viciously. Accepting myself as a basically worthwhile person (whether Susan likes me or not) will probably help me to relax around her and behave more like myself. Accepting myself will help me to reach my goal of being able to socialize with women I find attractive. Accepting myself feels a lot better because I'm not making myself depressed by putting myself down.
What arguments can I use to convince myself that even though I want this person's approval, I don't have to get it?	It doesn't make sense that, just because I really want Susan to like me, she has to do so. Just because I want something very much, it doesn't logically follow that I must get it. If Susan prefers Jack to me, that's disappointing, but it won't kill me. I can survive not getting what I want. I really like Susan, and I really want her to like me back. But if she doesn't, I can still go on to lead a happy and fulfilling life. I don't need Susan's approval to get on with my life. If Susan absolutely had to like me, she'd be deprived of her own free will. In reality, she has the ability to either like me or not. She has her own mind and will decide how she feels about me for herself.

Now complete Worksheet 18-6 to address how you seek the approval of others.

REMEMBER

Putting into regular practice the principles we outline in this chapter will help you to become emotionally healthy — and to stay that way.

WORKSHEET 18-6 My Other-Approval Account

Broad description of situation or event (think of a specific recent or typical event in which you sought other people's approval).	
Whose approval am I seeking in this situation?	
What specific type of approval am I seeking from this person?	
Am I putting myself down about any specific aspects of myself when I sense that I'm not getting approval?	
What arguments can I use to convince myself that accepting myself is a good idea even in the absence of approval from this person?	
What arguments can I use to convince myself that even though I want this person's approval, I don't have to get it?	

5 The Part of Tens

IN THIS PART . . .

It wouldn't be a *For Dummies* book without a Part of Tens. This part contains handy tips for working with professionals, getting better sleep, and renewing your motivation when you find it flagging.

IN THIS CHAPTER

» Knowing where to look for professional help

» Making the most of professional treatment

Chapter 19
Ten Tips for Working with Professionals

Despite your best efforts to get better using self-help methods like this workbook, you may find that you need to seek out some professional input. Your problems may be interfering with your ability to put self-help into practice, or maybe you feel that seeing a therapist will give you an added boost. Whatever your reasons for seeking out professional help, this chapter offers useful advice on choosing the best treatment strategy for you, as well as useful tips on making the most of your therapy.

Choosing the Right Type of Therapy for You

Psychiatrists and doctors are increasingly recommending cognitive behavioral therapy (CBT) treatment because scientific research proves its effectiveness. Its problem-solving approach and emphasis on helping you to become your own therapist also reduce relapse.

However, you may want to try out a different type of therapy even if you've found CBT beneficial. Perhaps you want to focus more on your past experiences or on your relationships, for example. A few of the more common types of therapy include the following:

» **Psychoanalytical therapy:** Developed by Sigmund Freud, it involves free association and places emphasis on your childhood relationships, particularly family dynamics. You're likely to be asked to commit to attending therapy sessions more than once a week for at least a year.

- **Psychodynamic therapy:** This type of therapy looks at how your past experiences and relationships influenced your development. It places a lot of emphasis on the past. It also tends to require long-term treatment.
- **Person-centered therapy:** Developed by Carl Rogers, it focuses very much on the relationship, or *alliance,* between client and therapist. A person-centered therapist doesn't direct the sessions but expects to be led by you.
- **Systemic therapy:** This type of therapy focuses on family systems and the roles individuals play within their relationships with others. It's often used for work with couples and families.
- **Interpersonal therapy:** This type of therapy is short-term and often used to treat depression. The treatment focuses on how you relate to others and ways to enhance and improve your relationships and social activity.

There are many other schools of therapy out there. Some therapists practice *integrative* or *eclectic therapy,* drawing from several approaches. In fact, one CBT therapist may practice quite differently from another, depending on which school of CBT they follow, so it can be worth asking.

WARNING

We recommend that you thoroughly research whatever type of therapy you choose and make sure that it's a genuine treatment protocol recognized by a professional body like the American Psychological Association (`www.apa.org`).

Knowing Who's Who in the Psychology World

Many different types of mental health professionals are able to offer general counseling. Counseling can be helpful, but if you have a specific disorder — such as depression, obsessive-compulsive disorder (OCD), or post-traumatic stress disorder (PTSD) — seeing a fully qualified therapist with experience dealing with your type of problem is best. Some counselors are specifically trained in a therapeutic orientation such as CBT, but asking clearly about specialist qualifications is still worthwhile.

TIP

Any therapist you see should hold a degree (ideally, a graduate degree) from a university or recognized training institute.

Following is a brief rundown of different professionals and the type of help they can offer:

- **Clinical psychologists** usually have studied a broad range of therapies and have a basic knowledge of applying them to specific problems. Often they have counseling training. Many may have knowledge of CBT, but not all have advanced training in it.
- **Counselors** generally are trained in listening and helping skills. They may hold a certificate in basic counseling or have been trained to deal with certain types of problems such as grief or addictions. Not all counselors have a psychology degree or particular knowledge of psychological problems.

- **Licensed clinical social workers (LCSWs)** may also add further training in CBT and practice as therapists.
- **Psychiatric nurses or nurse therapists** gain extra training to become CBT therapists in the UK.
- **Psychiatrists** are medically trained doctors who specialize in psychological disorders. Some are trained in CBT or another type of psychotherapy, but more often they conduct assessments and then refer you to a suitable therapist. They can prescribe medication and know more about the drugs used to treat psychiatric problems than general practitioners.
- **Psychotherapists** usually specialize in a school of psychotherapy such as CBT. Many have a psychology degree and in-depth knowledge of experience with psychological problems. The level of training and experience can vary widely, however.

Asking the Right Questions

If you ask yourself certain questions, such as the following, you may be clearer about what you want to ask your potential therapist:

- What do I want help with? What are my problems?
- How often do I want sessions? Weekly? Every other week?
- Do I prefer a female or male therapist?
- How much can I afford to pay?
- How far am I prepared to travel?
- How many sessions am I prepared to have?

Don't be worried about asking a potential therapist as many questions as you like, either during your first session or during an initial phone call. Ensuring that you have your questions answered in your early conversations is usually best. Sometimes a therapist may find it difficult to answer certain questions conclusively prior to assessment, such as how many sessions you're likely to need, but most will be able to give you a rough idea at least.

Looking in the Right Places for a Therapist

Doctors are probably the most reliable sources for finding a therapist. Most medical professionals only refer to therapists that they know and have referred to before. Recommendations from friends can be good, too, but make sure they have a similar problem to yours or that you're looking for the same things from a therapist as they are.

You can also look online for accredited or licensed CBT therapists, too. In the U.S., the website of *Psychology Today* (`www.psychologytoday.com/us/therapists`) is a great resource for finding therapists; you can filter by male or female, in person or online, the type of therapy they conduct (including CBT), and more. In the UK, properly trained therapists are accredited by the British Association for Behavioural and Cognitive Psychotherapies (`https://babcp.com`) or the UK Council for Psychotherapy (`www.psychotherapy.org.uk`).

Vetting Your Potential Therapist

WARNING

Unfortunately, some people advertise themselves as counselors or therapists without any professional training or qualifications.

Any therapist worth their salt won't take offence to any questions you ask about their experience or training. In fact, most professional psychotherapists will expect you to do so. Ask your prospective therapist which professional bodies they're accredited by or registered with, where they studied, and how long they've been practicing. New therapists can be very competent, but they may not have extensive experience dealing with your type of problem, so asking about this is worthwhile. If you're considering a CBT therapist, ask specifically about the extent and nature of their CBT training.

REMEMBER

Finding a therapist you can work with can sometimes take more than one attempt. This is far from unusual. Being too choosy or dropping a therapist the moment they say something you don't like can, of course, be a problem, but it's okay to try someone else if you feel you and your therapist just aren't a good fit.

Remaining Open-Minded about Medication

You may not be interested in taking medication to help you overcome your psychological or emotional troubles. Many people don't like taking medication and prefer to try to overcome their problems solely through therapy. Often this approach can work, and very frequently CBT on its own is enough to help you beat depression or anxiety. But sometimes even your best efforts won't be enough to resolve your problems.

Medication can help relieve some of your symptoms and enable you to more fully engage with and benefit from therapy. Even a low dose of the right type of medication can help take the edge off symptoms that may be blocking your progress with CBT.

REMEMBER

If you couldn't fight off an infection, you'd probably go to your doctor for antibiotics. Your mental health isn't very different from your physical health in this regard. There's no shame in taking medication to treat your symptoms.

TIP

Your doctor may be able to prescribe the kind of medication best suited to your description of your problem. If you aren't sure what medication you need, ask to be referred to a psychiatrist. Psychiatrists have specialist knowledge of this type of medication.

Working on Stuff between Sessions

Your therapist is likely to work with you to devise specific between-session tasks that help to further your understanding of core concepts. These tasks can also help you to face your fears, overcome your problematic behaviors, and strengthen healthy ways of thinking. Carrying out between-session work and reporting any problems with it (or positive results from it) to your therapist is in your best interest.

REMEMBER

Therapy sessions are usually only about 50 minutes long. You can make the most of treatment by working between sessions and preparing your thoughts before sessions.

TIP

Record the results of your between-session work. Think about any doubts, reservations, or confusion you may have about either therapy itself or your between-session work, and bring them up in the next session.

Discussing Issues during Sessions

Therapy can only really be useful if you're prepared to talk openly and honestly to your therapist. Although trained and experienced in all sorts of psychological problems, therapists aren't mind readers. We rely on you to provide us with the information we need to understand your difficulties.

You may feel a bit embarrassed or worried about telling your therapist about some of your thoughts or behaviors. Try to remember that your therapist is there not to judge you but to try to understand and offer you recognized techniques for dealing with your problems. Most experienced therapists are relatively unshockable. Remind yourself that your therapist has trained for years and met many people with problems very similar to your own.

Above all, your therapist is a human being first and a professional mental health worker second. Many of the thoughts and behaviors that you may want to discuss are common human experiences. Making a list of issues you feel you need to address prior to your first session may help. Then, if words fail you at the time, you can simply read out your list or hand it over to your therapist to read.

Use Worksheet 19-1 to write down issues that are leading you to seek therapy.

WORKSHEET 19-1 My Issue List

What are the key issues in my life that I want to discuss in therapy?	

Preparing for Therapy Sessions

In addition to working on therapeutic tasks between sessions and being open to discussing your issues during sessions, you can further prepare before sessions. Although you'll probably define your problems and goals with your therapist in the first few sessions, life can throw some curveballs your way, and you may find that your circumstances have changed since your first session. You can prepare for sessions by making brief notes about any changes in your circumstances, problems, or goals that your therapist may need to know about. Keeping all your therapy paperwork in a file or folder so you can easily bring it to sessions and review your work with your therapist can also be useful.

Setting Goals

CBT is a goal-directed therapy. Expect your therapist to listen to your description of your problems in the initial sessions and to ask you what your goals are regarding those problems. Thinking about not only your specific problematic emotions and behaviors but also how you want to change is a good idea. So, you may decide, for example, that you want to be more confident about your appearance, more assertive with your partner, sad but not depressed about the loss of your job, or nervous but not anxious about entering social situations. (See Chapter 8 for more guidance on goal setting.)

Use Worksheet 19-2 to record a list of goals in relation to your problems. Bring the completed list with you to your first therapy session.

REMEMBER

Your therapist can help you establish appropriate, realistic, and achievable goals.

WORKSHEET 19-2 My Goals

What are my problems?	
What are my goals for these problems? How do I want to feel/act differently?	

IN THIS CHAPTER

» Bedding down helpful sleep patterns

» Setting the scene for slumber

Chapter 20

Ten Tips for Getting a Good Night's Sleep

Many common psychological problems can lead to sleep disturbance of one kind or another. You may find it difficult to fall asleep, or you may wake up in the night and have trouble getting back to sleep. Sleep disturbance of any kind is unpleasant. In this chapter, we offer some tips to help increase your chances of getting a good night's rest.

Wear Yourself Out with Exercise

Perhaps you're an exception to the rule, but most of us don't get enough daily exercise. Exercise is important not only because it keeps you physically fit, but because it has a positive impact on mental fitness, too. When you exercise (especially quite vigorously), your brain releases "feel good" chemicals called *endorphins*. These little folks are good news for your general mood and can help promote relaxation.

Perhaps you've had the experience of spending a day gardening, at the beach, or hiking and felt very physically tired afterward. Chances are, you slept well that night. The combination of fresh air and physical exertion is a great recipe for restful sleep.

TIP

Try to increase the amount you exercise each day. Even small changes such as walking to the store instead of driving or taking the stairs instead of the elevator can make a difference. Ideally, you want to increase your heart rate (and really work up a sweat) through cardiovascular exercise such as running, swimming, or cycling at least three times per week.

TIP

Doing your more vigorous exercising early in the day is a good idea. If you exercise too close to bedtime, you may end up feeling physically "pumped" instead of relaxed. Suitable gentle exercises for the evening include yoga, Pilates, and walking.

Establish a Schedule

If you aren't sleeping well at night you may be tempted to try to catch up on sleep by getting up later or taking naps during the day. But ultimately, doing so can cement bad sleep habits rather than help to get your sleeping back on track.

TIP

If you're trying to restore a pattern to your sleep, try getting up and *out* of bed at the same time every day for at *least* two weeks, even weekends! This routine means *not* hitting the snooze button on the alarm. Also, resist napping during the day no matter how poorly you slept the night before. The idea is that your body will begin to feel sleepy at a regular time each night because you're getting up at a regular time and staying awake all day. You'll probably also find that (eventually) you fall asleep more easily when your head hits the pillow. You may feel uncomfortably tired for the first few days after you start sticking to a sleep schedule. In the long run, however, you'll benefit from establishing a better sleep pattern.

If you know that you tend to feel sleepy and want to nap at a certain point during the day, plan to be doing something active at this time.

Use Worksheet 20-1 to schedule your wakeup time and nap avoidance strategies.

WORKSHEET 20-1 My Sleep Schedule

My regular time for getting up and out of bed each day:	
Times I most often feel like napping:	
Things I can do instead of napping:	

Don't Lie in Bed Tossing and Turning

If you find it difficult to get to sleep or you wake up in the middle of the night and can't get back to sleep, you'll gain little from lying in bed bemoaning the fact. Give yourself 10 to 15 minutes to fall asleep, and if it doesn't happen, get up.

Try doing something not overly stimulating (including looking at screens) — in fact, doing something boring or monotonous is recommended. Sorting the laundry, ironing, reading a dull book, or doing something repetitive such as knitting are some ideas. Avoid alcoholic or caffeinated drinks. Have a cup of herbal tea or a warm milky drink instead. Try not to return to bed until you're genuinely sleepy and your eyelids are getting heavy.

WARNING

You may feel more tired the next day if you've been up a lot in the night or got to sleep late. However, over time, your sleep pattern will stabilize. Lying in bed tossing and turning can build up unhelpful associations of sleeplessness while you're in bed.

Take Care with Caffeine, Alcohol, and Late-Night Snacks

Some people are more sensitive to caffeine than others. Caffeine can stay in your system for a long time. So, even if you don't think that you're very sensitive to it, avoiding caffeine and other stimulants can be a good idea. Tea, coffee, soda, energy drinks, and even chocolate can contain caffeine. Try cutting out all these types of drinks from midafternoon onward.

A common strategy people use to help themselves get off to sleep is to have an alcoholic drink. Although this approach can often help with initially falling asleep, alcohol can make your sleep less deep and restorative, and make you more prone to waking up in the middle of the night, so it's best avoided.

Eating a heavy meal before bed can also initially make you feel sleepy but disturb your sleep. So, keep your evening snacks light.

Set a Bedtime Routine

If you were trying to soothe a child to sleep, you'd probably take away their noisy toys, give them a warm bath, put them in some comfy pajamas, read them a story or sing them a lullaby by the light of a soft lamp, and then tuck them in and say, "Sweet dreams," wouldn't you? Try giving yourself a similarly soothing bedtime routine. Many adults make the mistake of jumping into bed without giving themselves a chance to wind down.

Particularly if you're having sleep problems, using your bed *only* for sleep is important. Working on a laptop, watching TV, or even reading are activities you're better off doing elsewhere. (The one obvious exception to this rule is sex — you can keep doing that in bed.) The idea here is to build associations of getting into bed and going to sleep rather than associations of doing your tax return (not a relaxing activity for most people!).

TIP

Try reading or listening to soothing music or a soft radio program in a comfortable chair near your bed. But only get into bed when you feel ready for sleep.

Put pen to paper and properly plan out your peaceful pre-bedtime routine in Worksheet 20-2. Getting into a soothing bedtime routine can really help your body and mind to recognize that the day is done and it's time to shut down.

WORKSHEET 20-2 **My Bedtime Routine**

Regular time to start my bedtime routine:	
Relaxing and unwinding activities I can indulge in before bedtime:	

Cozy Up Your Sleeping Area

Is your bedroom a sleep-inducing place to be? If not, get cozying. Ideally your bedroom should hold strong associations for you of (surprise, surprise) sleeping! Remove excess clutter from your bedroom, keep your bed linens fresh and clean, invest in some comfortable (even sumptuous) sleepwear, and keep the temperature comfortable (on the cooler side). Take phones and other devices out of the room, or at least put them well out of reach. Think about how you might arrange a child's sleep area. Apply the same basic principles to your own bedroom.

Shed a Little (Less Blue) Light on the Subject

Our lives are now full of screens that, alongside the lights in our homes, can produce blue light. The problem is that our brains experience this as a cue that it's daytime — time to be awake. Not ideal when it's midnight and you really want to be asleep. If you can, set your devices to night mode, which automatically drops the amount of blue light produced. To really help screen out the blue light in your environment, try wearing blue-light glasses in the evening, or just put down the phone.

Set Sensible Sleep Expectations

Despite your efforts to set the scene for bedtime, you may find your thoughts working against you. This point is very important because the pressure you may be putting on yourself to sleep well or the expectations you may have about sleeping poorly can really affect your actual sleep outcome. If your sleep has been disturbed for some time, it's understandable that you may have thoughts such as "I've *got* to get some sleep tonight" or "I'll be up all night again" or "I can't cope on so little sleep anymore." Unfortunately, these types of thoughts can become self-fulfilling prophecies.

Many of the tips in this chapter are designed to help you set the optimum conditions for relaxation and sleep, but sleep itself is something that you can't force. No matter how uncomfortable it is, many people do cope on little or poor-quality sleep without disaster. So, try challenging your negative sleep expectations by telling yourself something such as "I don't know how I'll sleep tonight, so I'll just see how it goes" or "If I don't sleep well tonight, then I'll be tired tomorrow but I'll manage."

In reality, sleep is your body's natural response to fatigue. In fact, sleep is such a natural and automatic process that you don't need to *try* to get to sleep — you're better off just letting it happen spontaneously. So, although the principles we outline here are generally good for optimizing sleep, it's important to stay flexible and not apply them too strictly.

Recording your negative expectations or demands about your sleeping can be helpful. Then you can generate some more sensible sleep expectations to take the pressure off and allow sleep to come of its own volition. Try using Worksheet 20-3 to replace unhelpful thoughts with more helpful ones.

WORKSHEET 20-3 My Sensible Sleep Expectations

What are my negative sleep expectations/demands?	
What are some more realistic and constructive ways of thinking about my current sleep problems?	
What are my sensible sleep expectations?	

Leave Your Cares at the Bedroom Door

Throughout history, very few people have solved the world's problems while in bed. Bedtime is not the best time to embark on problem-solving. Many people with sleep disturbance unwittingly use bedtime as "worry time." Because worrying isn't a relaxing activity, it tends to seriously impede sleep. Putting your thoughts on hold for the night can be very difficult, but with practice, you can train yourself to do it!

Try setting aside half an hour (or less) before bedtime to run through your plan for the next day or to deal with any residual concerns from the current day. Then tell yourself to draw a line under your concerns until the next day. If worries return during sleep time, remind yourself that now is not the time to deal with them and that you will sort it out the next day. You can even use a little imagery exercise if you're so inclined: Stand in front of your bedroom doorway and do a brief shaking action — imagine that you're shaking off your worries before getting into bed and snuggling down.

TIP

Some people find practicing mindfulness meditation before bed helps them to sleep better. There is even evidence that it may reduce your anxiety in the morning. Take a look at Chapter 5 for an introduction to mindfulness and consider experimenting with a few minutes of practice before bed for a couple weeks.

IN THIS CHAPTER

» Staying motivated

» Normalizing ups and downs on the road to recovery

» Preserving an optimistic perspective

Chapter 21
Ten Reasons to Never Give Up

We wrote this book to equip you with core skills and techniques to help you overcome your personal problems. We fully expect that if you use the worksheets in this book, you'll benefit. That said, there are times when all your best efforts seem not to be enough. Don't despair! It's entirely normal and human to feel demotivated and disheartened from time to time. Many psychological problems are disruptive, consuming, and very stubborn opponents. In this chapter, we offer advice and encouragement to keep you on the road to recovery.

Setbacks Are Not Exceptional

Setbacks, relapses, and symptom reappearance are *normal.* In fact, if you recovered from anxiety, depression, an eating disorder, an addiction, obsessive-compulsive disorder (OCD), or virtually any psychological disturbance *without* a setback, *that* would be exceptional.

REMEMBER

Change is not linear. Recovery from an emotional, behavioral, or psychological problem rarely (if ever) goes steadily upward in a straight line. Sure, it would be nice if you just got better and better every day until you achieved full recovery, but that just isn't the way it normally works. And that's okay. You may as well expect the occasional hiccup — forewarned is forearmed!

TIP

Given that setbacks are normal and that change isn't linear, it's a good idea to accept the possibility of setbacks instead of living in fear of them. Try taking the following attitude toward possible setbacks: "I'd really prefer *not* to have a setback, but there is no reason that I shouldn't have one and if I do, I *will* get through it and back on track," or "I bet lots of other people have setbacks. This isn't a failing or a mistake, it's all part of being a human who is trying to improve their health." In fact, practicing a balanced and compassionate attitude toward your struggles is practicing the very thinking that will help you improve.

Have a go at Worksheet 21-1 to help you surmount setbacks.

WORKSHEET 21-1 Surmounting Setbacks

List the techniques that you used to overcome your problem. (The same techniques that worked the first time will work for setbacks!)	
List the progress you've made so far. Include changes to your daily activities and changes in your thinking and mood. (It's easy to forget how far you've come!)	
Take a moment to give yourself credit for your efforts thus far. When you're facing a setback, that's when you most need to pat yourself on the back. List at least three of the harder things you've done in order to help yourself get better.	
List a minimum of three people you can go to for support. Try to include at least one professional person like a doctor or therapist.	
Rate your current problem severity on a scale of 1 to 10. Next rate the severity of your problem *before* you started working on overcoming it. Compare the two ratings. (Even if your problem is only a few points less severe than when you first began, you've improved!)	Current rating:
	Rating at start of using CBT on this problem:
	Point difference:
Review your relapse prevention plan in Chapter 17. List three things from your plan that you can put into practice. For example, you may consider restarting or increasing medication if it has helped you before (with your doctor's advice, of course!).	

REMEMBER

Setbacks do not mean a return to square one. Often, what determines how long a setback lasts is how quickly you take action to arrest it. A realistically optimistic attitude toward overcoming setbacks also makes a big difference. That's why the Worksheet 21-1 and a relapse prevention plan are useful tools to have in your toolkit.

Recovery Requires Practice, Patience, and Persistence

We've been in this therapy game a long time, and we've never seen anybody get better overnight. Rome wasn't built in a day, and we'd be prepared to bet that it took a lot longer than a couple of months to construct. Yet there it is, a whopping great city. So if you follow the three P's (practice, patience, and persistence), you'll get there. After all, Rome did.

Small Achievements Add Up

Every little bit of progress you make counts in large amounts! Take notice of the small positive changes to your life. Have another look at Worksheet 21-1. When you're feeling disheartened, it's all too easy to discredit your achievements. So try making a fair and accurate assessment of your progress to date. Small changes can be very significant.

You Have Value in the World

No matter how you may be thinking about yourself during your low times, the world needs you! Every time you act in a socially responsible way, you're enhancing your environment. Whether you're smiling at a barista, recycling your trash, or doing something grander, your positive input adds to the world you live in. Do not underestimate your individual value and contribution to the world. Also remember that when you feel depressed or guilty or otherwise emotionally disturbed, you're probably not the best person to judge your value. Reserve your judgment for another day when you may have a more balanced and realistic view of yourself. Pay a visit to Chapter 12 for more info on how to accept yourself just as you are.

Nobody Is Perfect

Well, ain't that the truth? No one is perfectly happy, perfectly healthy, or perfect in any other way. As human beings, we're fundamentally designed to be flawed. Humans are prone to make mistakes, to sometimes behave self-destructively, and to occasionally do bad things. Instead of condemning yourself on the basis of your human imperfection, try treating yourself with some compassion and understanding as you would a friend. Perfection is an unachievable goal. Focus instead on selecting specific and realistic aspects of yourself for improvement. Do this *while* accepting yourself as perfectly imperfect — just like everybody else you know.

You May Feel Differently Tomorrow

Keep in mind that the way you *feel* influences the way you *think*. If today you're feeling depressed, anxious, or angry, for example, you're probably thinking negative, threatening, or anger-provoking thoughts. Your negative feelings can temporarily taint your view of life. Tomorrow you may feel differently, and you'll probably see the world in a much more favorable light.

TIP

If you're tempted to make a decision today (especially a major decision!) based on your current negative feelings, try holding off for a while. You may feel better tomorrow or next week and be better able to make a balanced, informed decision based on facts rather than on feelings.

You Can Always Try Other Options

Even if you have tried very hard to get past your problems and the payoffs still seem meager, you can try other things. Self-help may not be enough for you right now. You may want to try out some of the following options:

- **Medication:** Talk to your doctor and see what they have to say on the subject. Often medication can take the edge off your symptoms and enable you to more fully engage with either self-help or therapy sessions.
- **Support groups:** Many different types of support groups are available for a host of different types of problems. There are also online forums and websites that may be able to offer support.
- **Individual therapy:** Seeing a therapist for regular sessions may give you the extra boost you need. Self-help often works, but frequently, people find that seeing a therapist makes a big difference.
- **Other therapies:** Sometimes other types of therapy apart from CBT can be useful. Clearly, we think that CBT is highly effective, but that doesn't mean that other schools of therapy don't have value. Investigate your options by looking stuff up online, speaking to professionals, and asking for recommendations from friends.

  REMEMBER

  Any therapist you decide to see should be able to tell you their qualifications and be accredited with a recognized professional body. Accept nothing less.
- **Holistic therapies:** Massage, reflexology, acupuncture, and osteopathy are growing in recognition and can be used as adjuncts to CBT. Massage and reflexology can promote relaxation. Acupuncture is frequently used to help minimize cravings in addiction treatment. Osteopathy is a sophisticated muscular and skeletal treatment that may help resolve chronic pain and can promote overall well-being. Again, always be sure to see someone with a professional qualification.

Talking to Others Often Helps

If you're feeling discouraged with your progress, the temptation can often be to clam up and tell no one. But talking to others about it can help in the following ways:

- Friends or family may be able to offer much-needed encouragement.
- Others may be able to offer you practical help.
- Talking to others can give you a different perspective on your situation.
- Friends or family may help you to normalize your feelings and experiences by sharing some of their own.

Use Worksheet 21-2 to list people you can count on for support (you can list more than three!).

WORKSHEET 21-2 People I Can Turn to If the Going Gets Tough

1.

2.

3.

You Are Not Alone

Nope. You're not the only one. You're in this life gig with all the rest of us. No matter how alone you may be feeling, other people feel the same way, too. We can guarantee it! Everybody struggles from time to time, even doctors and therapists. That's because we're people first and professionals second (or third, or fourth, or fifth . . .). If you really were the only one with psychological problems, these books we've been writing wouldn't be selling so well and neither of us would have a job. So, instead of putting yourself on an island, come back to the mainland and rejoin the human race!

Change Is an Ongoing Process

Recovery is a process, not a one-off event. You'll be far better off thinking of your efforts to overcome your difficulties as a lifestyle shift rather than a finite endeavor. We humans all have to make an ongoing concerted effort to keep emotionally well. So although setting clear goals and putting a time frame around achieving them is great, be prepared to be flexible. It helps to make a distinction between long-, medium-, and short-term goals. (Turn to Chapter 8 for more on goal setting.)

REMEMBER

The main message here is that you are a vibrant, ever-changing, complex creature. Continuous growth and development is all part of being human.

Index

C

D

E

F

G

H

I

P

R

S

T

About the Authors

Rob Willson PhD, is a specialist cognitive behavioral therapist based in the UK, with more than 30 years of clinical experience. For the past 12 years, he has been the chair of the Body Dysmorphic Disorder Foundation (`https://bddfoundation.org`), the world's first charity exclusively devoted to the condition. Prior to building his own practice, Rob spent 12 years working at Priory Hospital North London, where he was a therapist and therapy services manager. He also trained and supervised numerous CBT therapists over a seven-year period at Goldsmiths College, University of London. He is regularly invited, around the UK, to train therapists and psychologists in cognitive behavioral therapy for body dysmorphic disorder and related disorders. He has co-authored several books, including *Overcoming Obsessive-Compulsive Disorder*, 2nd Edition, and *Overcoming Body Dysmorphic Disorder*, 2nd Edition (both published by Robinson).

Rhena Branch, BSc, MSc, Dip CBT, is an accredited CBT practitioner and holds a post-graduate CBT supervision qualification. Rhena has recently left her London practice to relocate to Norfolk. She now runs a private practice in Norwich. She lectured and supervised, alongside Professor Windy Dryden, on the MSc course in CBT/REBT at Goldsmith's College, University of London, for 14 years. She also lectured and supervised on the post-graduate CBT diploma at Anglia Ruskin University for three years. Rhena is currently an associate tutor in the psychology department at the University of East Anglia. She has written several books on CBT in addition to her *For Dummies* publications.

Authors' Acknowledgments

Many researchers, fellow therapists, and authors have influenced our understanding and practice of CBT over the years and, therefore, the content in this book. Founding fathers, Albert Ellis and Aaron T. Beck, of course, merit special mention. Others include: David Burns, David M. Clark, David A. Clarke, Ray DiGiuseppe, Paul Gilbert, Kevin Gournay, Mary-Anne Layden, Michael Neenan, Christine Padesky, Jacqueline Persons, Stanley Rachman, Paul Salkovskis, David Veale, Adrian Wells, and many more. Special thanks goes to Windy Dryden for his extensive writings and for teaching us both so much.

Finally, a genuine thank-you to all our clients, past and present, for allowing us to get to know you and learn from you.

Publisher's Acknowledgments

Associate Editor: Elizabeth Stilwell
Managing Editor: Ajith Kumar
Editor: Elizabeth Kuball
Technical Editor: Katie d'Ath, MSc RECBT
Production Editor: Magesh Elangovan
Cover Image: Elena/stock.adobe.com
Special Help: Carmen Krikorian, Kristie Pyles